Lecture Notes in Computer Science 4601

Commenced Publication in 1973
Founding and Former Series Editors:
Gerhard Goos, Juris Hartmanis, and Jan van Leeuwen

Stefano Spaccapietra   Paolo Atzeni
François Fages   Mohand-Saïd Hacid
Michael Kifer   John Mylopoulos
Barbara Pernici   Pavel Shvaiko
Juan Trujillo   Ilya Zaihrayeu (Eds.)

Journal on Data Semantics IX

Volume Editors

Stefano Spaccapietra, EPFL Lausanne, Switzerland
E-mail: stefano.spaccapietra@epfl.ch

Paolo Atzeni, Università Roma Tre, Italy
E-mail: atzeni@dia.uniroma3.it

François Fages, INRIA Rocquencourt, Le Chesnay Cedex, France
E-mail: Francois.Fages@inria.fr

Mohand-Saïd Hacid, Université Claude Bernard Lyon 1, Villeurbanne, France
E-mail: mshacid@bat710.univ-lyon1.fr

Michael Kifer, State University of New York at Stony Brook, USA
E-mail: kifer@cs.sunysb.edu

John Mylopoulos, University of Toronto, Ontario, Canada
E-mail: jm@cs.toronto.edu

Barbara Pernici, Politecnico di Milano DEI, Italy
E-mail: barbara.pernici@polimi.it

Pavel Shvaiko, University of Trento, Italy
E-mail: pavel@dit.unitn.it

Juan Trujillo, University of Alicante, Spain
E-mail: jtrujillo@dlsi.ua.es

Ilya Zaihrayeu, University of Trento, Italy
E-mail: ilya@dit.unitn.it

Library of Congress Control Number: 2007934988

CR Subject Classification (1998): H.2, H.3, I.2, H.4, C.2
LNCS Sublibrary: SL 3 – Information Systems and Application, incl. Internet/Web
and HCI

ISSN   1861-2032
ISBN-10   3-540-74982-9 Springer Berlin Heidelberg New York
ISBN-13   978-3-540-74982-0 Springer Berlin Heidelberg New York

Springer is a part of Springer Science+Business Media

springer.com

© Springer-Verlag Berlin Heidelberg 2007
Printed in Germany

Typesetting: Camera-ready by author, data conversion by Scientific Publishing Services, Chennai, India
Printed on acid-free paper   SPIN: 12124558   06/3180   5 4 3 2 1 0

The LNCS Journal on Data Semantics

Computerized information handling has changed its focus from centralized data management systems to decentralized data exchange facilities. Modern distribution channels, such as high-speed Internet networks and wireless communication infrastructure, provide reliable technical support for data distribution and data access, materializing the new, popular idea that data may be available to anybody, anywhere, anytime. However, providing huge amounts of data on request often turns into a counterproductive service, making the data useless because of poor relevance or inappropriate level of detail. Semantic knowledge is the essential missing piece that allows the delivery of information that matches user requirements. Semantic agreement, in particular, is essential to meaningful data exchange.

Semantic issues have long been open issues in data and knowledge management. However, the boom in semantically poor technologies, such as the Web and XML, has boosted renewed interest in semantics. Conferences on the Semantic Web, for instance, attract big crowds of participants, while ontologies on their own have become a hot and popular topic in the database and artificial intelligence communities.

Springer's LNCS *Journal on Data Semantics* aims at providing a highly visible dissemination channel for most remarkable work that in one way or another addresses research and development on issues related to the semantics of data. The target domain ranges from theories supporting the formal definition of semantic content to innovative domain-specific application of semantic knowledge. This publication channel should be of the highest interest to researchers and advanced practitioners working on the Semantic Web, interoperability, mobile information services, data warehousing, knowledge representation and reasoning, conceptual database modeling, ontologies, and artificial intelligence.

Topics of relevance to this journal include:

- Semantic interoperability, semantic mediators
- Ontologies
- Ontology, schema and data integration, reconciliation and alignment
- Multiple representations, alternative representations
- Knowledge representation and reasoning
- Conceptualization and representation
- Multi-model and multi-paradigm approaches
- Mappings, transformations, reverse engineering
- Metadata
- Conceptual data modeling
- Integrity description and handling
- Evolution and change
- Web semantics and semi-structured data
- Semantic caching

- Data warehousing and semantic data mining
- Spatial, temporal, multimedia and multimodal semantics
- Semantics in data visualization
- Semantic services for mobile users
- Supporting tools
- Applications of semantic-driven approaches

These topics are to be understood as specifically related to semantic issues. Contributions submitted to the journal and dealing with semantics of data will be considered even if they are not from the topics in the list.

While the physical appearance of the journal issues is like the books from the well-known Springer LNCS series, the mode of operation is that of a journal. Contributions can be freely submitted by authors and are reviewed by the Editorial Board. Contributions may also be invited, and nevertheless carefully reviewed, as in the case for issues that contain extended versions of best papers from major conferences addressing data semantics issues. Special issues, focusing on a specific topic, are coordinated by guest editors once the proposal for a special issue is accepted by the Editorial Board. Finally, it is also possible that a journal issue be devoted to a single text.

The journal published its first volume in 2003 (LNCS 2800). That initial volume, as well as volumes II (LNCS 3360), V (LNCS 3870), this volume, IX, together with the previous volume, VIII, represent the annual occurrence of a special issue devoted to publication of selected extended versions of best conference papers from conferences of the year before. Volumes III and VI were special issues on a dedicated topic. Volume III (LNCS 3534), coordinated by guest editor Esteban Zimányi, addressed Semantic-Based Geographical Information Systems, while volume VI (LNCS 4090), coordinated by guest editors Karl Aberer and Philippe Cudre-Mauroux, addressed Emergent Semantics. Volumes IV and VI were "normal" volumes, made up of spontaneous submissions on any of the topics of interest to the journal.

The Editorial Board comprises an Editor-in-Chief (with overall responsibility), a Co-editor-in-Chief, and several members. The Editor-in-Chief has a four-year mandate. Members of the board have a three-year mandate. Mandates are renewable and new members may be elected anytime.

We are happy to welcome you to our readership and authorship, and hope we will share this privileged contact for a long time.

Stefano Spaccapietra
Editor-in-Chief
http://lbdwww.epfl.ch/e/Springer/

JoDS Volume IX

To foster the dissemination of the best ideas and results, the *Journal on Data Semantics* (JoDS) pursues a policy that includes annually publishing extended versions of the best papers from selected conferences whose scope encompasses or intersects the scope of the journal.

This initiative is motivated by the difference in goals between conferences and journals. Conferences usually have a faster turnaround and a focused audience, but they have to enforce space limitation and a fixed time frame, with no chances for improving a paper by producing multiple versions. In contrast, journals offer more space, room for debate and refinement, and are usually considered the real archival venue.

Therefore, the publication of an extended version of a conference paper is a much appreciated opportunity for researchers to widely disseminate a significantly improved presentation of their work, where they can develop the appropriate motivations, reasoning, results and comparative analysis. Moreover, by gathering the best papers from various conferences, JoDS special issues provide a unique opportunity for researchers to find in a single publication every year the best of ongoing research in the field of data semantics.

For 2005, papers from the following six international conferences were invited:

- The Seventh International Conference on Data Warehousing and Knowledge Discovery (DaWaK 2005)
- The 3rd International Workshop on Principles and Practice of Semantic Web Reasoning (PPSWR 2005)
- The 1st International Workshop on Contexts and Ontologies, Theory, Practice and Applications (C&O 2005), joint event with the 25th National Conference on Artificial Intelligence (AAAI 2005)
- The 2nd International Workshop on Peer-to-Peer Knowledge Management (P2PKM 2005), joint event with the 2nd Annual International Conference on Mobile and Ubiquitous systems (Mobiquitous 2005)
- The 13th International Conference on Cooperative Information Systems, (CoopIS 2005) and the International Conference on Ontologies, Databases, and Applications of Semantics (ODBASE 2005), which both took place October 31 to November 4, 2005, Agia Napa, Cyprus

Papers from these conferences were invited based on their quality, relevance and significance, and the viability of extending their results. Extended versions prepared by authors were subject to the traditional two-round scholarly review process, and the authors were required to respond to all concerns expressed by the reviewers before papers were accepted.

The selection of CoopIS 2005 best papers eventually resulted in the acceptance of three papers. The paper "Semantic Matching: Algorithms and Implementation" by Giunchiglia, Yatskevich and Shvaiko provides a framework that views *match* as an operator that takes two graph-like structures and produces a mapping between the nodes of the graphs that correspond semantically to each other. The authors introduce model-based techniques at the structure level.

The paper "Semantic-Guided Clustering of Heterogeneous XML Schemas" by De Meo, Quattrone, Terracina and Ursino, investigates a semantic-based approach for clustering heterogeneous XML schemas. The proposed approach makes use of the semantics of the underlying schemas by capturing the interschema properties among concepts of the schemas. The experimental analysis shows that the approach is scalable.

The paper "A Formal Framework for Adaptive Access Control Models" by Rinderle and Reichert proposes a framework that is suitable for handling evolution of organizational models and related access rules. The paper introduces a set of well-defined operators for defining and capturing changes in organizational models. In addition, the framework allows adaptation of access rules when the model changes.

DaWak 2005 contributed its best paper, "Processing Sequential Patterns in Relational Databases," by Shang and Sattler. The paper proposes an efficient SQL- based algorithm to mine sequential patterns in relational database systems. The authors start by saying that traditionally data mining techniques have been applied on flat files instead of on databases due to the low performance and high cost associated with implementing data mining with SQL on relational databases. The authors claim that it is possible to achieve a reasonable performance by implementing association rule mining and sequential pattern mining with carefully tuned SQL formulations. To this extent, the authors depart from inefficient a-priori methods and propose an efficient SQL-based algorithm, called Prospad (PROjection Sequential PAttern Discovery), to mine sequential patterns in relational database systems. Prospad adopts the divide-and-conquer strategy and projects the sequence table into a set of frequent item-related projected tables. Experimental results show that the Prospad algorithm can get higher performance than k-way joins based on a-priori approaches, especially on large and dense datasets, although it has severe limitations in performance compared to in-memory PrefixSpan algorithms.

Two extended articles were selected from PPSWR 2005. The paper "A Tool for Evaluating Ontology Alignment Strategies" by Lambrix and Tan addresses the important issue of aligning different ontologies, so that multiple sources of information can be exploited altogether. The paper describes a framework for the comparative evaluation of ontology alignment strategies and their combinations, and reports on the performance of an implementation of this framework. The test cases used for the evaluation are composed of five biomedical ontologies. A detailed example shows the use of two matchers in combination.

The paper "SomeRDFS in the Semantic Web" by Adjiman, Goasdoué and Rousset envisions the Semantic Web as a huge peer data management system, where data on the Web are annotated by ontologies networked together by mappings. The paper describes the SomeRDFS peer data management system architecture, its data model, query language, and query answering algorithm based on query rewriting techniques that are formally justified in the paper.

The selection from C&O 2005 resulted in three extended papers being accepted for JoDS.

The paper "Putting Things in Context: A Topological Approach to Mapping Contexts to Ontologies" by Segev and Gal provides a framework that defines the relationship between contexts and ontologies by using topological structures. This work has been motivated by the needs of the eGovernment domain. In this approach ontologies are viewed as the result of a manual effort to model a domain, while contexts are automatically generated models. The uncertainty, which usually exists in automatic context extraction, is managed through the definition of distance among contexts and a ranking of ontology concepts with respect to a given context. The approach has been implemented and evaluated on two real-world data sets: Reuters news reports and RSS news headlines.

The paper "Context Dependency Management in Ontology Engineering: A Formal Approach" by De Leenheer, de Moor, and Meersman introduces a framework that uses lexical knowledge to manage context dependences in ontology engineering tasks. The formalization of the context dependency management is built on top of the DOGMA ontology-engineering framework. The proposed approach is validated by a case study of inter-organizational competency ontology engineering.

The paper "Encoding Classifications into Lightweight Ontologies" by Giunchiglia, Marchese and Zaihrayeu provides a theory of how to translate standard classifications, such as DMoz, into formal classifications, namely, graph structures where labels are written in a propositional concept language. Formal classifications turn out to be a form of lightweight ontologies. This allows reducing essential tasks on classifications, such as document classification and query answering, to reasoning about subsumption.

Four extended versions of ODBASE 2005 papers were granted acceptance. The paper "Creating Ontologies for Content Representation – The OntoSeed Suite," by Paslaru Bontas Simperl and Schlangen, proposes a natural language-based technique to help ontology engineers decide which concepts to model in any particular domain. Unlike other NLP-based techniques, this approach does not require in-depth linguistic expertise. Instead it relies on the Web for collecting the documents against which to compare domain-specific texts.

"Metadata Management in a Multiversion Data Warehouse," a paper by Wrembel and Bebel, deals with the problem of evolving data warehouses in the presence of changes in the schema of the underlying data sources. The paper proposes a solution, called multiversion data warehouse, which maintains extensive metadata about the external data sources.

The paper by Kensche, Quix, Chatti and Jarke, "GeRoMe: A Generic Role-Based Metamodel for Model Management," proposes a generic mechanism for describing data models. This approach assigns multiple roles to model elements and permits an accurate description of these elements using only a small number of roles and metaclasses. This contrasts favorably with metamodel languages that are based exclusively on metaclasses, since such languages may require an exponentially large number of metaclasses.

The paper "Security Ontology to Facilitate Web Service Description and Discovery" by Kim, Luo and Kang proposes an ontology for describing security requirements of Web services. The goal of such an ontology is to enable Web service discovery that meets a client's security requirements, such as protocols, objectives and credentials. The proposed ontology is more comprehensive and detailed than other similar ontologies.

Because of size limitations, eight of the 14 above-described papers were published in volume JoDS VIII. This volume contains the other six papers.

C&O 2005 Co-chair
Pavel Shvaiko, University of Trento, Italy

CoopIS 2005 PC Co-chairs
Mohand-Saïd Hacid, University Lyon 1, France
John Mylopoulos, University of Trento, Italy and University of Toronto, Canada
Barbara Pernici, Politecnico Milano, Italy

DAWAK 2005 Co-chair
Juan Trujillo, University of Alicante, Spain

ODBASE 2005 Co-chairs
Michael Kifer, State University of New York at Stony Brook, USA
Stefano Spaccapietra, EPFL, Switzerland

PPSWR 2005 Co-chair
François Fages, INRIA Rocquencourt, France

P2PKM Co-chair
Ilya Zaihrayeu, University of Trento, Italy

Reviewers

We would like to express our gratitude to the following colleagues who helped in the review process by contributing detailed reviews of the submitted papers and provided invaluable feedback to the authors and editors alike:

Jean-Marc Petit, INSA de Lyon, France
Dimitris Plexousakis, University of Crete, Greece
Axel Polleres, Universidad Rey Juan Carlos, Spain
David Robertson, The University of Edinburgh, UK
Marie-Christine Rousset, IMAG, France
Peter Pater-Schneider, Bell Labs, Murray Hill, USA
Marta Sabou, The Open University, UK
Vasile-Marian Scuturici, INSA de Lyon, France
Manuel Serrano, University of Castilla La Mancha, Spain
Sylvain Soliman, INRIA Rocquencourt, France
Heiner Stuckenschmidt, University of Mannheim, Germany
York Sure, University of Karlsruhe, Germany
Thodoros Topaloglou, University of Toronto, Canada
Farouk Toumani, Université Blaise Pascal, France
Athena Vakali, Aristotle University of Thessaloniki, Greece
Panos Vassiliadis, University of Ioannina, Greece
Holger Wache, Vrije Universiteit Amsterdam, The Netherlands
Howard Williams, Heriot-Watt University, Edinburgh, UK
Xing Xie, Microsoft Research, USA
Esteban Zimányi, Université Libre de Bruxelles, Belgium

JoDS Editorial Board

Table of Contents

Semantic Matching: Algorithms and Implementation*

Fausto Giunchiglia, Mikalai Yatskevich, and Pavel Shvaiko

Department of Information and Communication Technology,
University of Trento,
38050, Povo, Trento, Italy
{fausto,yatskevi,pavel}@dit.unitn.it

Abstract. We view *match* as an operator that takes two graph-like structures (e.g., classifications, XML schemas) and produces a mapping between the nodes of these graphs that correspond semantically to each other. *Semantic matching* is based on two ideas: (i) we discover mappings by computing *semantic relations* (e.g., equivalence, more general); (ii) we determine semantic relations by analyzing the *meaning* (concepts, not labels) which is codified in the elements and the structures of schemas. In this paper we present basic and optimized algorithms for semantic matching, and we discuss their implementation within the S-Match system. We evaluate S-Match against three state of the art matching systems, thereby justifying empirically the strength of our approach.

1 Introduction

Match is a critical operator in many well-known metadata intensive applications, such as schema/ontology integration, data warehouses, data integration, e-commerce, etc. The match operator takes two graph-like structures and produces a mapping between the nodes of the graphs that correspond semantically to each other.

Many diverse solutions of match have been proposed so far, see [43,11,40,42] for recent surveys, while some examples of individual approaches addressing the matching problem can be found in [1,2,5,6,10,11,13,16,30,32,33,35,39][1].We focus on a schema-based solution, namely a matching system exploiting only the schema information, thus not considering instances. We follow a novel approach called *semantic matching* [20]. This approach is based on two key ideas. The first is that we calculate mappings between schema elements by computing *semantic relations* (e.g., equivalence, more general, disjointness), instead of computing coefficients rating match quality in the [0,1] range, as it is the case in most previous approaches, see, for example, [11,13,32,39,35]. The second idea is that we determine semantic relations by analyzing the *meaning* (concepts, not labels) which is codified in the elements and the structures of schemas. In particular, labels at nodes, written in natural language, are automatically translated into propositional formulas which explicitly codify the labels' intended meaning. This allows us to translate the matching problem into a

---

* This article is an expanded and updated version of an earlier conference paper [23].

[1] See www.OntologyMatching.org for a complete information on the topic.

S. Spaccapietra et al. (Eds.): Journal on Data Semantics IX, LNCS 4601, pp. 1–38, 2007.

propositional validity problem, which can then be efficiently resolved using (sound and complete) state of the art propositional satisfiability (SAT) deciders, e.g., [31].

A vision of the semantic matching approach and some of its implementation were reported in [20,21,25]. In contrast to these works, this paper elaborates in more detail the element level and the structure level matching algorithms, providing a complete account of the approach. In particular, the main contributions are: (i) a new schema matching algorithm, which builds on the advances of the previous solutions at the element level by providing a library of element level matchers, and guarantees correctness and completeness of its results at the structure level; (ii) an extension of the semantic matching approach for handling attributes; (iii) an evaluation of the performance and quality of the implemented system, called S-Match, against other state of the art systems, which proves empirically the benefits of our approach. This article is an expanded and updated version of an earlier conference paper [23]. Therefore, three contributions mentioned above were originally claimed and substantiated in [23]. The most important extensions over [23] include a technical account of: (i) word sense disambiguation techniques, (ii) management of the inconsistencies in the matching tasks, and (iii) an in-depth discussion of the optimization techniques that improve the efficiency of the matching algorithm.

The rest of the paper is organized as follows. Section 2 introduces the semantic matching approach. It also provides an overview of four main steps of the semantic matching algorithm, while Sections 3,4,5,6 are devoted to the technical details of those steps. Section 7 discusses semantic matching with attributes. Section 8 introduces the optimizations that allow improving efficiency of the basic version of the algorithm. The evaluation results are presented in Section 9. Section 10 overviews the related work. Section 11 provides some conclusions and discusses future work.

2 Semantic Matching

In our approach, we assume that all the data and conceptual models (e.g., classifications, database schemas, ontologies) can be generally represented as graphs (see [20] for a detailed discussion). This allows for the statement and solution of a *generic (semantic) matching problem* independently of specific conceptual or data models, very much along the lines of what is done in Cupid [32] and COMA [11]. We focus on tree-like structures, e.g., classifications, and XML schemas. Real-world schemas are seldom trees, however, there are (optimized) techniques, transforming a graph representation of a schema into a tree representation, e.g., the graph-to-tree operator of Protoplasm [7]. From now on we assume that a graph-to-tree transformation can be done by using existing systems, and therefore, we focus on other issues instead.

The semantic matching approach is based on two key notions, namely:

- *Concept of a label,* which denotes the set of documents (data instances) that one would classify under a label it encodes;
- *Concept at a node,* which denotes the set of documents (data instances) that one would classify under a node, given that it has a certain label and that it is in a certain position in a tree.

Our approach can discover the following semantic relations between the *concepts at nodes* of two schemas: *equivalence* (=); *more general* ($\sqsupseteq$); *less general* ($\sqsubseteq$); *disjointness* ($\perp$). When none of the relations holds, the special *idk* (I do not know) [2] relation is returned. The relations are ordered according to decreasing binding strength, i.e., from the strongest (=) to the weakest (*idk*), with more general and less general relations having equal binding power. Notice that the strongest semantic relation always exists since, when holding together, more general and less general relations are equivalent to equivalence. The semantics of the above relations are the obvious set-theoretic semantics.

A *mapping element* is a 4-tuple $\langle ID_{ij}, a_i, b_j, R \rangle$, $i = 1,...,N_A$; $j = 1,...,N_B$ where ID_{ij} is a unique identifier of the given mapping element; a_i is the *i*-th node of the first tree, N_A is the number of nodes in the first tree; b_j is the *j*-th node of the second tree, N_B is the number of nodes in the second tree; and R specifies a semantic relation which may hold between the *concepts at nodes* a_i and b_j. *Semantic matching* can then be defined as the following problem: given two trees T_A and T_B compute the $N_A \times N_B$ mapping elements $\langle ID_{ij}, a_i, b_j, R' \rangle$, with $a_i \in T_A$, $i=1,...,N_A$; $b_j \in T_B$, $j =1,..., N_B$; and R' is the strongest semantic relation holding between the *concepts at nodes* a_i and b_j. Since we look for the $N_A \times N_B$ correspondences, the cardinality of mapping elements we are able to determine is 1:N. Also, these, if necessary, can be decomposed straightforwardly into mapping elements with the 1:1 cardinality.

Let us summarize the algorithm for semantic matching via a running example. We consider small academic courses classifications shown in Figure 1.

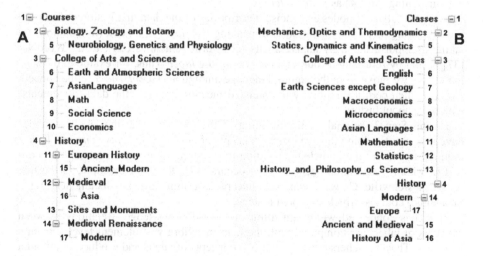

Fig. 1. Parts of two classifications devoted to academic courses

---

[2] Notice *idk* is an explicit statement that the system is unable to compute any of the declared (four) relations. This should be interpreted as either there is not enough background knowledge, and therefore, the system cannot explicitly compute any of the declared relations or, indeed, none of those relations hold according to an application.

Let us introduce some notation (see also Figure 1). Numbers are the unique identifiers of nodes. We use "C" for concepts of labels and concepts at nodes. Thus, for example, in the tree A, $C_{History}$ and C_4 are, respectively, the concept of the label *History* and the concept at node 4. Also, to simplify the presentation, whenever it is clear from the context we assume that the concept of a label can be represented by the label itself. In this case, for example, $C_{History}$ becomes denoted as *History*. Finally, we sometimes use subscripts to distinguish between trees in which the given concept of a label occurs. For instance, $History_A$, means that the concept of the label *History* belongs to the tree A.

The algorithm takes as input two schemas and computes as output a set of mapping elements in four macro steps:

- *Step 1:* for all labels L in two trees, compute concepts of labels, C_L.
- *Step 2:* for all nodes N in two trees, compute concepts at nodes, C_N.
- *Step 3:* for all pairs of labels in two trees, compute relations among C_L's.
- *Step 4:* for all pairs of nodes in two trees, compute relations among C_N's.

The first two steps represent the preprocessing phase, while the third and the fourth steps are the element level and structure level matching respectively[3]. It is important to notice that *Step 1* and *Step 2* can be done once, independently of the specific matching problem. *Step 3* and *Step 4* can only be done at run time, once the two trees which must be matched have been chosen. We also refer in the remainder of the paper to the element level matching (*Step 3*) as *label matching* and to the structure level matching (*Step 4*) as *node matching*.

We view labels of nodes as concise descriptions of the data that is stored under the nodes. During *Step 1*, we compute the meaning of a *label* at a node (in isolation) by taking as input a label, by analyzing its real-world semantics (e.g., using WordNet [37][4]), and by returning as output a *concept of the label*. Thus, for example, by writing $C_{History}$ we move from the natural language ambiguous label *History* to the concept $C_{History}$, which codifies explicitly its intended meaning, namely the data (documents) which are about history.

During *Step 2* we analyze the meaning of the *positions* that the labels of nodes have in a tree. By doing this we *extend* concepts of labels to *concepts at nodes*. This is required to capture the knowledge residing in the structure of a tree, namely the context in which the given concept of label occurs [17]. Thus, for example, in the tree A, when we write C_4 we mean the concept describing all the documents of the (academic) courses, which are about history.

Step 3 is concerned with acquisition of "world" knowledge. Relations between concepts of labels are computed with the help of a library of element level semantic matchers. These matchers take as input two concepts of labels and produce as output a

---

[3] Element level matching (techniques) compute mapping elements by analyzing schema entities in isolation, ignoring their relations with other entities. Structure-level techniques compute mapping elements by analyzing how schema entities appear together in a structure, see for more details [42,43].

[4] WordNet is a lexical database for English. It is based on *synsets* (or senses), namely structures containing sets of terms with synonymous meanings.

semantic relation (e.g., equivalence, more/less general) between them. For example, from WordNet [37] we can derive that *course* and *class* are synonyms, and therefore, $C_{Courses} = C_{Classes}$.

Step 4 is concerned with the computation of the relations between concepts at nodes. This problem cannot be resolved by exploiting static knowledge sources only. We have (from *Step 3*) background knowledge, codified as a set of relations between concepts of labels occurring in two trees. This knowledge constitutes the background theory (axioms) within which we reason. We need to find a semantic relation (e.g., equivalence, more/less general) between the concepts at any two nodes in two trees. However, these are usually complex concepts obtained by suitably combining the corresponding concepts of labels. For example, suppose we want to find a relation between C_4 in the tree A (which, intuitively, stands for the concept of courses of history) and C_4 in the tree B (which, intuitively, stands for the concept of classes of history). In this case, we should realize that they have the same extension, and therefore, that they are equivalent.

3 Step 1: Concepts of Labels Computation

Technically, the main goal of *Step 1* is to automatically translate ambiguous natural language labels taken from the schema elements' names into an internal logical language. We use a propositional description logic language[5] (L^C) for several reasons. First, given its set-theoretic interpretation, it "maps" naturally to the real world semantics. Second, natural language labels, e.g., in classifications, are usually short expressions or phrases having simple structure. These phrases can often be converted into a formula in L^C with no or little loss of meaning [18]. Third, a formula in L^C can be converted into an equivalent formula in a propositional logic language with boolean semantics. Apart from the atomic propositions, the language L^C includes logical operators, such as *conjunction* ($\sqcup$), *disjunction* ($\sqcap$), and *negation* ($\neg$). There are also comparison operators, namely *more general* ($\sqsupseteq$), *less general* ($\sqsubseteq$), and *equivalence* (=). The interpretation of these operators is the standard set-theoretic interpretation.

We compute concepts of labels according to the following four logical phases, being inspired by the work in [34].

1. *Tokenization.* Labels of nodes are parsed into tokens by a tokenizer which recognizes punctuation, cases, digits, stop characters, etc. Thus, for instance, the label *History and Philosophy of Science* becomes ⟨*history, and, philosophy, of, science*⟩. The multiword concepts are then recognized. At the moment the list of all multiword concepts in WordNet [37] is exploited here together with a heuristic which takes into account the natural language connectives, such as *and, or*, etc. For example, *Earth and Atmospheric Sciences* becomes ⟨*earth sciences, and,*

---

[5] A propositional description logic language (L^C) we use here is the description logic ALC language without the role constructor, see for more details [4]. Note, since we do not use roles, in practice we straightforwardly translate the natural language labels into propositional logic formulas.

atmospheric, sciences⟩ since WordNet contains senses for *earth sciences*, but not for *atmospheric sciences*.

2. *Lemmatization.* Tokens of labels are further lemmatized, namely they are morphologically analyzed in order to find all their possible basic forms. Thus, for instance, *sciences* is associated with its singular form, *science*. Also here we discard from further considerations some pre-defined meaningless (in the sense of being useful for matching) words, articles, numbers, and so on.

3. *Building atomic concepts.* WordNet is queried to obtain the senses of lemmas identified during the previous phase. For example, the label *Sciences* has the only one token *sciences*, and one lemma *science*. From WordNet we find out that *science* has two senses as a noun.

4. *Building complex concepts.* When existing, all tokens that are prepositions, punctuation marks, conjunctions (or strings with similar roles) are translated into logical connectives and used to build complex concepts out of the atomic concepts constructed in the previous phase. Thus, for instance, commas and conjunctions are translated into logical disjunctions, prepositions, such as *of* and *in,* are translated into logical conjunctions, and words like *except, without* are translated into negations. Thus, for example, the concept of label *History and Philosophy of Science* is computed as $C_{History\ and\ Philosophy\ of\ Science} = (C_{History} \sqcup C_{Philosophy}) \sqcap C_{Science}$, where $C_{Science} = \langle science, \{senses_{WN}\#2\}\rangle$ is taken to be the union of two WordNet senses, and similarly for *history* and *philosophy*. Notice that natural language *and* is converted into logical disjunction, rather than into conjunction (see [34] for detailed discussion and justification for this choice).

The result of *Step 1* is the logical formula for concept of label. It is computed as a full propositional formula were literals stand for atomic concepts of labels.

In Figure 2 we present the pseudo-code which provides an algorithmic account of how concepts of labels are built. In particular, the **buildCLab** function takes the tree of nodes `context` and constructs concepts of labels for each node in the tree. The nodes are preprocessed in the main loop in lines 220-350. Within this loop, first, the node label is obtained in line 240. Then, it is tokenized and lemmatized in lines 250 and 260, respectively. The (internal) loop on the lemmas of the node (lines 270-340) starts from stop words test in line 280. Then, WordNet is queried. If the lemma is in WordNet, its senses are extracted. In line 300, atomic concept of label is created and attached to the node by the **addACOLtoNode** function. In the case when WordNet returns no senses for the lemma, the special identifier SENSES_NOT_FOUND is attached to the atomic concept of label[6]. The propositional formula for the concept of label is iteratively constructed by **constructcLabFormula** (line 340). Finally, the logical formula is attached to the concept at label (line 350) and some sense filtering is performed by **elementLevelSenseFiltering**[7].

---

[6] This identifier is further used by element level semantic matchers in *Step 3* of the matching algorithm in order to determine the fact that the label (lemma) under consideration is not contained in WordNet, and therefore, there are no senses in WordNet for a given concept.

[7] The sense filtering problem is also known under the name of word sense disambiguation (WSD), see, e.g., [29].

```
Node struct of
               int nodeId;
               String label;
               String cLabel;
               String cNode;
               AtomicConceptAtLabel[] ACOLs;
AtomicConceptOfLabel struct of
               int id;
               String token;
               String[] wnSenses;
200. void buildCLab(Tree of Nodes context)
210.  String[] wnSenses;
220.  For each node in context
230.     String cLabFormula="";
240.     String nodeLabel=getLabel(node);
250.     String[] tokens=tokenize(nodeLabel);
260.     String[] lemmas=lematize(tokens);
270.     For each lemma in lemmas
280.        if (isMeaningful(lemma))
290.           if (!isInWordnet(lemma))
300.              addACOLtoNode(node, lemma, SENSES_NOT_FOUND);
310.           else
320.              wnSenses= getWNSenses(token);
330.              addACOLtoNode(node, lemma, wnSenses);
340.        cLabFormula=constructcLabFormula(cLabFormula, lemma);
350.     setcLabFormula(node, cLabFormula);
360.     elementLevelSenseFiltering(node);
```

Fig. 2. Concept of label construction pseudo code

The pseudo code in Figure 3 illustrates the sense filtering technique. It is used in order to filter out the irrelevant (for the given matching task) senses from concepts of labels. In particular, we look whether the senses of atomic concepts of labels within each concept of a label are connected by any relation in WordNet. If so, we discard all other senses from atomic concept of label. Otherwise we keep all the senses. For example, for the concept of label *Sites and Monuments* before the sense filtering step we have $\langle Sites, \{senses_{WN}\#4\}\rangle \sqcup \langle Monuments, \{senses_{WN}\#3\}\rangle$. Since the second sense of *monument* is a hyponym of the first sense of *site*, notationally $Monument\#2 \sqsubseteq Site\#1$, all the other senses are discarded. Therefore, as a result of this sense filtering step we have $\langle Sites, \{senses_{WN}\#1\}\rangle \sqcup \langle Monuments, \{senses_{WN}\#1\}\rangle$.

elementLevelSenseFiltering takes the node structure as input and discards the irrelevant senses from atomic concepts of labels within the node. In particular, it executes two loops on atomic concept of labels (lines 30-120 and 50-120). WordNet senses for the concepts are acquired in lines 40 and 70. Then two loops on the WordNet senses are executed in lines 80-120 and 90-120. Afterwards, checking whether the senses are connected by a WordNet relation is performed in line 100. If so, the senses are added to a special set, called *refined senses* set (lines 110, 120). Finally, the WordNet senses are replaced with the refined senses by **saveRefined-Senses**.

```
10.void elementLevelSenseFiltering(Node node)
20. AtomicConceptOfLabel[] nodeACOLs=getACOLs(node);
30. for each nodeACOL in nodeACOLs
40.  String[] nodeWNSenses=getWNSenses(nodeACOL);
50.  for each ACOL in nodeACOLs
60.   if (ACOL!=nodeACOL)
70.    String[] wnSenses=getWNSenses(ACOL);
80.     for each nodeWNSense in nodeWNSenses
90.      for each wnSense in wnSenses
100.        if (isConnectedbyWN(nodeWNSense, focusNodeWNSense))
110.         addToRefinedSenses(nodeACOL,nodeWNSense);
120.         addToRefinedSenses(focusNodeACOL, focusNodeWNSense);
130.    saveRefinedSenses(context);

140. void saveRefinedSenses(context)
150.   for each node in context
160.     AtomicConceptOfLabel[] nodeACOLs=getACOLs(node);
170.   for each nodeACOL in NodeACOLs
180.     if (hasRefinedSenses(nodeACOL))
190.       //replace original senses with refined
```

Fig. 3. The pseudo code of element level sense filtering technique

4   Step 2: Concepts at Nodes Computation

Concepts at nodes are written in the same propositional description logic language as concepts of labels. Classifications and XML schemas are hierarchical structures where the path from the root to a node uniquely identifies that node (and also its meaning). Thus, following an *access criterion* semantics [26], the logical formula for a concept at node is defined as a conjunction of concepts of labels located in the path from the given node to the root. For example, in the tree A, the concept at node four is computed as follows: $C_4 = C_{Courses} \sqcap C_{History}$.

Further in the paper we require the concepts at nodes to be consistent (satisfiable). The reasons for their inconsistency are negations in atomic concepts of labels. For example, natural language label *except_geology* is translated into the following logical formula $C_{except\_geology} = \neg C_{geology}$. Therefore, there can be a concept at node represented by a formula of the following type $C_{geology} \sqcap ... \sqcap \neg C_{geology}$, which is inconsistent. In this case the user is notified that the concept at node formula is unsatisfiable and asked to decide a more important branch, i.e., (s)he can choose what to delete from the tree, namely $C_{geology}$ or $C_{except\_geology}$. Notice that this does not sacrifice the system performance since this check is made within the preprocessing (i.e., off-line, when the tree is edited)[8]. Let us consider the following example: $C_N = ... \sqcap C_{Medieval} \sqcap C_{Modern}$. Here, concept at node formula contains two concepts of labels, which are as from WordNet disjoint. Intuitively, this means that the context talks about either *Medieval* or *Modern* (or there is implicit disjunction in the concept at node formula). Therefore,

---

[8] In general case the reasoning is as costly as in the case of propositional logic (i.e., deciding unsatisfiability of the concept is co-NP hard). In many real world cases (see [25] for more details) the corresponding formula is *Horn*. Thus, its satisfiability can be decided in linear time.

in such cases, the formula for concept at node is rewritten in the following way:
$C_N = (C_{Medieval} \sqcup C_{Modern}) \sqcap ...$

The pseudo code of the second step is presented in Figure 4. The **buildCNode** function takes as an input the tree of nodes with precomputed concepts of labels and computes as output the concept at node for each node in the tree. The sense filtering (line 620) is performed by **structureLevelSenseFiltering** in the way similar to the sense filtering approach used at the element level (as discussed in Figure 3). Then, the formula for the concept at node is constructed within **buildcNodeFormula** as conjunction of concepts of labels attached to the nodes in the path to the root. Finally, the formula is checked for unsatisfiability (line 640). If so, user is asked about the possible modifications in the tree structure or they are applied automatically, specifically implicit disjunctions are added between disjoint concepts (line 650).

```
600. void buildCNode(Tree of Node context)
610.   for each node in context
620.     structureLevelSenseFiltering (node, context);
630.     String cNodeFormula= buildcNodeFormula (node, context);
640.     if (isUnsatisifiable(cNodeFormula))
650.       updateFormula(cNodeFormula);
```

Fig. 4. Concepts at nodes construction pseudo code

Let us discuss how the structure level sense filtering operates. As noticed before, this technique is similar to the one described in Figure 3. The major difference is that the senses now are filtered not within the node label but within the tree structure. For all concepts of labels we collect all their ancestors and descendants. We call them a *focus* set. Then, all WordNet senses of atomic concepts of labels from the focus set are compared with the senses of the atomic concepts of labels of the concept. If a sense of atomic concept of label is connected by a WordNet relation with the sense taken from the focus set, then all other senses of these atomic concepts of labels are discarded. Therefore, as a result of sense filtering step we have (i) the WordNet senses which are connected with any other WordNet senses in the focus set or (ii) all the WordNet senses otherwise. After this step the meaning of concept of labels is reconciled with respect to the knowledge residing in the tree structure. The pseudo code in Figure 5 provides an algorithmic account of the structure level sense filtering procedure.

The **structureLevelSenseFiltering** function takes a node and a tree of nodes as input and refines the WordNet senses within atomic concepts of labels in the node with respect to the tree structure. First, atomic concepts at labels from the ancestor and descendant nodes are gathered into the focus set (line 420). Then, a search for pairwise relations between the senses attached to the atomic concepts of labels is performed (lines 440-520). These senses are added to the refined senses set (lines 530-540) and further **saveRefinedSenses** from Figure 3 is applied (line 550) in order to save the refined senses.

```
400.void structureLevelSenseFiltering (Node node, Tree of Nodes context)
410.  AtomicConceptOfLabel[] focusNodeACOLs;
420.  Node[] focusNodes=getFocusNodes(node, context);
430.  AtomicConceptOfLabel[] nodeACOLs=getACOLs(node);
440.  for each nodeACOL in nodeACOLss
450.    String[] nodeWNSenses=getWNSenses(nodeACOL);
460.    for each nodeWNSense in nodeWNSenses
470.      for each focusNode in focusNodes
480.        focusNodeACOLs=getACOLs(focusNode);
490.        for each focusNodeACOL in focusNodeACOLs
500.          String[] fNodeWNSenses=getWNSenses(focusNodeACOL);
510.          for each fNodeWNSense in nodeWNSenses
520.            if (isConnectedbyWN(nodeWNSense, fNodeWNSense))
530.              addToRefinedSenses(nodeACOL,nodeWNSense);
540.              addToRefinedSenses(focusNodeACOL, focusNodeWNSense);
550.  saveRefinedSenses(context);
```

Fig. 5. The pseudo code of structure level sense filtering technique

5   Step 3: Label Matching

5.1   A Library of Label Matchers

Relations between concepts of labels are computed with the help of a library of element level semantic matchers [24]. These matchers take as input two atomic concepts of labels and produce as output a semantic relation between them. Some of them are re-implementations of well-known matchers used in Cupid [32] and COMA [11]. The most important difference is that our matchers ultimately return a semantic relation, rather than an affinity level in the [0,1] range, although sometimes using customizable thresholds.

Our label matchers are briefly summarized in Table 1. The first column contains the names of the matchers. The second column lists the order in which they are executed. The third column introduces the matchers' approximation level. The relations produced by a matcher with the first approximation level are always correct. For example, *name* $\sqsupseteq$ *brand* as returned by *WordNet*. In fact, according to WordNet *name* is a hypernym (superordinate word) of *brand*. Notice that *name* has 15 senses and *brand* has 9 senses in WordNet. We use sense filtering techniques to discard the irrelevant senses, see Sections 3 and 4 for details. The relations produced by a matcher with the second approximation level are likely to be correct (e.g., *net* = *network*, but *hot* = *hotel* by *Prefix*). The relations produced by a matcher with the third approximation level depend heavily on the context of the matching task (e.g., *cat* = *dog* by *Extended gloss comparison* in the sense that they are both *pets*). Note, matchers by default are executed following the order of increasing approximation level. The fourth column reports the matchers' type. The fifth column describes the matchers' input.

We have three main categories of matchers: *string-*, *sense-* and *gloss- based* matchers. String-based matchers exploit string comparison techniques in order to produce the semantic relation, while sense-based exploit the structural properties of the WordNet hierarchies and gloss-based compare two textual descriptions (*glosses*) of WordNet senses. Below, we discuss in detail some matchers from each of these categories.

Table 1. Element level semantic matchers implemented so far

Matcher name	Execution Order	Approximation level	Matcher type	Schema info
Prefix	2	2	String-based	Labels
Suffix	3	2		
Edit distance	4	2		
N-gram	5	2		
Text Corpus	13	3		Labels + Corpus
WordNet	1	1	Sense-based	WordNet senses
Hierarchy distance	6	3		
WordNet Gloss	7	3	Gloss-based	WordNet senses
Extended WordNet Gloss	8	3		
Gloss Comparison	9	3		
Extended Gloss Comparison	10	3		
Semantic Gloss Comparison	11	3		
Extended semantic gloss comparison	12	3		

5.1.1 Sense-Based Matchers

We have two sense-based matchers. Let us discuss how the *WordNet* matcher works. As it was already mentioned, WordNet [37] is based on *synsets* (or senses), namely structures containing sets of terms with synonymous meanings. For example, the words *night, nighttime* and *dark* constitute a single synset. Synsets are connected to one another through explicit (lexical) semantic relations. Some of these relations (hypernymy, hyponymy for nouns and hypernymy and troponymy for verbs) constitute *kind-of* and *part-of* (holonymy and meronymy for nouns) hierarchies. For instance, *tree* is a kind of *plant*. Thus, *tree* is hyponym of *plant* and *plant* is hypernym of *tree*. Analogously, from *trunk* being a part of *tree* we have that *trunk* is meronym of *tree* and *tree* is holonym of *trunk*.

The *WordNet* matcher translates the relations provided by WordNet to semantic relations according to the following rules:

- A $\sqsubseteq$ B, if A is a hyponym, meronym or troponym of B;
- A $\sqsupseteq$ B, if A is a hypernym or holonym of B;
- A = B, if they are connected by synonymy relation or they belong to one synset (*night* and *nighttime* from the example above);
- A $\perp$ B, if they are connected by antonymy relation or they are the siblings in the *part of* hierarchy.

5.1.2 String-Based Matchers

We have five string-based matchers. Let us discuss how the *Edit distance* matcher works. It calculates the number of simple editing operations (delete, insert and replace) over the label's characters needed to transform one string into another, normalized by the length of the longest string. The result is a value in [0,1]. If the value exceeds a given threshold (0.6 by default) the equivalence relation is returned, otherwise, *Idk* is produced.

5.1.3 Gloss-Based Matchers

We have six gloss-based matchers. Let us discuss how the *Gloss comparison* matcher works. The basic idea behind this matcher is that the number of the same words occurring in the two WordNet glosses increases the similarity value. The equivalence relation is returned if the number of shared words exceeds a given threshold (e.g., 3). *Idk* is produced otherwise. For example, suppose we want to match *Afghan hound* and *Maltese dog* using the gloss comparison strategy. Notice, although these two concepts are breeds of dog, WordNet does not have a direct lexical relation between them, thus the *WordNet* matcher would fail in this case. However, the glosses of both concepts are very similar. *Maltese dog* is defined as a breed of toy dogs having a long straight silky white coat. *Afghan hound* is defined as a tall graceful breed of hound with a long silky coat; native to the Near East. There are 4 shared words in both glosses, namely breed, long, silky, coat. Hence, the two concepts are taken to be equivalent.

5.2 The Label Matching Algorithm

The pseudo code implementing *Step 3* is presented in Figure 6. The label matching algorithm produces (with the help of matchers of Table 1) a matrix of relations between all the pairs of atomic concepts of labels from both trees.

```
700. String[][] fillCLabMatrix(Tree of Nodes source, target);
710. String[][] cLabsMatrix;
720. String[] matchers;
730. int i,j;
740. matchers=getMatchers();
750. for each sourceAtomicConceptOfLabel in source
760.   i=getACoLID(sourceAtomicConceptOfLabel);
770.   for each targetAtomicConceptOfLabel in target
780.     j= getACoLID(targetAtomicConceptOfLabel);
790.     cLabsMatrix[i][j]=getRelation(matchers,
                    sourceAtomicConceptOfLabel,targetAtomicConceptOfLabel);
795. return cLabsMatrix
800. String getRelation(String[] matchers,
                              AtomicConceptOfLabel source, target)
810.   String matcher;
820.   String relation="Idk";
830.   int i=0;
840.   while ((i<sizeof(matchers))&&(relation=="Idk"))
850.     matcher= matchers[i];
860.     relation=executeMatcher(matcher,source,target);
870.     i++;
880.   return relation;
```

Fig. 6. Label matching pseudo code

fillCLabMatrix takes as input two trees of nodes. It produces as output the matrix of semantic relations holding between the atomic concepts of labels in both trees. First, the element level matchers of Table 1, which are to be executed (based on the configuration settings), are acquired in line 740. Then, for each pair of atomic concepts of labels in both trees, semantic relations holding between them are determined by using the **getRelation** function (line 790).

getRelation takes as input an array of *matchers* and two atomic concepts of labels. It returns the semantic relation holding between this pair of atomic concepts of labels according to the element level matchers. These label matchers are executed (line 860) until the semantic relation different from *Idk* is produced. Notice that execution order is defined by the *matchers* array.

The result of *Step 3* is a matrix of the relations holding between atomic concepts of labels. A part of this matrix for the example in Figure 1 is shown in Table 2.

Table 2. *cLabsMatrix:* matrix of relations among the atomic concepts of labels

A \ B	Classes	History	Modern	Europe
Courses	=	idk	idk	idk
History	idk	=	idk	idk
Medieval	idk	idk	⊥	idk
Asia	idk	idk	idk	⊥

6 Step 4: Node Matching

During this step, we initially reformulate the tree matching problem into a set of node matching problems (one problem for each pair of nodes). Finally, we translate each node matching problem into a propositional validity problem. Let us first discuss in detail the tree matching algorithm. Then, we consider the node matching algorithm.

6.1 The Tree Matching Algorithm

The tree matching algorithm is concerned with decomposition of the tree matching task into a set of node matching tasks. It takes as input two preprocessed trees obtained as a result of *Steps 1,2* and a matrix of semantic relations holding between the atomic concepts of labels in both trees obtained as a result of *Step 3*. It produces as output the matrix of semantic relations holding between concepts at nodes in both trees. The pseudo code in Figure 7 illustrates the tree matching algorithm.

```
900.String[][] treeMatch(Tree of Nodes source, target, String[][]
cLabsMatrix)
910. Node sourceNode,targetNode;
920. String[][]cNodesMatrix, relMatrix;
930. String axioms, context_A, context_B;
940. int i,j;
960. For each sourceNode in source
970.   i=getNodeId(sourceNode);
980.   context_A=getCnodeFormula (sourceNode);
990.   For each targetNode in target
1000.     j=getNodeId(targetNode);
1010.     context_B=getCnodeFormula (targetNode);
1020.     relMatrix=extractRelMatrix(cLabsMatrix, sourceNode,
                                                 targetNode);
1030.     axioms=mkAxioms(relMatrix);
1040.     cNodesMatrix[i][j]=nodeMatch(axioms,context_A,context_B);
1050. return cNodesMatrix;
```

Fig. 7. The pseudo code of the tree matching algorithm

treeMatch takes two trees of *Nodes* (*source* and *target*) and the matrix of relations holding between atomic concepts of labels (*cLabsMatrix*) as input. It starts from two loops over all the nodes of source and target trees in lines 960-1040 and 990-1040. The node matching problems are constructed within these loops. For each node matching problem we take a pair of propositional formulas encoding concepts at nodes and relevant relations holding between the atomic concepts of labels using the **getCnodeFormula** and **extractRelMatrix** functions respectively. The former are memorized as $context_A$ and $context_B$ in lines 980 and 1010. The latter are memorized in *relMatrix* in line 1020. In order to reason about relations between concepts at nodes, we build the premises (*axioms*) in line 1030. These are a conjunction of the concepts of labels which are related in *relMatrix*. For example, the semantic relations in Table 2, which are considered when we match C_4 in the tree A and C_4 in the tree B are $Classes_B = Courses_A$ and $History_B = History_A$. In this case *axioms* is $(Classes_B \leftrightarrow Courses_A) \wedge (History_B \leftrightarrow History_A)$. Finally, in line 1040, the semantic relations holding between the concepts at nodes are calculated by **node-Match** and are reported as a bidimensional array (*cNodesMatrix*). A part of this matrix for the example in Figure 1 is shown in Table 3.

Table 3. *cNodesMatrix*: matrix of relations among the concepts at nodes (matching result)

A \ B	C_1	C_4	C_{14}	C_{17}
C_1	$=$	$\sqsupseteq$	$\sqsupseteq$	$\sqsupseteq$
C_4	$\sqsubseteq$	$=$	$\sqsupseteq$	$\sqsupseteq$
C_{12}	$\sqsubseteq$	$\sqsubseteq$	$\perp$	$\perp$
C_{16}	$\sqsubseteq$	$\sqsubseteq$	$\perp$	$\perp$

6.2 The Node Matching Algorithm

Each node matching problem is converted into a propositional validity problem. Semantic relations are translated into propositional connectives using the rules described in Table 4 (second column).

Table 4. The relationship between semantic relations and propositional formulas

$rel(a,b)$	Translation of $rel(a, b)$ into propositional logic	Translation of Eq. 2 into Conjunctive Normal Form
$a = b$	$a \leftrightarrow b$	*N/A*
$a \sqsubseteq b$	$a \to b$	$axioms \wedge context_A \wedge \neg context_B$
$a \sqsupseteq b$	$b \to a$	$axioms \wedge context_B \wedge \neg context_A$
$a \perp b$	$\neg(a \wedge b)$	$axioms \wedge context_A \wedge context_B$

The criterion for determining whether a relation holds between concepts of nodes is the fact that it is entailed by the premises. Thus, we have to prove that the following formula:

$$(axioms) \to rel(context_A, context_B), \tag{1}$$

is valid, namely that it is *true* for all the truth assignments of all the propositional variables occurring in it. *axioms*, *context$_A$*, and *context$_B$* are as defined in the tree matching algorithm. *rel* is the semantic relation that we want to prove holding between *context$_A$* and *context$_B$*. The algorithm checks the validity of Eq. 1 by proving that its negation, i.e., Eq. 2, is unsatisfiable.

$$axioms \wedge \neg \; rel(context_A, context_B) \qquad (2)$$

Table 4 (third column) describes how Eq. 2 is translated before testing each semantic relation. Notice that Eq. 2 is in Conjunctive Normal Form (CNF), namely it is a conjunction of disjunctions of atomic formulas. The check for equivalence is omitted in Table 4, since $A=B$ holds if and only if $A \sqsubseteq B$ and $A \sqsupseteq B$ hold, i.e., both *axioms∧context$_A$∧¬context$_B$* and *axioms∧context$_B$∧¬context$_A$* are unsatisfiable formulas.

We assume the labels of nodes and the knowledge derived from element level semantic matchers to be all globally consistent. Under this assumption the only reason why we get an unsatisfiable formula is because we have found a match between two nodes. In fact, *axioms* cannot be inconsistent by construction. Consistency of *context$_A$* and *context$_B$* is checked in the preprocessing phase (see, Section 4 for details). However, *axioms* and *contexts* (for example, *axioms∧context$_A$*) can be mutually inconsistent. The situation occurs, for example, when *axioms* entails negation of the variable occurring in the *context*. In this case, the concepts at nodes are disjoint. In order to guarantee the correct behavior of the algorithm we perform the disjointness test first. It does not influence the algorithm correctness in general but allow us to obtain the correct result in this special case.

Let us consider the pseudo code of a basic node matching algorithm, see Figure 8. In line 1110, **nodeMatch** constructs the formula for testing disjointness. In line 1120, it converts the formula into CNF, while in line 1130 it checks the CNF formula for unsatisfiability. If the formula is unsatisfiable the disjointness relation is returned.

```
1100.String nodeMatch(String axioms, context_A, context_B)
1110.  formula= And(axioms, context_A, context_B);
1120.  formulaInCNF=convertToCNF(formula);
1130.  boolean isOpposite= isUnsatisfiable(formulaInCNF);
1140.  if (isOpposite)
1150.    return "⊥";
1160.  String formula=And(axioms,context_A,Not(context_B));
1170.  String formulaInCNF=convertToCNF(formula);
1180.  boolean isLG=isUnsatisfiable(formulaInCNF)
1190.  formula=And(axioms, Not(context_A), context_B);
1200.  formulaInCNF=convertToCNF(formula);
1210.  boolean isMG= isUnsatisfiable(formulaInCNF);
1220.  if (isMG && isLG)
1230.    return "=";
1240.  if (isLG)
1250.    return "⊑";
1260.  if (isMG)
1270.    return "⊒";
1280.  return "Idk";
```

Fig. 8. The pseudo code of the node matching algorithm

Then, the process is repeated for the less and more general relations. If both relations hold, then the equivalence relation is returned (line 1220). If all the tests fail, the *idk* relation is returned (line 1280). In order to check the unsatisfiability of a propositional formula in a basic version of our **NodeMatch** algorithm we use the standard DPLL-based SAT solver [31].

From the example in Figure 1, trying to prove that C_4 in the tree B is less general than C_4 in the tree A, requires constructing the following formula:

$$((Classes_B \leftrightarrow Courses_A) \wedge (History_B \leftrightarrow History_A)) \wedge$$

$$(Classes_B \wedge History_B) \wedge \neg (Courses_A \wedge History_A)$$

The above formula turns out to be unsatisfiable, and therefore, the less general relation holds. Notice, if we test for the more general relation between the same pair of concepts at nodes, the corresponding formula would be also unsatisfiable. Thus, the final relation retuned by the **NodeMatch** algorithm for the given pair of concepts at nodes is the equivalence.

7 Semantic Matching with Attributes

So far we have focused on classifications, which are simple class hierarchies. If we deal with, e.g., XML schemas, their elements may have attributes, see Figure 9.

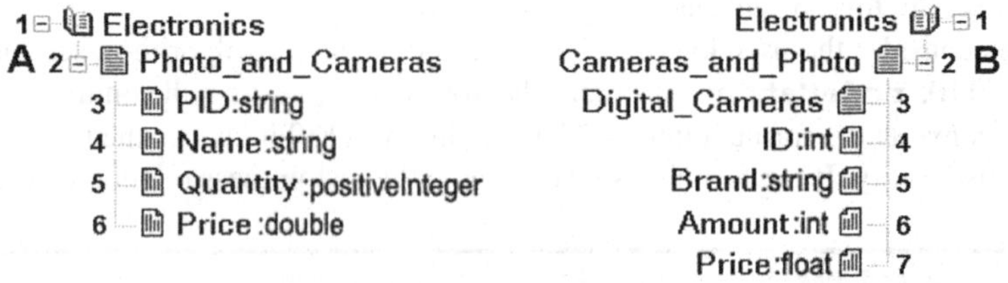

1⊟ 🕮 Electronics
A 2⊟ 📄 Photo_and_Cameras
3 ┈ 📄 PID:string
4 ┈ 📄 Name:string
5 ┈ 📄 Quantity:positiveInteger
6 ┈ 📄 Price:double

Electronics 📖 ⊟1
Cameras_and_Photo 📄 ⊟2 B
Digital_Cameras 📄 3
ID:int 📄 4
Brand:string 📄 5
Amount:int 📄 6
Price:float 📄 7

Fig. 9. Two simple XML schemas

Attributes are ⟨*attribute–name, type*⟩ pairs associated with elements. Names for the attributes are usually chosen such that they describe the roles played by the domains in order to ease distinguishing between their different uses. For example, in the tree A, the attributes *PID* and *Name* are defined on the same domain *string*, but their intended use are the internal (unique) product identification and representation of the official products' names, respectively. There are no strict rules telling us when data should be represented as elements, or as attributes, and obviously there is always more than one way to encode the same data. For example, in the tree A, *PIDs* are encoded as *strings*, while in the tree B, *IDs* are encoded as *ints*. However, both attributes serve for the same purpose of the unique products' identification. These observations suggest two possible ways to perform semantic matching with attributes: (i) taking into account datatypes, and (ii) ignoring datatypes.

The semantic matching approach is based on the idea of matching concepts, not their direct physical implementations, such as elements or attributes. If names of attributes and elements are abstract entities, therefore, they allow for building arbitrary concepts out of them. Instead, datatypes, being concrete entities, are limited in this sense. Thus, a plausible way to match attributes using the semantic matching approach is to discard the information about datatypes. In order to support this claim, let us consider both cases in turn.

7.1 Exploiting Datatypes

In order to reason with datatypes we have created a *datatype ontology*, O_D, specified in OWL [45]. It describes the most often used XML schema built-in datatypes and relations between them. The backbone taxonomy of O_D is based on the following rule: *the is-a relationship holds between two datatypes if and only if their value spaces are related by set inclusion.* Some examples of axioms of O_D are: float $\sqsubseteq$ double, int $\perp$ string, anyURI $\sqsubseteq$ string, and so on. Let us discuss how datatypes are plugged within the four macro steps of the algorithm.

Steps 1,2. Compute concepts of labels and nodes. In order to handle attributes, we extend propositional description logics with the quantification construct and datatypes. Thus, we compute concepts of labels and concepts at nodes as formulas in the description logics $ALC(D)$ language [38]. For example, in the tree A in Figure 9, C_4, namely, the concept at node describing all the string data instances which are the names of electronic photography products is encoded as follows: $Electronics_A \sqcap (Photo_A \sqcap Cameras_A) \sqcap \exists Name_A.string$.

Step 3. Compute relations among concepts of labels. In this step we extend our library of element level matchers by adding a *Datatype* matcher. It takes as input two datatypes, it queries O_D and retrieves a semantic relation between them. For example, from axioms of O_D, the *Datatype* matcher can learn that float $\sqsubseteq$ double, and so on.

Step 4. Compute relations among concepts at nodes. In the case of attributes, the node matching problem is translated into an $ALC(D)$ formula, which is further checked for its unsatisfiability using sound and complete procedures. Notice that in this case we have to test for modal satisfiability, not propositional satisfiability. The system we use is Racer [27]. From the example in Figure 9, trying to prove that C_7 in the tree B is less general than C_6 in the tree A, requires constructing the following formula:

$$((Electronics_A = Electronics_B) \sqcap (Photo_A = Photo_B) \sqcap$$
$$(Cameras_A = Cameras_B) \sqcap (Price_A = Price_B) \sqcap (float \sqsubseteq double)) \sqcap$$
$$(Electronics_B \sqcap (Cameras_B \sqcup Photo_B) \sqcap \exists Price_B.float) \sqcap \neg$$
$$(Electronics_A \sqcap (Photo_A \sqcup Cameras_A) \sqcap \exists Price_A.double)$$

It turns out that the above formula is unsatisfiable. Therefore, C_7 in the tree B is less general than C_6 in the tree A. However, this result is not what the user expects. In fact, both C_6 in the tree A and C_7 in the tree B describe prices of electronic products, which are photo cameras. The storage format of *prices* in A and B (i.e., *double* and *float* respectively) is not an issue at this level of detail.

Thus, another semantic solution of taking into account datatypes would be to build abstractions out of the datatypes, e.g., float, double, decimal should be abstracted to type numeric, while token, name, normalizedString should be abstracted to type string, and so on. However, even such abstractions do not improve the situation, since we may have, for example, an *ID* of type numeric in the first schema, and a conceptually equivalent *ID*, but of type string, in the second schema. If we continue building such abstractions, we result in having that numeric is equivalent to string in the sense that they are both datatypes.

The last observation suggests that for the semantic matching approach to be correct, we should assume that all the datatypes are equivalent. Technically, in order to implement this assumption, we should add corresponding axioms (e.g., float = double) to the premises of Eq. 1. On the one hand, with respect to the case of not considering datatypes (see, Section 7.2), such axioms do not affect the matching result from the quality viewpoint. On the other hand, datatypes make the matching problem computationally more expensive by requiring to handle the quantification construct.

7.2 Ignoring Datatypes

In this case, information about datatypes is discarded. For example, ⟨*Name, string*⟩ becomes *Name*. Then, the semantic matching algorithm builds concepts of labels out of attributes' names in the same way as it does in the case of elements' names, and so on. Finally, it computes mapping elements using the algorithm of Section 6. A part of the cNodesMatrix with relations holding between attributes for the example in Figure 9 is presented in Table 5. Notice that this solution allows a mappings' computation not only between the attributes, but also between attributes and elements.

Table 5. Attributes: the matrix of semantic relations holding between concepts of nodes (the matching result) for Figure 9

A　　　　B	C_4	C_5	C_6	C_7
C_3	=	*idk*	*idk*	*idk*
C_4	*idk*	⊒	*idk*	*idk*
C_5	*idk*	*idk*	=	*idk*
C_6	*idk*	*idk*	*idk*	=

The task of determining mappings typically represents a first step towards the ultimate goal of, for example, data translation, query mediation, agent communication, and so on. Although information about datatypes will be necessary for accomplishing an ultimate goal, we do not discuss this issue any further since in this paper we concentrate only on the mappings discovery task.

8 Efficient Semantic Matching

The node matching problem in semantic matching is a CO-NP hard problem, since it is reduced to the validity problem for the propositional calculus. In this section we present a set of optimizations for the node matching algorithm. In particular, we show that when dealing with *conjunctive concepts at nodes*, i.e., the concept at node is a conjunction (e.g., C_7 in the tree A in Figure 1 is defined as $Asian_A \sqcap Languages_A$), the node matching tasks can be solved in linear time. When we have *disjunctive concepts at nodes*, i.e., the concept at node contains both conjunctions and disjunctions in any order (e.g., C_3 in the tree B in Figure 1 is defined as $College_B \sqcap (Arts_B \sqcup Sciences_B)$), we use techniques allowing us to avoid the exponential space explosion which arises due to the conversion of disjunctive formulas into CNF. This modification is required since all state of the art SAT deciders take CNF formulas in input.

8.1 Conjunctive Concepts at Nodes

Let us make some observations with respect to Table 4 (Section 6.2). The first observation is that the *axioms* part remains the same for all the tests, and it contains only clauses with two variables. In the worst case, it contains $2 \times n_A \times n_B$ clauses, where n_A and n_B are the number of atomic concepts of labels occurred in $context_A$ and $context_B$, respectively. The second observation is that the formulas for testing less and more general relations are very similar and they differ only in the negated context formula (e.g., in the test for less general relation $context_B$ is negated). This means that Eq. 2 contains one clause with n_B variables plus n_A clauses with one variable. In the case of disjointness test $context_A$ and $context_B$ are not negated. Therefore, formula Eq. 2 contains $n_A + n_B$ clauses with one variable.

8.1.1 The Node Matching Problem by an Example

Let us suppose that we want to match C_{16} in the tree A and C_{17} in the tree B in Figure 1. The relevant semantic relations between atomic concepts of labels are presented in Table 2. Thus, *axioms* is as follows:

$$(course_A \leftrightarrow class_B) \wedge (history_A \leftrightarrow history_B) \wedge$$
$$\neg (medieval_A \wedge modern_B) \wedge \neg (asia_A \wedge europe_B) \tag{3}$$

which, when translated in CNF, becomes:

$$(\neg course_A \vee class_B) \wedge (course_A \vee \neg class_B) \wedge (\neg history_A \vee history_B) \wedge$$
$$(history_A \vee \neg history_B) \wedge (\neg medieval_A \vee \neg modern_B) \wedge (\neg asia_A \vee \neg europe_B) \tag{4}$$

As from *Step 2*, $context_A$ and $context_B$ are constructed by taking the conjunction of the concepts of labels in the path from the node under consideration to the root. Therefore, $context_A$ and $context_B$ are:

$$course_A \wedge history_A \wedge medieval_A \wedge asia_A \tag{5}$$

$$class_B \wedge history_B \wedge modern_B \wedge europe_B \tag{6}$$

while their negations are:

$$\neg course_A \vee \neg history_A \vee \neg medieval_A \vee \neg asia_A \tag{7}$$

$$\neg class_B \vee \neg history_B \vee \neg modern_B \vee \neg europe_B \tag{8}$$

So far we have concentrated on atomic concepts of labels. The propositional formulas remain structurally the same if we move to conjunctive concepts at labels. Let consider the following example:

| 1 ⊟ Course of history | Classes history ⊟ 1 |
| A 2   Medieval Asia | Modern Europe   2 B |

Fig. 10. Two simple classifications (obtained by modifying, pruning the example in Figure 1)

Suppose we want to match C_2 in the tree A and C_2 in the tree B in Figure 10. Axioms required for this matching task are as follows: $(course_A \leftrightarrow class_B) \land (history_A \leftrightarrow history_B) \land (medieval_A \sqsubseteq modern_B) \land (asia_A \sqsubseteq europe_B)$. If we compare them with those of Eq. 3 and Eq.4, which represent axioms for the above considered example in Figure 1, we find out that they are the same. Furthermore, as from *Step 2*, the propositional formulas for $context_A$ and $context_B$ are the same for atomic and for conjunctive concepts of labels as long as they "globally" contain the same formulas. In fact, concepts at nodes are constructed by taking the conjunction of concepts at labels. Splitting a concept of a label with two conjuncts into two atomic concepts has no effect on the resulting matching formula. The matching result for the matching tasks in Figure 10 is presented in Table 6.

Table 6. The matrix of relations between concepts at nodes (matching result) for Figure 10

A ╲ B	C_1	C_2
C_1	=	⊒
C_2	⊑	⊥

8.1.2 Optimizations

Tests for less and more general relations. Using the observations in the beginning of Section 8.1 concerning Table 4, Eq. 2, with respect to the tests for less/more general relations, can be represented as follows:

$$\overbrace{\underset{q=0}{\overset{n*m}{\bigwedge}}(\neg A_s \lor B_t) \land \underset{w=0}{\overset{n*m}{\bigwedge}}(A_k \lor \neg B_l) \land \underset{v=0}{\overset{n*m}{\bigwedge}}(\neg A_p \lor \neg B_r) \land}^{Axioms} \overbrace{\underset{i=1}{\overset{n}{\bigwedge}} A_i}^{Context_A} \land \overbrace{\underset{j=1}{\overset{m}{\bigvee}} \neg B_j}^{\neg Context_B} \tag{9}$$

where n is the number of variables in $context_A$, m is the number of variables in $context_B$. The A_i's belong to $context_A$, and the B_j's belong to $context_B$. s, k, p are in the $[0..n]$ range, while t, l, r are in the $[0..m]$ range. q, w and v define the number of particular clauses. *Axioms* can be empty. Eq. 9 is composed of clauses with one or two variables plus one clause with possibly more variables (the clause corresponding to the negated context). The key observation is that the formula in Eq. 9 is *Horn*, i.e., each clause contains at most one positive literal. Therefore, its satisfiability can be decided in linear time by the *unit resolution rule* [9]. Notice, that DPLL-based SAT solvers require quadratic time in this case [47].

In order to understand how the linear time algorithm works, let us prove the unsatisfiability of Eq. 9 in the case of matching C_{16} in the tree A and C_{17} in the tree B in Figure 1. In this case, Eq. 9 is as follows:

$$(\neg course_A \vee class_B) \wedge (course_A \vee \neg class_B) \wedge (\neg history_A \vee history_B) \wedge$$
$$(history_A \vee \neg history_B) \wedge (\neg medieval_A \vee \neg modern_B) \wedge (\neg asia_A \vee \neg europe_B) \wedge$$
$$course_A \wedge history_A \wedge medieval_A \wedge asia_A \wedge \tag{10}$$
$$(\neg class_B \vee \neg history_B \vee \neg modern_B \vee \neg europe_B)$$

In Eq.10, the variables from $context_A$ are written in bold face. First, we assign *true* to all unit clauses occurring in Eq. 10 positively. Notice these are all and only the clauses in $context_A$. This allows us to discard the clauses where $context_A$ variables occur positively (in this case: $course_A \vee \neg class_B$, $history_A \vee \neg history_B$). The resulting formula is as follows:

$$class_B \wedge history_B \wedge \neg modern_B \wedge \neg europe_B \wedge$$
$$(\neg class_B \vee \neg history_B \vee \neg modern_B \vee \neg europe_B) \tag{11}$$

Eq. 11 does not contain any variable derived from $context_A$. Notice that, by assigning *true* to $class_B$, $history_B$ and *false* to $modern_B$, $europe_B$ we do not derive a contradiction. Therefore, Eq. 10 is satisfiable. In fact, a (Horn) formula is unsatisfiable if and only if the empty clause is derived (and it is satisfiable otherwise).

Let us consider again Eq. 11. For this formula to be unsatisfiable, all the variables occurring in the negation of $context_B$ ($\neg class_B \vee \neg history_B \vee \neg modern_B \vee \neg europe_B$ in our example) should occur positively in the unit clauses obtained after resolving *axioms* with the unit clauses in $context_A$ ($class_B$ and $history_B$ in our example). For this to happen, for any B_j in $context_B$ there must be a clause of form $\neg A_i \vee B_j$ in *axioms*, where A_i is a formula of $context_A$. Formulas of the form $\neg A_i \vee B_j$ occur in Eq. 9 if and only if we have the axioms of form $A = B_j$ and $A_i \sqsubseteq B_j$. These considerations suggest the following algorithm for testing satisfiability:

- Step 1. Create an array of size m. Each entry in the array stands for one B_j in Eq. 9.
- Step 2. For each axiom of type $A_i = B_j$ and $A_i \sqsubseteq B_j$ mark the corresponding B_j.
- Step 3. If all the B_j's are marked, then the formula is unsatisfiable.

To complete the analysis, let us now suppose that we have not "*europe*", but "*except europe*" as a node of the tree depicted in Figure 1. This means that $context_B$ contains the negated variable $\neg europe_B$. Eq. 10 in this case is rewritten as follows:

$$(\neg course_A \vee class_B) \wedge (course_A \vee \neg class_B) \wedge (\neg history_A \vee history_B) \wedge$$
$$(history_A \vee \neg history_B) \wedge (\neg medieval_A \vee \neg modern_B) \wedge (\neg asia_A \vee \neg europe_B) \wedge$$
$$course_A \wedge history_A \wedge medieval_A \wedge asia_A \wedge \tag{12}$$
$$(\neg class_B \vee \neg history_B \vee \neg modern_B \vee europe_B)$$

Suppose that we have replaced all the occurrences of $\neg europe_B$ and $europe_B$ in the formula with $europe_{nB}$ and $\neg europe_{nB}$ respectively. In fact, we replace the variable with the new one which represents its negation. Notice that this replacement does not change the satisfiability properties of the formula. Truth assignment satisfying the new formula will satisfy the original formula after inverting the truth value of the new variable (*europe$_{nB}$* in our example). Notice also that the replacement changed the clause with *europe$_B$* variable in *axioms* (*$\neg asia_A \lor europe_{nB}$* in Eq. 13).

$$(\neg course_A \lor class_B) \land (course_A \lor \neg class_B) \land (\neg history_A \lor history_B) \land$$
$$(history_A \lor \neg history_B) \land (\neg medieval_A \lor \neg modern_B) \land (\neg asia_A \lor europe_{nB}) \land \tag{13}$$
$$course_A \land history_A \land medieval_A \land asia_A \land$$
$$(\neg class_B \lor \neg history_B \lor \neg modern_B \lor \neg europe_{nB})$$

Let us assign to *true* the unit clauses occurring in Eq. 13 positively. This allows us to discard a number of clauses. A simplified formula is depicted as Eq. 14.

$$class_B \land history_B \land \neg modern_B \land europe_B \land$$
$$(\neg class_B \lor \neg history_B \lor \neg modern_B \lor \neg europe_{nB}) \tag{14}$$

This formula is satisfiable by assigning *class$_B$*, *history$_B$*, *europe$_B$* to *true* and *modern$_B$* to *false*. Therefore, less general relation does not hold between the concept at node *Asia* and the concept at node *Except Europe*.

In order to construct an optimized algorithm for determining satisfiability of Eq. 13 let us compare Eq. 10 and Eq. 13. The parts of the formula representing contexts are the same. The differences are in axioms part of the formula and they are introduced by a variable replacement. Let us analyze how the replacement of the variable with its negations influences various classes of clauses in axioms, see Table 7.

Table 7. The correspondence between axioms and clauses

Axioms	$A_i \sqsubseteq B_j$ $A_i = B_j$	$B_j \sqsubseteq A_i$ $A_i = B_j$	$A_i \perp B_j$
The classes of propositional clauses With two variables	$\neg A_i \lor B_j$	$A_i \lor \neg B_j$	$\neg A_i \lor \neg B_j$
The classes of clauses after replacement of A_i with its negation A_{ni}	$A_{ni} \lor B_j$	$\neg A_{ni} \lor \neg B_j$	$A_{ni} \lor \neg B_j$
The classes of clauses after replacement of B_j with its negation B_{nj}	$\neg A_i \lor \neg B_{nj}$	$A_i \lor B_{nj}$	$\neg A_i \lor B_{nj}$
The classes of clauses after replacement of A_i and B_j with their negations A_{ni} and B_{ni} respectively	$A_{ni} \lor \neg B_j$	$\neg A_{ni} \lor B_j$	$A_{ni} \lor B_j$

Let us concentrate on three classes of propositional clauses depicted in the second row of Table 7. As from Eq. 9, we have only these classes of clauses in *axioms*. The axioms from which the particular class of clauses can be derived are described in the first column. Rows 2-5 demonstrate how the replacement of variables with its negation influences the clause. The first observation from Table 7 is that the new class of clauses ($A_i \lor B_j$) is introduced in *axioms*. The variables derived from both *context$_A$* and *context$_B$* occur in these clauses positively. This means that the clauses of form $A_i \lor B_j$ are discarded from the formula after unit propagation and cannot influence its satisfiability properties. The second observation is that all other clauses in Eq. 13 belong to the same classes as ones in Eq. 10. Therefore, the general observation made for Eq. 10 (namely, the formula is satisfiable if and only if there are clauses $\neg A_i \lor B_j$ in *axioms* for any B_j in *context$_B$*) holds for Eq. 13. As from Table 7, we have the clauses $\neg A_i \lor B_j$ in Eq. 13 in three cases:

- There are axioms $A_i = B_j$ and $A_i \sqsubseteq B_j$, where A_i and B_j occur in *contexts* of the original formula positively.

- There are axioms $A_i = B_j$ and $B_j \sqsubseteq A_i$, where A_i and B_j occur in *contexts* of the original formula negatively.
- There are axioms $A_i \perp B_j$, where A_i occurs in *context_A* of the original formula positively and B_j occurs in *context_B* of the original formula negatively.

These considerations suggest the following algorithm for testing the satisfiability (notice Step1 and Step 3 remain the same as in the previous version):

- Step 1. Create an array of size m. Each entry in the array stands for one B_j in Eq. 9.
- Step 2a. If A_i and B_j occur positively in *context_A* and *context_B* respectively, for each axiom $A_i{=}B_j$ and $A_i \sqsubseteq B_j$ mark the corresponding B_j.
- Step 2b. If A_i and B_j occur negatively in *context_A* and *context_B* respectively, for each axiom $A_i{=}B_j$ and $B_j \sqsubseteq A_i$ mark the corresponding B_j.
- Step 2c. If B_j occurs negatively in *context_B* and A_i occurs positively in *context_A* for each axiom $A_i \perp B_j$ mark the corresponding B_j.
- Step 3. If all the B_j's are marked, then the formula is unsatisfiable.

The pseudo code of the optimized algorithm is presented in Figure 11.

```
1155.  if (contextA and contextB are conjunctive)
1156.    isLG=fastHornUnsatCheck (contextA, contextB, axioms, "⊑", "⊒");
1157.    isMG=fastHornUnsatCheck (contextB, contextA, axioms, "⊒", "⊑");
1158.  else

1500.boolean fastHornUnsatCheck(String context, neg_context, axioms,
rel, neg_rel)
1510.  int m=getNumOfVar(String neg_context);
1520.  boolean array[m];
1530.  for each axiom in axioms
1540.   String Ai= getFirstVariable(axiom);
1550.   String Bj= getSecondVariable(axiom);
1560.   int j=getNumberInContext(Bj);
1570.   if((occurs_positevely (Ai, context))&&
                          (occurs_positevely (Bj, neg_context)))
1580.    if((getAType(axiom)="=")||(getAType(axiom)=rel))
1590.     array[j]=true;
1600.   if ((occurs_negatively (Ai, context))&&
                          (occurs_negatively (Bj, neg_context)))
1610.    if((getAType(axiom)="=")||(getAType(axiom)=neg_rel))
1620.     array[j]=true;
1630.   if ((occurs_positevely (Ai, context))&&
                          (occurs_negatively (Bj, neg_context)))
1640.    if(getAType(axiom)="⊥")
1650.     array[j]=true;
1660.  for (i=0; i<m; i++)
1670.   if (!array[i])
1680.    return false;
1690.  return true;
```

Fig. 11. Optimization pseudo code of tests for less and more general relations

Thus, **nodeMatch** can be modified as in Figure 11 (the numbers on the left indicate where the new code must be positioned). **fastHornUnsatCheck** implements the three steps above. Step 1 is performed in lines (1510-1520). Then, a loop on *axioms* (lines 1530-1650) implements Step 2. The final loop (lines 1660-1690) implements Step 3.

Disjointness test. Using the same notation as before in this section, Eq. 2 with respect to the disjointness test can be represented as follows:

$$\overbrace{\overset{n*m}{\underset{q=0}{\bigwedge}}(\neg A_s \vee B_t) \wedge \overset{n*m}{\underset{w=0}{\bigwedge}}(A_k \vee \neg B_l) \wedge \overset{n*m}{\underset{v=0}{\bigwedge}}(\neg A_p \vee \neg B_r)}^{Axioms} \wedge \overbrace{\overset{n}{\underset{i=1}{\bigwedge}} A_i}^{Context_A} \wedge \overbrace{\overset{m}{\underset{j=1}{\bigwedge}} B_j}^{Context_B} \tag{15}$$

For example, the formula for testing disjointness between C_{16} in the tree A and C_{17} in the tree B in Figure 1 is as follows:

$$(\neg course_A \vee class_B) \wedge (course_A \vee \neg class_B) \wedge (\neg history_A \vee history_B) \wedge$$
$$(history_A \vee \neg history_B) \wedge (\neg medieval_A \vee \neg modern_B) \wedge (\neg asia_A \vee \neg europe_B) \wedge \tag{16}$$
$$course_A \wedge history_A \wedge medieval_A \wedge asia_A \wedge class_B \wedge history_B \wedge modern_B \wedge europe_B$$

Eq. 16 is Horn, and thus, similarly to Eq. 10, the satisfiability of this formula can be decided by the unit propagation rule. After assigning *true* to all the variables in *context$_A$* and propagating the results we obtain the following formula:

$$class_B \wedge history_B \wedge \neg modern_B \wedge \neg europe_B \wedge class_B \wedge history_B \wedge modern_B \wedge europe_B \tag{17}$$

If we further unit propagate *class$_B$* and *history$_B$* (this means that we assign them to *true*), then we obtain the contradiction $modern_B \wedge \neg modern_B \wedge europe_B \wedge \neg europe_B$. Therefore, the formula is unsatisfiable. This contradiction arises because ($\neg$*medieval$_A$* $\vee \neg$*modern$_B$*) and ($\neg$*asia$_A$* $\vee \neg$*europe$_B$*) occur in Eq. 16, which, in turn, are derived (as from Table 4) from the disjointness axioms $modern_B \bot medieval_A$ and $asia_A \bot europe_B$. In fact, all the clauses in Eq. 15 contain one positive literal except for the clauses in *axioms* corresponding to disjointness relations. Thus, the key intuition here is that if there are no disjointness axioms, then Eq. 15 is satisfiable. However, if there is a disjointness axiom, atoms occurring there are also ensured to be either in *context$_A$* or in *context$_B$*, hence, Eq. 15 is unsatisfiable. Therefore, the optimization consists of just checking the presence/absence of disjointness axioms in *axioms*.

To complete the analysis suppose that we have negated variable in *context$_B$* in the same fashion as described in the example with negations given before in this section. Then, Eq. 16 can be rewritten as follows:

$$(\neg course_A \vee class_B) \wedge (course_A \vee \neg class_B) \wedge (\neg history_A \vee history_B) \wedge$$
$$(history_A \vee \neg history_B) \wedge (\neg medieval_A \vee \neg modern_B) \wedge (\neg asia_A \vee \neg europe_B) \wedge \tag{18}$$
$$course_A \wedge history_A \wedge medieval_A \wedge asia_A \wedge class_B \wedge history_B \wedge modern_B \wedge \neg europe_B$$

As in the case of less general relation all the occurrences of the negated variable are replaced with a new variable representing its negation (i.e., $\neg europe_B$ and $europe_B$ are replaced by $europe_{nB}$ and $\neg europe_{nB}$ respectively), see Eq. 19.

$$(\neg course_A \vee class_B) \wedge (course_A \vee \neg class_B) \wedge (\neg history_A \vee history_B) \wedge$$
$$(history_A \vee \neg history_B) \wedge (\neg medieval_A \vee \neg modern_B) \wedge (\neg asia_A \vee europe_{nB}) \wedge \qquad (19)$$
$$course_A \wedge history_A \wedge medieval_A \wedge asia_A \wedge class_B \wedge history_B \wedge modern_B \wedge europe_{nB}$$

After the unit propagation of the variables derived from $context_A$ we obtain

$$class_B \wedge history_B \wedge \neg modern_B \wedge europe_{nB} \wedge class_B \wedge history_B \wedge modern_B \wedge europe_{nB} \qquad (20)$$

Eq. 20 is satisfiable. This means that the concept at node *Asia* is not disjoint with the concept at node *Except Europe*. The replacement introduces the new class of clauses $A_i \vee B_j$. However, such clauses are discarded after the unit propagation, and therefore, do not influence the satisfiability of the formula. As from Table 7, all other clauses introduced after the replacement belong to the same classes as ones in Eq. 16. This means that the major observation made in this section, namely the fact that the satisfiability of Eq. 16 can be decided by checking the presence/absence of the clauses of form $\neg A_i \vee \neg B_j$ holds for Eq. 19. As from Table 7, we have the clauses of form $\neg A_i \vee \neg B_j$ in Eq. 19 in the following three cases:

– There are axioms of form $A_i \perp B_j$, where both A_i and B_j occur in *contexts* of the original formula positively.
– There are axioms of form $B_j \sqsubseteq A_i$ and $A_i = B_j$, where A_i occurs negatively in $context_A$ of the original formula and B_j occurs positively in $context_B$ of the original formula.
– There are axioms of form $A_i \sqsubseteq B_j$ and $A_i = B_j$, where A_i occurs positively in $context_A$ of the original formula and B_j occurs negatively in $context_B$ of the original formula.

Thus, the pseudo code of **nodeMatch** should be modified as shown in Figure 12.

```
1105.if (context_A and context_B are conjunctive)
1106.  isOpposite=optimizedUnsatTestForDisjointness (axioms, context_A,
context_B);
1107.else

1300. optimizedUnsatTestForDisjointness (axioms, context_A, context_B);
1310. for each axiom in axioms
1320.   String A_i= getFirstVariable(axiom);
1330.   String B_j= getSecondVariable(axiom);
1340.   if ((occurs_positively (A_i, context_A))&&
                              (occurs_positively (B_j, context_B)))
1350.    if (getAType(axiom)="⊥")
1360.      return true;
1370.    if ((occurs_negatively (A_i, context_A))&&
                              (occurs_positively (B_j, context_B)))
1380.    if((getAType(axiom)="=")||(getAType(axiom)="⊒"))
1390.      return true;
1400.    if ((occurs_positevely (A_i, context_A))&&
                              (occurs_negatively (B_j, context_B)))
1410.    if((getAType(axiom)="=")||(getAType(axiom)="⊑"))
1420.      return true;
1430. return false;
```

Fig. 12. Disjointness test optimization pseudo code

optimizedUnsatTestForDisjointness check three conditions listed above. The first condition is checked in lines 1340-1360. In lines 1370-1390 the second condition is checked. Finally, the third condition is checked in lines 1400-1420.

8.2 Disjunctive Concepts at Nodes

8.2.1 The Node Matching Problem by an Example

Now, we allow for the concepts at nodes to contain conjunctions and disjunctions in any order. Suppose, we want to match C_5 in the tree A and C_5 in the tree B in Figure 1. The relevant part of `cLabsMatrix` is shown in Table 8.

Table 8. `cLabsMatrix:` matrix of relations among the atomic concepts of labels

A ＼ B	Classes	Mechanics	Optics	Statistics	Dynamics	Kinematics
Courses	=					
Biology						
Zoology						
Botany						
Neurobiology						
Genetics						
Physiology						

As from Table 4, the *axioms* is as follows:

$$(course_A \leftrightarrow class_B) \tag{21}$$

Eq.21 in CNF then becomes:

$$(\neg course_A \lor class_B) \land (course_A \lor \neg class_B) \tag{22}$$

As from *Step 2*, $context_A$ and $context_B$ are:

$$class_B \land (mechanics_B \lor optics_B \lor thermodynamics_B) \land \\ (statics_B \lor dynamics_B \lor kinematics_B) \tag{23}$$

$$course_A \land (biology_A \lor zoology_A \lor botany_A) \land \\ (neurobiology_A \lor genetics_A \lor physiology_A) \tag{24}$$

The negations of $context_A$ and $context_B$, in turn, are:

$$\neg class_B \lor (\neg mechanics_B \land \neg optics_B \land \neg thermodynamics_B) \lor \\ (\neg statics_B \land \neg dynamics_B \land \neg kinematics_B) \tag{25}$$

$$\neg course_A \lor (\neg biology_A \land \neg zoology_A \land \neg botany_A) \lor \\ (\neg neurobiology_A \land \neg genetics_A \land \neg physiology_A) \tag{26}$$

The matching result for this task is presented in Table 9.

Table 9. `cNodesMatrix`: matrix of relations among the concepts at nodes (matching result)

A \ B	C_1	C_2	C_5
C_1	=	idk	idk
C_2	idk	idk	idk
C_5	idk	idk	idk

8.2.2 Optimizations

As from Table 4, *axioms* is the same for all the tests. However, $context_A$ and $context_B$ may contain any number of disjunctions. Some of them are coming from the concepts of labels, while others may appear from the negated $context_A$ or $context_B$ (e.g., see tests for less/more general relations). Thus, for instance, as from Table 4 in case of test for less general relation we obtain the following formula:

$$(\neg course_A \vee class_B) \wedge (course_A \vee \neg class_B) \wedge (mechanics_B \vee optics_B \vee$$
$$thermodynamics_B) \wedge (statics_B \vee dynamics_B \vee kinematics_B) \wedge ((\neg biology_A \wedge \qquad (27)$$
$$\neg zoology_A \wedge \neg botany_A) \vee (\neg neurobiology_A \wedge \neg genetics_A \neg physiology_A))$$

With disjunctive concepts at nodes, Eq. 2 is a full propositional formula and no hypothesis can be made on its structure. As a consequence, its satisfiability must be tested using a standard DPLL SAT solver. Thus, for instance, CNF conversion of Eq. 27 is as follows:

$$(\neg course_A \vee class_B) \wedge (course_A \vee \neg class_B) \wedge (mechanics_B \vee optics_B \vee thermody\text{-}$$
$$namics_B) \wedge (statics_B \vee dynamics_B \vee kinematics_B) \wedge ((\neg course_A \vee \neg biol\text{-}$$
$$ogy_A \vee \neg neurobiology_A) \wedge (\neg course_A \vee \neg biology_A \vee \neg genetics_A) \wedge (\neg course_A \vee$$
$$\neg biology_A \vee \neg physiology_A) \wedge (\neg course_A \vee \neg zoology_A \vee \neg neurobiology_A) \wedge (\neg \qquad (28)$$
$$course_A \vee \neg zoology_A \vee \neg genetics_A) \wedge (\neg course_A \vee \neg zoology_A \vee \neg physiology_A) \wedge$$
$$(\neg course_A \vee \neg botany_A \vee \neg neurobiology_A) \wedge (\neg course_A \vee \neg botany_A \vee \neg genet\text{-}$$
$$ics_A) \wedge (\neg course_A \vee \neg botany_A \vee \neg physiology_A))$$

In order to avoid the space explosion, which may arise when converting a formula into CNF (see for instance Eq. 28), we apply a set of structure preserving transformations [41,19]. The main idea is to replace disjunctions occurring in the original formula with newly introduced variables and explicitly state that these variables imply the subformulas they substitute. Consider for instance Eq. 27. We obtain:

$$(\neg course_A \vee class_B) \wedge (course_A \vee \neg class_B) \wedge (mechan\text{-}$$
$$ics_B \vee optics_B \vee thermodynamics_B) \wedge (statics_B \vee dynamics_B \vee kinematics_B) \wedge$$
$$new_1 \wedge new_2 \wedge (new_1 \rightarrow \neg biology_A \vee \neg zoology_A \vee \neg car_A) \wedge \qquad (29)$$
$$(new_2 \rightarrow \neg neurobiology_A \vee \neg genetics_A \vee \neg physiology_A)$$

where new_1 and new_2 stand for newly introduced variables. Eq. 29 is converted into CNF as follows:

$$(\neg course_A \vee class_B) \wedge (course_A \vee \neg class_B) \wedge (mechan\text{-}$$
$$ics_B \vee optics_B \vee thermodynamics_B) \wedge (statics_B \vee dynamics_B \vee kinematics_B) \wedge$$
$$new_1 \wedge new_2 \wedge (\neg new_1 \vee \neg biology_A \vee \neg zoology_A \vee \neg car_A) \wedge \qquad (30)$$
$$(\neg new_2 \vee \neg neurobiology_A \vee \neg genetics_A \vee \neg physiology_A)$$

Notice that the size of the propositional formula in CNF grows linearly with respect to number of disjunctions in original formula. To account for this optimization in **nodeMatch** all calls to **convertToCNF** are replaced with calls to **optimizedConvertToCNF**, (see Figure 13):

```
1120. formulaInCNF=optimizedConvertToCNF(formula);
...
1170. formulaInCNF=optimizedConvertToCNF(formula);
...
1200. formulaInCNF=optimizedConvertToCNF(formula);
```

Fig. 13. The CNF conversion optimization pseudo code

9 Evaluation

In this section, we present the performance and quality evaluation of the matching system we have implemented, called S-Match. In particular, we evaluate basic and optimized versions of our system, called (S-Match$_B$) and (S-Match) respectively, against three state of the art matchers, namely Cupid [32], COMA [11][9], and SF [35] as implemented in Rondo [36]. All the systems under consideration are fairly comparable because they are all schema-based. They differ in the specific matching techniques they use and in the way they compute mappings.

9.1 Evaluation Set-Up

The evaluation was performed on seven matching tasks from different application domains, see Table 10. There are three matching tasks from a business domain (#1,3,5). The first business example (#1) describes two company profiles: a Standard one (mini) and Yahoo Finance (mini), while, #5, represents their full versions. The third business example (#3) deals with BizTalk[10] purchase order schemas. There is one matching task from an academy domain (#2). It describes courses taught at Cornell University (mini) and at the University of Washington (mini). Finally, there are three matching tasks on general topics (#4,6,7) as represented by the well-known web directories, such as Google[11], Yahoo[12], and Looksmart[13]. Table 10 provides some indicators of the complexity of these test cases[14].

The reference mappings (also called expert mappings) for some of these problems (namely for the tasks #1,2,3) were established manually. Then, the results computed

---

[9] We thank to Phil Bernstein, Hong Hai Do, and Erhard Rahm for providing us with Cupid and COMA. In the evaluation we use the version of COMA described in [11]. A newer version of the system COMA++ exists but we do not have it.

[10] http://www.microsoft.com/biztalk/

[11] http://www.google.com/Top/

[12] http://dir.yahoo.com/

[13] http://www.looksmart.com/

[14] Source files and description of the schemas tested can be found at our project web-site, experiments section: http://www.dit.unitn.it/~accord/

Table 10. Some indicators of the complexity of the test cases

#	Matching task	Max. depth	# nodes	# labels	Concepts at nodes
1	*Yahoo(mini)-Standard(mini)*	2/2	10/16	22/45	Conjunctive Disjunctive
2	*Cornell-Washington*	3/3	34/39	62/64	Conjunctive Disjunctive
3	*CIDX – Excel*	3/3	34/39	56/58	Conjunctive Disjunctive
4	*Looksmart-Yahoo*	10/8	140/74	222/101	Conjunctive Disjunctive
5	*Yahoo-Standard*	3/3	333/115	965/242	Conjunctive Disjunctive
6	*Google-Yahoo*	11/11	561/665	722/945	Conjunctive Disjunctive
7	*Google-Looksmart*	11/16	706/1081	1048/1715	Conjunctive Disjunctive

by the systems have been compared with expert mappings. It is worth noticing that the task of creation of expert mappings is an error-prone and a time consuming one. Even if for the moment of writing this paper we have created expert mappings for the biggest matching tasks (#6,7) of Table 10, we do not report these findings in this paper. Addressing in full detail the emerged issues along that process as well as the matching results achieved is out of scope of this paper, see for some details [3,22]. Thus, in this evaluation study we focus mostly on the performance characteristics of S-Match, involving large matching tasks, namely schemas with hundreds and thousands of nodes. Notice, scalability properties of matching systems is among the most important problems of schema matching (in general) these days, see e.g., [7,12]. Quality characteristics of the S-Match results which are presented here address only medium size schemas. We acknowledge that a large-scale quality evaluation is also of high importance. However, we view it as a separate direction, requiring (beyond some preliminary results of [3,22]) further in-depth investigations. Thus, we pose it as future work.

There are three further observations that ensure a fair (qualitative) comparative study. The first observation is that Cupid, COMA, and Rondo can discover only the mappings which express similarity between schema elements. Instead, S-Match, among others, discovers the disjointness relation which can be interpreted as strong dissimilarity in terms of other systems under consideration. Therefore, we did not take into account the disjointness relations when specifying the expert mappings. The second observation is that, since S-Match returns a matrix of relations, while all other systems return a list of the best mappings, we used some filtering rules. More precisely we have the following two rules: (i) discard all the mappings where the relation is *idk*; (ii) return always the *core* relations, and discard relations whose existence is *implied* by the core relations. Finally, whether S-Match returns the equivalence or subsumption relations does not affect the quality indicators. What only matters is the presence of the mappings standing for those relations.

As match quality measures we have used the following indicators: *precision, recall, overall,* and *F-measure. Precision* varies in the [0,1] range; the higher the value, the smaller the set of wrong mappings (false positives) which have been computed. *Precision* is a correctness measure. *Recall* varies in the [0,1] range; the higher the value, the smaller the set of correct mappings (true positives) which have not found. *Recall* is a completeness measure. *F-measure* varies in the [0,1] range. The version computed here is the harmonic mean of *precision* and *recall*. It is a global measure of the matching quality, growing with it. *Overall* is an estimate of the post match efforts needed for adding false negatives and removing false positives. *Overall* varies in the [-1, 1] range; the higher it is, the less post-match efforts are needed. As a performance measure we have used *time*. It estimates how fast systems are when producing mappings fully automatically. Time is very important for us, since it shows the ability of matching systems to scale up.

In our experiments each test has two degrees of freedom: *directionality* and *use of oracles*. By directionality we mean here the direction in which mappings have been computed: from the first schema to the second one (forward direction), or vice versa (backward direction). We report the best results obtained with respect to directionality, and use of oracles allowed. We were not able to plug a thesaurus in Rondo, since the version we have is standalone, and it does not support the use of external thesauri. Thesauri of S-Match, Cupid, and COMA were expanded with terms necessary for a fair competition (e.g., expanding *uom* into *unitOfMeasure*, a complete list is available at the URL in footnote 14).

All the tests have been performed on a P4-1700, with 512 MB of RAM, with the Windows XP operating system, and with no applications running but a single matching system. The systems were limited to allocate no more than 512 MB of memory. All the tuning parameters (e.g., thresholds, combination strategies) of the systems were taken by default (e.g., for COMA we used *NamePath* and *Leaves* matchers combined in the *Average* strategy) for all the tests. S-Match was also used in default configuration, e.g., threshold for string-based matchers was 0.6. This threshold has been defined after experimentation on several schema matching tasks (see for details the URL in footnote 14). Finally, all the element level matchers of the third approximation level (e.g., gloss-based matchers) were not involved in the evaluation since all the matching tasks under consideration were successfully resolved by the matchers of Table 1 which belong to the first and the second approximation levels; see [22] for the preliminary evaluation results of matchers belonging to the third approximation level as well as for the tasks where they are useful.

9.2 Evaluation Results

We present the time performance results for all the tasks of Table 10, while quality results, as from the previous discussion are possible to estimate only for some of the matching tasks (#1,2,3). The evaluation results for the matching problems #1,2,3 are shown in Figure 14.

For example, in Figure 14.2, since all the labels at nodes in the given test case were correctly encoded into propositional formulas, all the quality measures of S-Match reach their highest values. In fact, as discussed before, the propositional SAT solver is correct and complete. This means that once the element level matchers have found all and only the mappings, S-Match will return all of them and only the correct ones.

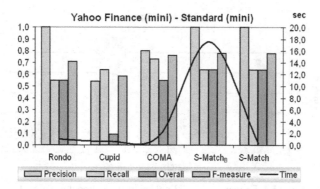

Fig. 14.1. Evaluation results: Yahoo Finance (mini) vs. Standard (mini), test case #1

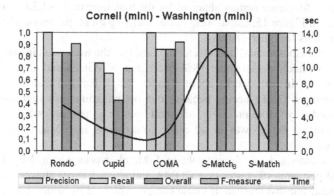

Fig. 14.2. Evaluation results: Cornell (mini) vs. Washington (mini), test case #2

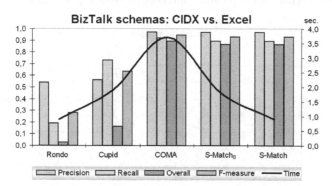

Fig. 14.3. Evaluation results: CIDX vs. Excel, test case #3

For a pair of BizTalk schemas: CIDX vs. Excel, S-Match performs as good as COMA and outperforms other systems in terms of quality indicators. Also, the optimized version of S-Match works more than 4 times faster than COMA, more than 2 times faster than Cupid, and as fast as Rondo.

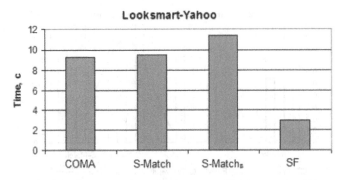

Fig. 15.1. Execution times: Looksmart vs. Yahoo, test case #4

The time performance results obtained for the matching tasks #4,5,6,7 of Table 10 are presented in Figure 15. Cupid went out of memory on all the tasks. Therefore, we present the results for other systems.

In the case of Looksmart-Yahoo matching problem the trees contain about hundred nodes each. S-Match works about 18% faster than S-Match$_B$ and about 2% slower than COMA. SF, in turn, works about 3 times faster than S-Match. The relatively poor improvement (18%) occurs because our optimizations are implemented in a straightforward way. More precisely, on small trees (e.g., test case #4) a big constant factor[15] dominates the growth of all other components in S-Match computational complexity formula.

On Yahoo-Standard matching problem S-Match works about 40% faster than S-Match$_B$. It performs 1% faster than COMA and about 5 times slower than SF. The relatively small improvement in this case can be explained by noticing that the maximum depth in both trees is 3 and that the average number of labels at nodes is about 2. The optimizations cannot significantly influence the system performance.

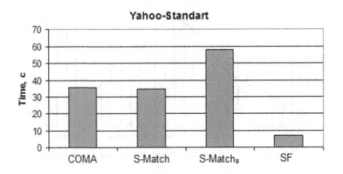

Fig. 15.2. Execution times: Yahoo vs. Standard, test case #5

The next two matching problems are much bigger than the previous ones. They contain hundreds and thousands of nodes. On these trees SF went out of memory.

---

[15] This is also known in the literature as an implementational constant.

Therefore, we provide the results only for the other systems. In the case of Google-Yahoo matching task S-Match is more than 6 times faster than S-Match$_B$. COMA performs about 5 times slower than the optimized version. These results suggest that the optimizations described in this paper are better suited for big trees. In the case of the biggest matching problem, involving Google-Looksmart, S-Match performs about 9 times faster than COMA, and about 7 times faster than S-Match$_B$.

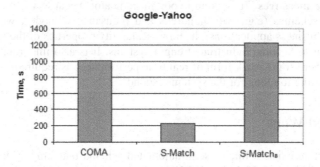

Fig.15.3. Execution times: Google vs. Yahoo, test case #6

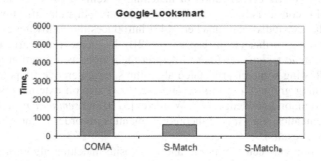

Fig. 15.4. Execution times: Google vs. Looksmart, test case #7

Having considered matching tasks of Table 10, we conclude that S-Match performs (in terms of execution time) slightly slower than COMA and SF on the schemas with one up to three hundred of nodes (see, Figures 15.1-15.2). At the same time, S-Match is considerably faster on the schemas with more than five hundreds nodes (see, Figures 15.3-15.4), thereby indicating system scalability.

9.3 Evaluation Summary

Quality measures. Since most matching systems return similarity coefficients, rather than semantic relations, our qualitative analysis was based on the measures developed for those systems. Therefore, we had to omit information about the type of relations S-Match returns, and focus only on the number of present/absent mappings. We totally discarded from our considerations the disjointness relation, however, its value should not be underestimated, because this relation reduces the search space.

We pose a large-scale qualitative evaluation of the system as future work. Thus, in our evaluation we have focused only on the overall qualitative system results, hence, not discussing exhaustively element level matchers, e.g., by showing impact of each of them on the matching results (see, for some preliminary results [22]). Also, it is worth mentioning that, e.g., string-based matchers, have already been extensively evaluated in [11,44].

Performance measures. *Time* is an important indicator, because when matching industrial-size schemas (e.g., with hundreds and thousands of nodes, which is quite typical for e-business applications), it shows scalability properties of the matchers and their potential to become industrial-strength systems. It is also important in web applications, where some weak form of real time performance is required (to avoid having a user waiting too long for the system respond).

10   Related Work

At present, there exists a line of semi-automated schema matching systems, see, for instance [5,10,13,14,32,30,35,39,49,28,46]. A good survey and a classification of matching approaches up to 2001 is provided in [42], an extension of its schema-based part and a user-centric classification of matching systems is provided in [43], while the work in [14] considers both [42, 43] as well as some other classifications.

In particular, for individual matchers, [43] introduces the following criteria which allow for detailing further (with respect to [42]), the element and structure level of matching: *syntactic techniques* (these interpret their input as a function of their sole structures following some clearly stated algorithms, e.g., iterative fix point computation for matching graphs), *external techniques* (these exploit external resources of a domain and common knowledge, e.g., WordNet [37]), and *semantic techniques* (these use formal semantics, e.g., model-theoretic semantics, in order to interpret the input and justify their results).

The distinction between the hybrid and composite matching algorithms of [42] is useful from an architectural perspective. [43] extends this work by taking into account how the systems can be distinguished in the matter of considering the mappings and the matching task, thus representing the end-user perspective. In this respect, the following criteria are proposed: *mappings as solutions* (these systems consider the matching problem as an optimization problem and the mapping is a solution to it, e.g., [13,35]); *mappings as theorems* (these systems rely on semantics and require the mapping to satisfy it, e.g., the approach proposed in this paper); *mappings as likeness clues* (these systems produce only reasonable indications to a user for selecting the mappings, e.g., [32,11]).

Let us consider the closest to S-Match schema-based state of the art systems in light of the above criteria.

Rondo. The Similarity Flooding (SF) [35] approach, as implemented in Rondo [36], utilizes a hybrid matching algorithm based on the ideas of similarity propagation. Schemas are presented as directed labeled graphs. The algorithm exploits only syntactic techniques at the element and structure level. It starts from the string-based comparison (common prefixes, suffixes tests) of the nodes' labels to obtain an initial mapping which is further refined within the fix-point computation. SF considers the mappings as a solution to a clearly stated optimization problem.

Cupid. Cupid [32] implements a hybrid matching algorithm comprising syntactic techniques at the element (e.g., common prefixes, suffixes tests) and structure level (e.g., tree matching weighted by leaves). It also exploits external resources, in particular, a precompiled thesaurus. Cupid falls into the mappings as likeness clues category.

COMA. COMA [11] is a composite schema matching system which exploits syntactic and external techniques. It provides a library of matching algorithms; a framework for combining obtained results, and a platform for the evaluation of the effectiveness of the different matchers. The matching library is extensible, it contains 6 elementary matchers, 5 hybrid matchers, and one reuse-oriented matcher. Most of them implement string-based techniques (affix, n-gram, edit distance, etc.); others share techniques with Cupid (tree matching weighted by leaves, thesauri look-up, etc.); reuse-oriented is a completely novel matcher, which tries to reuse previously obtained results for entire new schemas or for its fragments. Distinct features of COMA with respect to Cupid, are a more flexible architecture and a possibility of performing iterations in the matching process. COMA falls into the mappings as likeness clues category.

Reduction of semantic heterogeneity is typically performed in two steps. So far, we have concentrated on the first step, namely on determining correspondences between semantically related entities. The second step is the ultimate goal of the matching exercise, which can be *data translation, query answering,* and so on. Here, mappings are taken as input and are analyzed in order to generate, e.g., query expressions that automatically translate/exchange data instances between the information sources, see, for example, [16,48]. Notice that taking as input semantic relations, instead of coefficients in the [0,1] range, potentially enables, e.g., data translation systems to produce better results, since, for example, in such systems as Clio [16], the fist step is to interpret the correspondences by giving them a clear semantics.

11 Conclusions

We have presented a new semantic schema matching algorithm and its optimizations. Our solution builds on top of the past approaches at the element level and introduces a novel (with respect to schema matching) techniques, namely model-based techniques, at the structure level. We conducted a comparative evaluation of our approach implemented in the S-Match system against three state of the art systems. The results empirically prove the strength of our approach.

Future work includes development of an *iterative* and *interactive* semantic matching system. It will improve the quality of the mappings by iterating and by focusing user's attention on the critical points where his/her input is maximally useful. S-Match works in a top-down manner, and hence, mismatches among the top level elements of schemas can imply further mismatches between their descendants. Therefore, next steps include development of a *robust* semantic matching algorithm. Also, we are planning to extend the semantic matching approach by computing the *overlapping relation* (with the intersection semantics). This relation might be useful when, e.g., input schemas encode a domain of interest at different levels of details. Finally, we are going to develop a *testing methodology* which is able to estimate quality of the mappings between schemas with hundreds and thousands of nodes. Initial steps have already been done; see for details [3]. Here, the key issue is that in these cases, specifying expert mappings manually is neither desirable nor feasible task, thus a semi-automatic approach is needed. Comparison of matching algorithms on large real-world schemas from different application domains will also be performed *extensively*.

References

1. Atzeni, P., Cappellari, P., Bernstein, P.: Model-independent schema and data translation. In: Proceedings of EDBT, pp. 368–385 (2006)
2. Atzeni, P., Cappellari, P., Bernstein, P.: Modelgen: model independent schema translation. In: Proceedings of ICDE, pp. 1111–1112 (2005)
3. Avesani, P., Giunchiglia, F., Yatskevich, M.: A large scale taxonomy mapping evaluation. In: Gil, Y., Motta, E., Benjamins, V.R., Musen, M.A. (eds.) ISWC 2005. LNCS, vol. 3729, pp. 67–81. Springer, Heidelberg (2005)
4. Baader, F., Calvanese, D., McGuinness, D.L., Nardi, D., Patel-Schneider, P.F. (eds.): The Description Logic Handbook. Cambridge University Press, Cambridge (2002)
5. Bergamaschi, S., Castano, S., Vincini, M.: Semantic integration of semistructured and structured data sources. SIGMOD Record, pp. 54–59 (1999)
6. Bouquet, P., Serafini, L., Zanobini, S.: Semantic coordination: A new approach and an application. In: Fensel, D., Sycara, K.P., Mylopoulos, J. (eds.) ISWC 2003. LNCS, vol. 2870, pp. 130–145. Springer, Heidelberg (2003)
7. Bernstein, P., Melnik, S., Petropoulos, M., Quix, C.: Industrial-strength schema matching. SIGMOD Record 33(4), 38–43 (2004)
8. Davis, M., Longemann, G., Loveland, D.: A machine program for theorem proving. Journal of the ACM 5(7) (1962)
9. Davis, M., Putnam, H.: A computing procedure for quantification theory. Journal of the ACM 7, 201–215 (1960)
10. Dhamankar, R., Lee, Y., Doan, A., Halevy, A., Domingos, P.: iMAP: Discovering complex semantic matches between database schemas. In: Proceedings of SIGMOD, pp. 383–394 (2004)
11. Do, H.H., Rahm, E.: COMA - a system for flexible combination of schema matching approaches. In: Bressan, S., Chaudhri, A.B., Lee, M.L., Yu, J.X., Lacroix, Z. (eds.) CAiSE 2002 and VLDB 2002. LNCS, vol. 2590, pp. 610–621. Springer, Heidelberg (2003)
12. Doan, A., Halevy, A.: Semantic integration research in the database community: A brief survey. AI Magazine, Special Issue on Semantic Integration (2005)
13. Euzenat, J., Valtchev, P.: Similarity-based ontology alignment in OWL-lite. In: Proceedings of ECAI, pp. 333–337 (2004)
14. Euzenat, J., Shvaiko, P.: Ontology matching. Springer (to appear)
15. Gal, A., Anaby-Tavor, A., Trombetta, A., Montesi, D.: A framework for modeling and evaluating automatic semantic reconciliation. The VLDB Journal 14(1), 50–67 (2005)
16. Haas, L.M., Hernandez, M.A., Ho, H., Popa, L., Roth, M.: Clio grows up: from research prototype to industrial tool. In: Proceedings of SIGMOD, pp. 805–810 (2005)
17. Giunchiglia, F.: Contextual reasoning. Epistemologia, special issue on "I Linguaggi e le Macchine" XVI, 345–364 (1993)

18. Giunchiglia, F., Marchese, M., Zaihrayeu, I.: Encoding Classifications into Lightweight Ontologies. In: Sure, Y., Domingue, J. (eds.) ESWC 2006. LNCS, vol. 4011, pp. 80–94. Springer, Heidelberg (2006)
19. Giunchiglia, E., Sebastiani, R.: Applying the Davis-Putnam procedure to non-clausal formulas. In: Proceedings of AI*IA, pp. 84–94 (1999)
20. Giunchiglia, F., Shvaiko, P.: Semantic matching. The Knowledge Engineering Review Journal 18(3), 265–280 (2003)
21. Giunchiglia, F., Shvaiko, P., Yatskevich, M.: S-Match: an algorithm and an implementation of semantic matching. In: Bussler, C.J., Davies, J., Fensel, D., Studer, R. (eds.) ESWS 2004. LNCS, vol. 3053, pp. 61–75. Springer, Heidelberg (2004)
22. Giunchiglia, F., Shvaiko, P., Yatskevich, M.: Discovering Missing Background Knowledge in Ontology Matching. In: Proceedings of ECAI, pp. 382–386 (2006)
23. Giunchiglia, F., Shvaiko, P., Yatskevich, M.: Semantic schema matching. In: Proceedings of CoopIS, pp. 347–365 (2005)
24. Giunchiglia, F., Yatskevich, M.: Element level semantic matching. In: McIlraith, S.A., Plexousakis, D., van Harmelen, F. (eds.) ISWC 2004. LNCS, vol. 3298, Springer, Heidelberg (2004)
25. Giunchiglia, F., Yatskevich, M., Giunchiglia, E.: Efficient semantic matching. In: Gómez-Pérez, A., Euzenat, J. (eds.) ESWC 2005. LNCS, vol. 3532, pp. 272–289. Springer, Heidelberg (2005)
26. Guarino, N.: The role of ontologies for the Semantic Web (and beyond). Technical report, Laboratory for Applied Ontology, ISTC-CNR (2004)
27. Haarslev, V., Moller, R., Wessel, M.: RACER: Semantic middleware for industrial projects based on RDF/OWL, http://www.sts.tu-harburg.de/ r.f.moeller/racer/
28. He, B., Chang, K.C.-C.: Automatic Complex Schema Matching across Web Query Interfaces: A Correlation Mining Approach. ACM Transactions on Database Systems 31(1), 346–395 (2006)
29. Ide, N., Veronis, J.: Word Sense Disambiguation: the state of the art. Computational linguistics 24(1), 1–40 (1998)
30. Kang, J., Naughton, J.F.: On schema matching with opaque column names and data values. In: Proceedings of SIGMOD, pp. 205–216 (2003)
31. Le Berre, D.: SAT4J: A satisfiability library for Java, http://www.sat4j.org/
32. Madhavan, J., Bernstein, P., Rahm, E.: Generic schema matching with Cupid. In: Proceedings of VLDB, pp. 49–58 (2001)
33. Madhavan, J., Bernstein, P., Doan, A., Halevy, A.: Corpus-based schema matching. In: Proceedings of ICDE, pp. 57–68 (2005)
34. Magnini, B., Serafini, L., Speranza, M.: Making explicit the semantics hidden in schema models. In: Fensel, D., Sycara, K.P., Mylopoulos, J. (eds.) ISWC 2003. LNCS, vol. 2870, Springer, Heidelberg (2003)
35. Melnik, S., Garcia-Molina, H., Rahm, E.: Similarity Flooding: A versatile graph matching algorithm. In: Proceedings of ICDE, pp. 117–128 (2002)
36. Melnik, S., Rahm, E., Bernstein, P.: Rondo: A programming platform for generic model management. In: Proceedings of SIGMOD, pp. 193–204 (2003)
37. Miller, A.G.: WordNet: A lexical database for English. Communications of the ACM 38(11), 39–41 (1995)
38. Pan, J.Z.: Description Logics: reasoning support for the Semantic Web. PhD thesis, School of Computer Science, The University of Manchester (2004)

39. Modica, G.A., Gal, A., Jamil, H.M.: The use of machine-generated ontologies in dynamic information seeking. In: Batini, C., Giunchiglia, F., Giorgini, P., Mecella, M. (eds.) CoopIS 2001. LNCS, vol. 2172, pp. 433–448. Springer, Heidelberg (2001)
40. Noy, N.: Semantic Integration: A survey of ontology-based approaches. SIGMOD Record 33(4), 65–70 (2004)
41. Plaisted, D., Greenbaum, S.: A structure-preserving clause form translation. Journal of Symbolic Computation (2), 293–304 (1986)
42. Rahm, E., Bernstein, P.: A survey of approaches to automatic schema matching. The VLDB Journal 10(4), 334–350 (2001)
43. Shvaiko, P., Euzenat, J.: A survey of schema-based matching approaches. Journal on Data Semantics IV, 146–171 (2005)
44. Stoilos, G., Stamou, G.B., Kollias, S.D.: A String Metric for Ontology Alignment. In: Gil, Y., Motta, E., Benjamins, V.R., Musen, M.A. (eds.) ISWC 2005. LNCS, vol. 3729, pp. 624–637. Springer, Heidelberg (2005)
45. Smith, M.K., Welty, C., McGuinness, D.L.: OWL web ontology language guide. Technical report, World Wide Web Consortium (W3C) (February 10, 2004), http://www.w3.org/TR/2004/REC-owl-guide-20040210/
46. Su, W., Wang, J., Lochovsky, F.: Holistic Schema Matching for Web Query Interface. In: Proceedings of EDBT, pp. 77–94 (2006)
47. Tsetin, G.: On the complexity proofs in propositional logics. Seminars in Mathematics 8 (1970)
48. Velegrakis, Y., Miller, J., Popa, L.: Preserving mapping consistency under schema changes. The VLDB Journal 13(3), 274–293 (2004)
49. Ziegler, P., Kiefer, C., Sturm, C., Dittrich, K., Bernstein, A.: Detecting Similarities in Ontologies with the SOQA-SimPack Toolkit. In: Proceedings of EDBT, pp. 59–76 (2006)

Semantics-Guided Clustering of Heterogeneous XML Schemas

Pasquale De Meo[1], Giovanni Quattrone[1],
Giorgio Terracina[2], and Domenico Ursino[1]

[1] DIMET, Università Mediterranea di Reggio Calabria, Via Graziella, Località Feo di
Vito, 89060 Reggio Calabria, Italy
[2] Dipartimento di Matematica, Università della Calabria, Via Pietro Bucci, 87036
Rende (CS), Italy
demeo@unirc.it, quattrone@unirc.it,
terracina@mat.unical.it, ursino@unirc.it

Abstract. In this paper we illustrate an approach for clustering semantically heterogeneous XML Schemas. The proposed approach is driven
by the semantics of the involved Schemas that is defined by means of the
interschema properties existing among concepts represented therein; interschema properties taken into account by our approach are synonymies
(indicating that two concepts have the same meaning), hyponymies (denoting that a concept has a more specific meaning than another one), and
overlappings (indicating that two concepts are neither synonyms nor one
hyponym of the other, but represent, to some extent, the same reality).
An important feature of our approach consists of its capability of being
integrated with almost all the clustering algorithms already proposed in
the literature. Both a theoretical and an experimental analysis on the
complexity of our approach are presented in the paper. They show that
our approach is scalable and particularly suited in application contexts
characterized by a great number and a large variety of XML Schemas.

1 Introduction

Clustering is the process of grouping a set of physical or abstract objects into
classes of similar objects, called *clusters* [21], in such a way that those objects
belonging to the same cluster are as similar as possible, whereas those ones
belonging to different clusters are as dissimilar as possible.

Clustering has its roots in many areas, including Data Mining, Statistics,
Biology and Machine Learning. Its applications are extremely various and range
from Economy to Finance, from Biology to Sociology, and so on. Clustering can
play a key role also in the Web; in fact, in this scenario, numerous applications
that largely benefit of clustering have been proposed [6,8].

In the Web context, a specific activity in which clustering can play a key role
consists of grouping semantically heterogeneous information sources. In fact, currently, both the number and the semantic heterogeneity of information sources

S. Spaccapietra et al. (Eds.): Journal on Data Semantics IX, LNCS 4601, pp. 39–81, 2007.

available on the Web are strongly increasing. As a consequence, it appears extremely important the definition of approaches for clustering them into homogeneous classes.

On the contrary, as for data representation format and data exchange, the World Wide Web Consortium foretells a certain uniformity for the future and, to this purpose, proposes the usage of the XML language.

The growing importance of both clustering and XML stimulated, in the past, various researchers to study clustering techniques for XML sources [9,27,33,36]. Many of these techniques were "structural", i.e., they aimed at defining groups of structurally similar XML sources [9,33]. Clearly, the structural similarity (resp., dissimilarity) of two information sources is an indicator of their semantic similarity (resp., dissimilarity); however, often, it could be not sufficient [3,15,34]. As an example, consider a list of orders (i.e., a list of products bought by a customer in a commercial transaction); in an XML Schema this list could be represented in very different ways. In a first representation we could have an element, `order`, containing two sub-elements, `product` and `customer`; in a second representation we could have three elements, `product`, `customer` and `order`, at the same level, and we could implement their relationships by means of `key/keyref` constructs. Clearly, these two representations would lead to documents extremely different from a structural point of view; nonetheless, these documents might be extremely similar from a semantic standpoint.

In the literature various methods for defining information source semantics have been proposed; one of the most commonly adopted methods is based on the exploitation of the so-called *interschema properties*, [2,3,34,38], i.e., terminological and structural relationships existing among concepts belonging to different information sources. The most important interschema properties are synonymies (indicating that two concepts have the same meaning), homonymies (denoting that two concepts have different meanings, yet having the same name), hyponymies/hypernymies (indicating that a concept has a more specific meaning than another one) and overlappings (denoting that two concepts are neither synonyms nor one hyponym of the other, but represent, to some extent, the same reality).

In order to better understand the importance of interschema properties, consider the following example. Let S_1 be an XML Schema concerning vegetables and let S_2 be an XML Schema about factories; assume that both S_1 and S_2 contain the element "plant". If we consider only their name, we could erroneously conclude that the element "plant" of S_1 and the element "plant" of S_2 represent the same concept; on the contrary, if we consider their semantics, we could state that an interschema property (i.e., an homonymy) holds between these two elements and, consequently, that they represent different concepts.

In the literature some approaches for clustering XML sources, taking into account their semantic similarities, have been proposed too [27,36]. However, in these approaches, source similarity is determined by considering only concept similarities that, in the context of interschema properties, correspond to synonymies. In our opinion they are extremely interesting; however, they could be further refined if, in addition to synonymies, also other interschema properties, such as hyponymies and overlappings, would be considered.

This paper aims at providing a contribution in this setting; in fact, it presents an approach for clustering semantically heterogeneous information sources; the proposed approach takes not only synonymies, but also hyponymies and over-lappings, into account.

In order to clarify the importance of hyponymies and overlappings in the clustering process, consider the following example. Let S_1 be an XML Schema having an element **house**, described by four sub-elements, namely **bedroom**, **bathroom**, **kitchen** and **garden**. Let S_2 be an XML Schema containing the element **firstfloor**, characterized by the sub-elements **kitchen** and **lounge**, and the element **secondfloor**, characterized by the sub-elements **garden**, **bedroom**, **bathroom** and **garret**. Now, neither **firstfloor** nor **secondfloor** would be recognized as synonymous with **house** and, consequently, the corresponding portions of schemas would be considered completely distinct by a clustering approach taking only synonymies into account. However, both **firstfloor** and **secondfloor** should be considered overlapping with **house**, since the information content of **house** is distributed over them. As a consequence, a clustering approach taking also overlappings into account would recognize that there is a form of similarity also in these portions of S_1 and S_2 and, hence, would compute more refined clusters.

We point out that the present paper has not been conceived for defining a new clustering algorithm; on the contrary, it aims at allowing the application, to our reference context, of most of the existing clustering algorithms. As a matter of fact, in the literature, a great number of clustering algorithms, characterized by extremely various features, already exists, and other ones will be presumably proposed in the future. As a consequence, allowing the application of all these algorithms to our reference context would provide the user with the availability of a large variety of clustering tools, characterized by different peculiarities.

The key for reaching such a result is the exploitation of the so called *Dissimilarity Matrix* [21]; this is, in fact, the data structure which almost all the clustering algorithms already proposed in the literature operate upon. The rows and the columns of this matrix represent the objects to cluster; its generic element $M[i, j]$ denotes the distance, i.e., the dissimilarity, between the objects i and j. Generally, $M[i, j]$ is a non-negative number that is as closer to 0 as i and j are similar.

Our approach exploits interschema properties for finding the dissimilarity degree between two XML Schemas and, consequently, for constructing the Dissimilarity Matrix. Since some clustering algorithms require the involved objects to be represented as points in a metric space (see Section 3.5), in order to allow the applicability of the maximum possible number of clustering algorithms to our reference context, we define the dissimilarity among XML Schemas by exploiting a suitable euclidean space.

The outline of the paper is as follows: Section 2 describes a technique for extracting interschema properties. Section 3 provides a detailed description of the proposed approach. The experiments we have carried out for evaluating its performance are presented in Section 4. Some possible applications are described in Section 5. Related works are examined in Section 6. Finally, in Section 7, we draw our conclusions.

2   Preliminaries

As pointed out in the Introduction, the clustering approach we are presenting in this paper requires interschema properties concerning involved sources to be provided as input. These properties might be derived by applying any approach proposed in the literature for this purpose (see, for example, [3,14,17,31,34,38]). In order to illustrate the main features of an interschema property extraction task, in this section we describe an approach for deriving interschema properties; this approach has been already presented in detail in [11]. Interschema properties we are considering in this paper are synonymies, hyponymies/hyperonymies and overlappings.

The interschema property extraction approach we are introducing in this section is specialized for XML, almost automatic, semantic, and takes the intensional component of the involved XML sources into account. It is based on the observation that, given two concepts belonging to different information sources, an interesting and powerful way for determining their semantics consists of examining their *neighborhoods*, since the concepts and the relationships which they are involved in contribute to define their meaning [38]. In addition, it exploits two further indicators for defining the semantics of involved data sources in a more precise fashion; these indicators are the *types* and the *cardinalities* of the elements and the attributes belonging to the XML Schemas into consideration.

In XML Schemas, concepts are expressed by elements or attributes. Since, for the interschema property extraction task, it does not appear relevant to distinguish concepts represented by elements from concepts represented by attributes, we introduce the term *x-component* for denoting an element or an attribute in an XML Schema.

In order to compute the neighborhood of an x-component, it is necessary to define a "Semantic Distance" between two x-components of the same schema; this distance considers how much the corresponding x-components are semantically related. To this purpose we introduce some boolean functions that allow the strength of the relationship existing between two x-components x_ν and x_μ of an XML Schema S to be determined. These functions are:

- $veryclose(x_\nu, x_\mu)$, that returns *true* if and only if: *(i)* $x_\mu = x_\nu$, or *(ii)* x_μ is an attribute of x_ν, or *(iii)* x_μ is a simple sub-element of x_ν;
- $close(x_\nu, x_\mu)$, that returns *true* if and only if: *(i)* x_μ is a complex sub-element of x_ν, or *(ii)* x_μ is an element of S and there exists a `keyref` constraint stating that an attribute of x_ν refers to a `key` attribute of x_μ;
- $near(x_\nu, x_\mu)$, that returns *true* if and only if either $veryclose(x_\nu, x_\mu) = true$ or $close(x_\nu, x_\mu) = true$;

– $reachable(x_\nu, x_\mu)$, that returns $true$ if and only if there exists a sequence of $distinct$ x-components $x_1, x_2, \ldots, x_n$ such that: $x_1 = x_\nu$, $near(x_1, x_2) = near(x_2, x_3) = \ldots = near(x_{n-1}, x_n) = true$, $x_n = x_\mu$.

The exploitation of the functions introduced above allows each pair $\langle x_\nu, x_\mu \rangle$ of an XML Schema to be associated with a coefficient called $Connection\ Cost$. It is a measure of the correlation degree existing between x_ν and x_μ and indicates how much the concept expressed by x_ν is semantically close to the concept represented by x_μ; in other words, it represents the ability of the concept associated with x_μ to characterize the concept associated with x_ν. More formally, the Connection Cost from x_ν to x_μ, denoted by $CC(x_\nu, x_\mu)$, is defined as:

$$CC(x_\nu, x_\mu) = \begin{cases} 0 & \text{if } veryclose(x_\nu, x_\mu) = true \\ 1 & \text{if } close(x_\nu, x_\mu) = true \\ C_{\nu\mu} & \text{if } reachable(x_\nu, x_\mu) = true \text{ and } near(x_\nu, x_\mu) = false \\ \infty & \text{if } reachable(x_\nu, x_\mu) = false \end{cases}$$

Here $C_{\nu\mu} = min_{x_\alpha} \left(CC(x_\nu, x_\alpha) + CC(x_\alpha, x_\mu) \right)$ for each x_α such that $reachable(x_\nu, x_\alpha) = reachable(x_\alpha, x_\mu) = true$.

Finally, given a non-negative integer i, we define the ith neighborhood of an x-component x_ν of an XML Schema S as the set of x-components of S having a Connection Cost from x_ν lesser than or equal to i. More formally, the ith neighborhood of x_ν is defined as:

$$nbh(x_\nu, i) = \{x_\mu |\ x_\mu \text{ is an x-component of } S, CC(x_\nu, x_\mu) \leq i\}$$

In order to verify if an interschema property holds between two x-components, our approach compares their neighborhoods, their cardinalities and their data types. In addition, it exploits a thesaurus storing lexical synonymies holding among the terms of a language; specifically, it uses the English language and WordNet [32]. If necessary, different (possibly already defined) domain-specific thesauruses might be exploited.

Since neighborhood comparison plays a key role in the interschema property extraction task, we first introduce it and, then, illustrate the property extraction task in detail.

2.1   Neighborhood Comparison

Given two x-components x_ν and x_μ, belonging to different XML Schemas, and two corresponding neighborhoods $nbh(x_\nu, v)$ and $nbh(x_\mu, v)$, there could exist different relationships between them.

Specifically, three possible relationships, namely $similarity$, $comparability$ and $generalization$, could be taken into account. All of them are derived by computing suitable objective functions on the maximum weight matching associated with a bipartite graph obtained from the x-components of $nbh(x_\nu, v)$ and $nbh(x_\mu, v)$.

In the following we indicate by $BG(x_\nu, x_\mu, v) = \langle NSet(x_\nu, x_\mu, v), ESet(x_\nu, x_\mu, v) \rangle$ the bipartite graph associated with $nbh(x_\nu, v)$ and $nbh(x_\mu, v)$; when it is not confusing, we shall use the notation $BG(v)$ instead of $BG(x_\nu, x_\mu, v)$. In $BG(v)$, $NSet(v) = PSet(v) \cup QSet(v)$ represents the set of nodes; there is a node in $PSet(v)$ (resp., $QSet(v)$) for each x-component of $nbh(x_\nu, v)$ (resp., $nbh(x_\mu, v)$). $ESet(v)$ is the set of edges; there is an edge between $p \in PSet(v)$ and $q \in QSet(v)$ if: (i) a lexical synonymy between the names of the x-components x_p and x_q, associated with p and q, is stored in the reference thesaurus; (ii) the cardinalities of x_p and x_q are *compatible*; (iii) their data types are *compatible* (this last condition must be verified only if x_p and x_q are attributes or simple elements). Here, the cardinalities of two x-components are considered compatible if the intersection of the intervals defined by them is not empty. Compatibility rules associated with data types are analogous to the corresponding ones valid for high level programming languages.

The maximum weight matching for $BG(v)$ is the set $ESet'(v) \subseteq ESet(v)$ of edges such that, for each node $x \in PSet(v) \cup QSet(v)$, there is *at most one* edge of $ESet'(v)$ incident onto x and $|ESet'(v)|$ is maximum (for algorithms solving the maximum weight matching problem, see [18]).

Neighborhood Similarity. Intuitively, two neighborhoods (and, more in general, two sets of objects) are considered similar if most of their components are similar.

For determining if $nbh(x_\nu, v)$ and $nbh(x_\mu, v)$ are similar, we construct $BG(x_\nu, x_\mu, v)$ and, then, we compute the objective function $\phi_{BG(v)} = \frac{2|ESet'(v)|}{|PSet(v)| + |QSet(v)|}$. Here $|ESet'(v)|$ represents the number of matches associated with $BG(v)$, as well as the number of similarities involving $nbh(x_\nu, v)$ and $nbh(x_\mu, v)$. $2|ESet'(v)|$ indicates the number of matching nodes in $BG(v)$, as well as the number of similar x-components present in $nbh(x_\nu, v)$ and $nbh(x_\mu, v)$. $|PSet(v)| + |QSet(v)|$ denotes the total number of nodes in $BG(v)$, as well as the total number of x-components associated with $nbh(x_\nu, v)$ and $nbh(x_\mu, v)$. Finally, $\phi_{BG(v)}$ represents the share of matching nodes in $BG(v)$, as well as the share of similar x-components present in $nbh(x_\nu, v)$ and $nbh(x_\mu, v)$.

We say that $nbh(x_\nu, v)$ and $nbh(x_\mu, v)$ are similar if, given the bipartite graph $BG(v)$, $\phi_{BG(v)} > \frac{1}{2}$; such an assumption derives from the consideration that two sets of objects can be considered similar if the number of similar components is greater than the number of the dissimilar ones or, in other words, if the number of similar components is greater than half of the total number of components.

It is possible to prove that the worst case time complexity for determining if $nbh(x_\nu, v)$ and $nbh(x_\mu, v)$ are similar is $O(p^3)$, where p is the maximum between $|nbh(x_\nu, v)|$ and $|nbh(x_\mu, v)|$.

Neighborhood Comparability. Intuitively, two neighborhoods $nbh(x_\nu, v)$ and $nbh(x_\mu, v)$ are comparable if there exist at least two (quite large) subsets $XSet_\nu$ of $nbh(x_\nu, v)$ and $XSet_\mu$ of $nbh(x_\mu, v)$ that are similar. Similarity between $XSet_\nu$ and $XSet_\mu$ is computed by constructing a bipartite graph $\overline{BG}(XSet_\nu, XSet_\mu)$ starting from the x-components of $XSet_\nu$ and $XSet_\mu$, and by computing $\phi_{\overline{BG}}$ in a way analogous to that we have seen previously. Comparability is a weaker property w.r.t. similarity. As a matter of fact, if two neighborhoods are similar, they are also comparable. However, it could happen that two neighborhoods are not similar but they are comparable because they have quite large similar subsets.

More formally, two neighborhoods $nbh(x_\nu, v)$ and $nbh(x_\mu, v)$ are comparable if there exist two subsets, $XSet_\nu$ of $nbh(x_\nu, v)$ and $XSet_\mu$ of $nbh(x_\mu, v)$, such that: (i) $|XSet_\nu| > \frac{1}{2}|nbh(x_\nu, v)|$; (ii) $|XSet_\mu| > \frac{1}{2}|nbh(x_\mu, v)|$; (iii) $\phi_{\overline{BG}}(XSet_\nu, XSet_\mu) > \frac{1}{2}$. In this definition, conditions (i) and (ii) guarantee that $XSet_\nu$ and $XSet_\mu$ are representative (i.e., quite large); we assume that this happens if they involve more than half of the components of the corresponding neighborhoods; condition (iii) guarantees that $XSet_\nu$ and $XSet_\mu$ are similar.

It is possible to prove that: (i) the worst case time complexity for determining if $nbh(x_\nu, v)$ and $nbh(x_\mu, v)$ are comparable is $O(p^3)$, where p is the maximum between $|nbh(x_\nu, v)|$ and $|nbh(x_\mu, v)|$; (ii) if $nbh(x_\nu, v)$ and $nbh(x_\mu, v)$ are similar, then they are also comparable.

Neighborhood Generalization. Consider two neighborhoods α and β and assume that: (1) they are not similar; (2) most of the x-components of β match with x-components of α; (3) most of the x-components of α do not match with x-components of β. If all these conditions hold, then it is possible to conclude that the reality represented by α is richer than that represented by β and, consequently, that α is more specific than β or, conversely, that β is more general than α. The following definition formalizes this reasoning.

Let x_ν and x_μ be two x-components belonging to different XML Schemas. We say that $nbh(x_\nu, v)$ is more specific than $nbh(x_\mu, v)$ (and, consequently, that $nbh(x_\mu, v)$ is more general than $nbh(x_\nu, v)$) if: (i) they are not similar, and (ii) the objective function $\varphi_{BG}(x_\nu, x_\mu, v) = \frac{|ESet'(v)|}{|QSet(v)|}$, associated with the bipartite graph $BG(v)$, is greater than $\frac{1}{2}$; here, $BG(v)$ has been previously defined, $ESet'(v)$ represents the set of matching edges associated with BG whereas $QSet(v)$ is the set of nodes of BG corresponding to the x-components of $nbh(x_\mu, v)$.

The reasoning underlying this definition derives from the observation that $\varphi_{BG}(x_\nu, x_\mu, v)$ represents the share of x-components belonging to $nbh(x_\mu, v)$ matching with the x-components of $nbh(x_\nu, v)$. If this share is sufficiently high then most of the x-components of $nbh(x_\mu, v)$ match with the x-components of $nbh(x_\nu, v)$ (condition (2)) but, since $nbh(x_\nu, v)$ and $nbh(x_\mu, v)$ are not similar (condition (1)), most of the x-components of $nbh(x_\nu, v)$ do not match with the x-components of $nbh(x_\mu, v)$ (condition (3)). As a consequence, it is possible to conclude that $nbh(x_\nu, v)$ is more specific than $nbh(x_\mu, v)$.

It is possible to prove that the worst case time complexity for determining if $nbh(x_\nu, v)$ is more specific than $nbh(x_\mu, v)$ is $O(p^3)$, where p is the maximum between $|nbh(x_\nu, v)|$ and $|nbh(x_\mu, v)|$.

2.2 Interschema Property Derivation

As previously pointed out, in order to verify if an interschema property holds between two x-components x_ν and x_μ, belonging to different XML Schemas, it is necessary to examine their neighborhoods. Specifically, first it is necessary to consider $nbh(x_\nu, 0)$ and $nbh(x_\mu, 0)$ and to verify if they are comparable. In the affirmative case, it is possible to conclude that x_ν and x_μ refer to analogous "contexts" and, presumably, define comparable concepts. As a consequence, the pair $\langle x_\nu, x_\mu \rangle$ is marked as *candidate* for an interschema property. However, observe that $nbh(x_\nu, 0)$ (resp., $nbh(x_\mu, 0)$) takes only attributes and simple sub-elements of x_ν (resp., x_μ) into account; as a consequence, it considers quite a limited context. If a higher severity level is required, it is necessary to verify that other neighborhoods of x_ν and x_μ are comparable before marking the pair $\langle x_\nu, x_\mu \rangle$ as candidate. Such a reasoning is formalized by the following definition.

Definition 1. Let S_1 and S_2 be two XML Schemas. Let x_ν (resp., x_μ) be an x-component of S_1 (resp., S_2). Let u be a severity level. We say that *the pair $\langle x_\nu, x_\mu \rangle$ is candidate for an interschema property at the severity level u if $nbh(x_\nu, v)$ and $nbh(x_\mu, v)$ are comparable for each v such that $0 \le v \le u$.*   □

It is possible to prove that the worst case time complexity for verifying if $\langle x_\nu, x_\mu \rangle$ is a candidate pair at the severity level u is $O(u \times p^3)$, where p is the maximum between $|nbh(x_\nu, u)|$ and $|nbh(x_\mu, u)|$.

Now, in order to verify if a synonymy, a hyponymy or an overlapping holds, at the severity u, for a *candidate pair* $\langle x_\nu, x_\mu \rangle$ it is necessary to examine the neighborhoods of x_ν and x_μ and to determine the relationship holding among them. Specifically:

- A synonymy holds between x_ν and x_μ at the severity level u if $nbh(x_\nu, v)$ and $nbh(x_\mu, v)$ are similar for each v such that $0 \le v \le u$.
- x_ν is said a hyponym of x_μ at the severity level u if $nbh(x_\nu, v)$ is more specific than $nbh(x_\mu, v)$, for each v such that $0 \le v \le u$.
- An overlapping holds between x_ν and x_μ at the severity level u if: *(i)* x_ν and x_μ are not synonymous; *(ii)* neither x_ν is a hyponym of x_μ nor x_μ is a hyponym of x_ν.

The previous assumptions derive from the following considerations: *(i)* if two x-components are comparable at the severity level u and their neighborhoods are also similar, then it is possible to conclude that they represent the same concept and, consequently, they can be considered synonymous; *(ii)* if two x-components are comparable at the severity level u but the neighborhoods of one of them, say x_ν, are more specific than the neighborhoods of the other, say x_μ, then it is possible to conclude that x_ν has a more specific meaning than x_μ or, in other words, that x_ν is a hyponym of x_μ; *(iii)* if two x-components are comparable at the severity level u but neither their neighborhoods are similar nor the neighborhoods of one of them are more specific than the neighborhoods of the other, then it is possible to conclude that they represent partially similar concepts and, consequently, that an overlapping holds between them.

As for the computational complexity of the interschema property derivation, it is possible to state that the worst case time complexity for computing synonymies, hyponymies and overlappings at the severity level u is $O(u \times p^3)$, where p is the maximum between $|nbh(x_\nu, u)|$ and $|nbh(x_\mu, u)|$.

Finally, it is possible to prove that the worst case time complexity for deriving all interschema properties holding between two XML Schemas S_1 and S_2 at the severity level u is $O(u \times q^3 \times m^2)$, where q is the maximum cardinality of a neighborhood of S_1 or S_2 and m is the maximum between the number of complex elements of S_1 and the number of complex elements of S_2.

3 Description of the Proposed Approach

3.1 Introduction

As pointed out in the Introduction, the main focus of the proposed approach is the clustering of semantically heterogeneous XML Schemas.

Our approach receives: *(i)* a set $SchemaSet = \{S_1, S_2, \ldots, S_n\}$ of XML Schemas to cluster; *(ii)* a dictionary IPD storing the interschema properties (synonymies, hyponymies/hypernymies and overlappings) involving concepts belonging to Schemas of $SchemaSet$.

IPD is constructed by applying the approach for the interschema property derivation illustrated in Section 2.2. In the following we shall assume that IPD is sorted on the basis of the names of the involved elements and attributes; if this is not the case, our approach preliminarily applies a suitable sorting algorithm on it.

Before providing a detailed description of the behaviour of our approach, it is necessary to introduce some definitions that will be largely exploited in the following.

Let S_i be an XML Schema. As introduced in Section 2, an *x-component* of S_i is an element or an attribute of S_i; it is characterized by its name, its typology (stating if it is a simple element, a complex element or an attribute) and its data type. The set of x-components of S_i is called $XCompSet(S_i)$. In the following we shall denote with $P = \sum_{i=1}^{n} |XCompSet(S_i)|$ the total number of x-components belonging to the Schemas of $SchemaSet$.

We define now some functions that will be extremely useful in the following; they receive two x-components x_ν and x_μ and return a boolean value; these functions are:

- *identical*(x_ν, x_μ), that returns *true* if and only if x_ν and x_μ are two synonymous x-components having the same name, the same typology and the same data type;
- *verystrong*(x_ν, x_μ), that returns *true* if and only if x_ν and x_μ are two synonymous x-components having the same typology but different names or different data types;
- *strong*(x_ν, x_μ), that returns *true* if and only if x_ν and x_μ are two synonymous x-components having different typologies;
- *hweak*(x_ν, x_μ), that returns *true* if and only if x_ν and x_μ are related by an hyponymy property;
- *oweak*(x_ν, x_μ), that returns *true* if and only if x_ν and x_μ are related by an overlapping property.

Proposition 1. Let $SchemaSet = \{S_1, S_2, \ldots, S_n\}$ be a set of XML Schemas; let P be the total number of x-components relative to the Schemas of $SchemaSet$; finally, let x_ν and x_μ be two x-components belonging to two distinct Schemas of $SchemaSet$. The computation of the functions $identical(x_\nu, x_\mu)$, $verystrong(x_\nu, x_\mu)$, $strong(x_\nu, x_\mu)$, $hweak(x_\nu, x_\mu)$ and $oweak(x_\nu, x_\mu)$ costs $O(\log P)$.

Proof. Observe that at most one kind of interschema properties can exist between two x-components of different Schemas. As a consequence, the maximum cardinality of IPD is $O(P^2)$. The computation of each function mentioned above implies the search of the corresponding pair in IPD. Since this dictionary is ordered, it is possible to apply the binary search on it. This costs $O(\log(P^2)) = O(2 \log P) = O(\log P)$.   □

Starting from the functions defined previously, it is possible to construct the following support dictionaries:

- *Identity Dictionary* ID, defined as:

  $ID = \{\langle x_\nu, x_\mu \rangle \mid x_\nu, x_\mu \in \bigcup_{i=1}^{n} XCompSet(S_i), identical(x_\nu, x_\mu) = true\};$

- *Very Strong Similarity Dictionary* $VSSD$, defined as:

  $VSSD = \{\langle x_\nu, x_\mu \rangle \mid x_\nu, x_\mu \in \bigcup_{i=1}^{n} XCompSet(S_i), verystrong(x_\nu, x_\mu) = true\};$

- *Strong Similarity Dictionary* SSD, defined as:

  $SSD = \{\langle x_\nu, x_\mu \rangle \mid x_\nu, x_\mu \in \bigcup_{i=1}^{n} XCompSet(S_i), strong(x_\nu, x_\mu) = true\};$

- *HWeak Similarity Dictionary* $HWSD$, defined as:

  $HWSD = \{\langle x_\nu, x_\mu \rangle \mid x_\nu, x_\mu \in \bigcup_{i=1}^{n} XCompSet(S_i), hweak(x_\nu, x_\mu) = true\};$

- *OWeak Similarity Dictionary* $OWSD$, defined as:

  $OWSD = \{\langle x_\nu, x_\mu \rangle \mid x_\nu, x_\mu \in \bigcup_{i=1}^{n} XCompSet(S_i), oweak(x_\nu, x_\mu) = true\}.$

The construction of these dictionaries is carried out in such a way that they are always ordered w.r.t. the names of the involved x-components.

Proposition 2. Let $SchemaSet = \{S_1, S_2, \ldots, S_n\}$ be a set of XML Schemas; let P be the total number of x-components relative to the Schemas of $SchemaSet$. The construction of ID, $VSSD$, SSD, $HWSD$ and $OWSD$ costs $O(P^2 \times \log P)$.

Proof. The construction of each dictionary is carried out by verifying the corresponding function for each of the $O(P^2)$ pairs of x-components. Proposition 1 states that this task costs $O(\log P)$; as a consequence, the total cost of the construction of all dictionaries is $O(P^2 \times \log P)$.   □

3.2   Example

Consider the set of XML Schemas $SchemaSet = \{S_1, S_2, S_3, S_4, S_5\}$ shown in Figures 1, 2, 3, 4 and 5, respectively. The pairs of complex elements stored in the corresponding Interschema Property Dictionary are shown in Table 1[1].

The complex elements of $SchemaSet$ belonging to ID, $VSSD$, $HWSD$ and $OWSD$[2] are the following[3]:

$$ID = \{\langle \text{shop}_{[S_3]}, \text{shop}_{[S_4]} \rangle\}$$

$$VSSD = \{\langle\text{customer}_{[S_3]}, \text{client}_{[S_4]}\rangle, \langle\text{music}_{[S_3]}, \text{composition}_{[S_4]}\rangle,$$
$$\langle\text{shop}_{[S_3]}, \text{store}_{[S_5]}\rangle, \langle\text{shop}_{[S_4]}, \text{store}_{[S_5]}\rangle, \langle\text{subject}_{[S_1]}, \text{course}_{[S_2]}\rangle\}$$

$$HWSD = \{\langle\text{student}_{[S_1]}, \text{PhDstudent}_{[S_2]}\rangle\}$$

$$OWSD = \{\langle\text{composition}_{[S_4]}, \text{CD}_{[S_5]}\rangle, \langle\text{lecturer}_{[S_1]}, \text{professor}_{[S_2]}\rangle,$$
$$\langle\text{music}_{[S_3]}, \text{CD}_{[S_5]}\rangle\}$$

As an example, the pair $\langle$ shop$_{[S_3]}$, shop$_{[S_4]}$ $\rangle$ belongs to ID because shop$_{[S_3]}$ and shop$_{[S_4]}$ have the same name, the same typology, the same data type and a synonymy between them is registered in IPD. Analogously, the pair $\langle$ subject$_{[S_1]}$, course$_{[S_2]}$ $\rangle$ belongs to $VSSD$ because a synonymy between subject$_{[S_1]}$ and course$_{[S_2]}$ is registered in IPD but these elements have different names. The other properties stored in $VSSD$, $HWSD$ and $OWSD$ have been determined by applying analogous reasonings.

3.3   Construction of the Dissimilarity Matrix

As specified in the Introduction, one of the key features of our approach is the construction of the Dissimilarity Matrix. In fact, once this structure has been constructed, it is possible to apply on it a large variety of clustering algorithms already proposed in the literature. In order to allow the application of the maximum possible number of clustering algorithms, we have decided to exploit a metrics for measuring the dissimilarity between two XML Schemas.

Since involved XML Schemas could be semantically heterogeneous and since we want to group them on the basis of their relative semantics, our definition of metrics must necessarily be very different from the classical ones; specifically, in our case, it must be strictly dependent on the interschema properties that are the way we exploit for defining inter-source semantics.

---

[1] Due to space constraints, in this example, and in the following ones, we show only properties concerning complex elements and disregard those ones involving simple elements and attributes.

[2] Note that SSD is not shown here because each of its tuples refers to attributes or simple elements.

[3] Here and in the following, whenever necessary, we use the notation $x_{[S]}$ for indicating the x-component x of the XML Schema S.

```
<?xml version="1.0" encoding="UTF-8"?>
<xs:schema xmlns:xs="http://www.w3.org/2001/XMLSchema">
    <xs:element name="lecturer">
        <xs:complexType>
            <xs:attribute name="identifier" type="xs:ID"/>
            <xs:attribute name="name" type="xs:string"/>
            <xs:attribute name="cultural_area" type="xs:string"/>
            <xs:attribute name="subjects" type="xs:IDREFS"/>
            <xs:attribute name="start_date" type="xs:date"/>
            <xs:attribute name="end_date" type="xs:date"/>
            <xs:attribute name="salary" type="xs:integer"/>
            <xs:attribute name="contracts" type="xs:string"/>
        </xs:complexType>
    </xs:element>
    <xs:element name="student">
        <xs:complexType>
            <xs:attribute name="identifier" type="xs:ID"/>
            <xs:attribute name="name" type="xs:string"/>
            <xs:attribute name="enrollment_year" type="xs:integer"/>
            <xs:attribute name="attends" type="xs:IDREFS"/>
        </xs:complexType>
    </xs:element>

    <xs:element name="subject">
        <xs:complexType>
            <xs:attribute name="identifier" type="xs:ID"/>
            <xs:attribute name="name" type="xs:string"/>
            <xs:attribute name="argument" type="xs:string"/>
            <xs:attribute name="duration" type="xs:integer"/>
            <xs:attribute name="attended_by" type="xs:IDREF"/>
            <xs:attribute name="teached_by" type="xs:IDREFS"/>
        </xs:complexType>
    </xs:element>
    <!-- Declaration of root -->
    <xs:element name="university">
        <xs:complexType>
            <xs:sequence>
                <xs:element ref="lecturer" maxOccurs="unbounded"/>
                <xs:element ref="student" maxOccurs="unbounded"/>
                <xs:element ref="subject" maxOccurs="unbounded"/>
            </xs:sequence>
        </xs:complexType>
    </xs:element>
</xs:schema>
```

Fig. 1. The XML Schema S_1

```
<?xml version="1.0" encoding="UTF-8"?>
<xs:schema xmlns:xs="http://www.w3.org/2001/XMLSchema">
    <xs:element name="professor">
        <xs:complexType>
            <xs:attribute name="identifier" type="xs:ID"/>
            <xs:attribute name="name" type="xs:string"/>
            <xs:attribute name="type" type="xs:string"/>
            <xs:attribute name="cultural_area" type="xs:string"/>
            <xs:attribute name="courses" type="xs:IDREFS"/>
            <xs:attribute name="projects" type="xs:string"/>
            <xs:attribute name="roles" type="xs:string"/>
            <xs:attribute name="references" type="xs:string"/>
        </xs:complexType>
    </xs:element>
    <xs:element name="PhDstudent">
        <xs:complexType>
            <xs:attribute name="identifier" type="xs:ID"/>
            <xs:attribute name="name" type="xs:string"/>
            <xs:attribute name="enrollment_year" type="xs:integer"/>
            <xs:attribute name="advisor" type="xs:string"/>
            <xs:attribute name="thesis" type="xs:string"/>
            <xs:attribute name="research_interests" type="xs:string"/>
            <xs:attribute name="refrences" type="xs:string"/>
        </xs:complexType>
    </xs:element>

    <xs:element name="course">
        <xs:complexType>
            <xs:attribute name="identifier" type="xs:ID"/>
            <xs:attribute name="name" type="xs:string"/>
            <xs:attribute name="argument" type="xs:string"/>
            <xs:attribute name="duration" type="xs:integer"/>
            <xs:attribute name="responsible" type="xs:IDREF"/>
            <xs:attribute name="program" type="xs:string"/>
            <xs:attribute name="number_of_students"
                type="xs:integer"/>
            <xs:attribute name="lecture_hall" type="xs:string"/>
        </xs:complexType>
    </xs:element>
    <!-- Declaration of root -->
    <xs:element name="department">
        <xs:complexType>
            <xs:sequence>
                <xs:element ref="professor" maxOccurs="unbounded"/>
                <xs:element ref="PhDstudent" maxOccurs="unbounded"/>
                <xs:element ref="course" maxOccurs="unbounded"/>
            </xs:sequence>
        </xs:complexType>
    </xs:element>
</xs:schema>
```

Fig. 2. The XML Schema S_2

```
<?xml version="1.0" encoding="UTF-8"?>
<xs:schema xmlns:xs="http://www.w3.org/2001/XMLSchema">
    <xs:element name="customer">
        <xs:complexType>
            <xs:attribute name="SSN" type="xs:string" use="required"/>
            <xs:attribute name="firstName" type="xs:string"/>
            <xs:attribute name="lastName" type="xs:string"/>
            <xs:attribute name="address" type="xs:string"/>
            <xs:attribute name="gender" type="xs:string"/>
            <xs:attribute name="birthDate" type="xs:date"/>
            <xs:attribute name="profession" type="xs:string"/>
            <xs:attribute name="purchases" type="xs:IDREFS"/>
        </xs:complexType>
    </xs:element>
    <xs:element name="music">
        <xs:complexType>
            <xs:attribute name="code" type="xs:ID" use="required"/>

            <xs:attribute name="artist" type="xs:string"/>
            <xs:attribute name="title" type="xs:string"/>
            <xs:attribute name="pubYear" type="xs:integer"/>
            <xs:attribute name="genre" type="xs:string"/>
            <xs:attribute name="support" type="xs:string"/>
        </xs:complexType>
    </xs:element>
    <!-- Definition of root element -->
    <xs:element name="shop">
        <xs:complexType>
            <xs:sequence>
                <xs:element ref="customer" maxOccurs="unbounded"/>
                <xs:element ref="music" maxOccurs="unbounded"/>
            </xs:sequence>
        </xs:complexType>
    </xs:element>
</xs:schema>
```

Fig. 3. The XML Schema S_3

```
<?xml version="1.0" encoding="UTF-8"?>                <xs:attribute name="title" type="xs:string"/>
<xs:schema xmlns:xs="http://www.w3.org/2001/XMLSchema">  <xs:attribute name="song" type="xs:string"/>
    <xs:element name="client">                        <xs:attribute name="year" type="xs:integer"/>
        <xs:complexType>                              <xs:attribute name="genre" type="xs:string"/>
            <xs:attribute name="SSN" type="xs:string" use="required"/>  </xs:complexType>
            <xs:attribute name="firstName" type="xs:string"/>  </xs:element>
            <xs:attribute name="lastName" type="xs:string"/>  <!-- Definition of root element -->
            <xs:attribute name="address" type="xs:string"/>  <xs:element name="shop">
            <xs:attribute name="phone" type="xs:string"/>      <xs:complexType>
            <xs:attribute name="email" type="xs:string"/>        <xs:sequence>
            <xs:attribute name="purchases" type="xs:IDREFS"/>      <xs:element ref="client" maxOccurs="unbounded"/>
        </xs:complexType>                                         <xs:element ref="composition" maxOccurs="unbounded"/>
    </xs:element>                                             </xs:sequence>
    <xs:element name="composition">                        </xs:complexType>
        <xs:complexType>                                 </xs:element>
            <xs:attribute name="id" type="xs:ID"/>      </xs:schema>
            <xs:attribute name="artist" type="xs:string"/>
```

Fig. 4. The XML Schema S_4

```
<?xml version="1.0" encoding="UTF-8"?>                <xs:attribute name="firstName" type="xs:string"/>
<xs:schema xmlns:xs="http://www.w3.org/2001/XMLSchema">  <xs:attribute name="lastName" type="xs:string"/>
    <xs:element name="CD">                            <xs:attribute name="address" type="xs:string"/>
        <xs:complexType>                              <xs:attribute name="email" type="xs:string"/>
            <xs:attribute name="id" type="xs:string" use="required"/>  <xs:attribute name="web_address" type="xs:string"/>
            <xs:attribute name="title" type="xs:string"/>  <xs:attribute name="music_CDs" type="xs:IDREFS"/>
            <xs:attribute name="year" type="xs:integer"/>  </xs:complexType>
            <xs:attribute name="artist" type="xs:IDREF"/>  </xs:element>
            <xs:attribute name="genre" type="xs:string"/>  <!-- Definition of root element -->
            <xs:attribute name="price" type="xs:integer"/>  <xs:element name="store">
            <xs:sequence>                                <xs:complexType>
                <xs:element name="song" type="xs:string"     <xs:sequence>
                    maxOccurs="unbounded"/>                    <xs:element ref="artist" maxOccurs="unbounded"/>
            </xs:sequence>                                     <xs:element ref="CD" maxOccurs="unbounded"/>
        </xs:complexType>                                   </xs:sequence>
    </xs:element>                                         </xs:complexType>
    <xs:element name="artist">                         </xs:element>
        <xs:complexType>                             </xs:schema>
            <xs:attribute name="SSN" type="xs:ID"/>
```

Fig. 5. The XML Schema S_5

Table 1. The pairs of complex elements stored in the Interschema Property Dictionary associated with S_1, S_2, S_3, S_4 and S_5

First x-component	Second x-component	semantic relationship
university$_{[S_1]}$	department$_{[S_2]}$	overlapping
lecturer$_{[S_1]}$	professor$_{[S_2]}$	overlapping
student$_{[S_1]}$	PhDstudent$_{[S_2]}$	hyponymy
subject$_{[S_1]}$	course$_{[S_2]}$	synonymy
customer$_{[S_3]}$	client$_{[S_4]}$	synonymy
music$_{[S_3]}$	composition$_{[S_4]}$	synonymy
shop$_{[S_3]}$	shop$_{[S_4]}$	synonymy
shop$_{[S_3]}$	store$_{[S_5]}$	synonymy
music$_{[S_3]}$	CD$_{[S_5]}$	overlapping
shop$_{[S_4]}$	store$_{[S_5]}$	synonymy
composition$_{[S_4]}$	CD$_{[S_5]}$	overlapping

Our notion of metrics is based on a suitable, multi-dimensional euclidean space. It has P dimensions, one for each x-component of the involved XML Schemas; in the following it will be denoted by the symbol $\Re^P$.

An XML Schema S_i can be represented in $\Re^P$ by means of a point $Q_i \equiv [q_1^i, q_2^i, \ldots, q_\nu^i, \ldots, q_P^i]$. The value of the generic coordinate q_ν^i is obtained by means of the following formula:

$$q_\nu^i = \xi(x_\nu) \cdot \psi(x_\nu, S_i, ID, VSSD, SSD, HWSD, OWSD)$$

$\xi(x_\nu)$ discriminates the complex elements w.r.t. the simple ones and the attributes. This is necessary because a complex element is presumably more characterizing than either a simple element or an attribute for defining the semantics of a concept. ξ is defined in the following way:

$$\xi(x_\nu) = \begin{cases} 1 & \text{if } x_\nu \text{ is a complex element} \\ \gamma & \text{if } x_\nu \text{ is either a simple element or an attribute} \end{cases}$$

Here, γ belongs to the real interval $[0, 1]$.

$\psi(x_\nu, S_i, ID, VSSD, SSD, HWSD, OWSD)$ indicates how much S_i is capable of representing the semantics expressed by the concept associated with x_ν; it is defined as follows:

$$\psi(x_\nu, S_i, ID, VSSD, SSD, HWSD, OWSD) =$$
$$\begin{cases} 1 & \text{if } x_\nu \in XCompSet(S_i) \\ \alpha_I & \text{if } x_\nu \notin XCompSet(S_i), \exists\, x_\mu \in XCompSet(S_i) \mid \langle x_\nu, x_\mu \rangle \in ID \\ \alpha_{VS} & \text{if } x_\nu \notin XCompSet(S_i), \exists\, x_\mu \in XCompSet(S_i) \mid \langle x_\nu, x_\mu \rangle \in VSSD \\ \alpha_S & \text{if } x_\nu \notin XCompSet(S_i), \exists\, x_\mu \in XCompSet(S_i) \mid \langle x_\nu, x_\mu \rangle \in SSD \\ \alpha_{HW} & \text{if } x_\nu \notin XCompSet(S_i), \exists\, x_\mu \in XCompSet(S_i) \mid \langle x_\nu, x_\mu \rangle \in HWSD \\ \alpha_{OW} & \text{if } x_\nu \notin XCompSet(S_i), \exists\, x_\mu \in XCompSet(S_i) \mid \langle x_\nu, x_\mu \rangle \in OWSD \\ 0 & \text{otherwise} \end{cases}$$

Here, α_I, α_{VS}, α_S, α_{HW} and α_{OW} belong to the real interval $[0, 1]$. An experimental study on the optimal values for α_I, α_{VS}, α_S, α_{HW}, α_{OW} and γ is illustrated in Section 4.3.

Proposition 3. Let $SchemaSet = \{S_1, S_2, \ldots, S_n\}$ be a set of XML Schemas; let P be the total number of x-components relative to the Schemas of $SchemaSet$. Let S_i be a Schema of $SchemaSet$. The worst case time complexity for determining the point Q_i associated with S_i in $\Re^P$ is $O(|XCompSet(S_i)| \times P \times \log P)$.

Proof. In order to determine Q_i, functions ξ and ψ must be evaluated for each dimension of $\Re^P$. Let us consider the νth dimension. The cost of ξ is constant. ψ requires to perform a search in ID, $VSSD$, SSD, $HWSD$ and $OWSD$ for each x-component of S_i. Since these dictionaries are ordered, this search can be performed in $O(\log P)$. As a consequence, the total cost of the function ψ is $O(|XCompSet(S_i)| \times \log P)$.

This evaluation must be repeated for each of the P dimensions; as a consequence, the total cost for determining Q_i is $O(|XCompSet(S_i)| \times P \times \log P)$. $\square$

Corollary 1. Let $SchemaSet = \{S_1, S_2, \ldots, S_n\}$ be a set of XML Schemas; let P be the total number of x-components relative to the Schemas of $SchemaSet$. The worst case time complexity for determining, in $\Re^P$, the points associated with all Schemas of $SchemaSet$ is $O\left(\left(\sum_{i=1}^{n} |XCompSet(S_i)|\right) \times P \times \log P\right) = O(P^2 \times \log P)$. □

We are now able to introduce our notion of distance between two XML Schemas and, consequently, to construct the Dissimilarity Matrix. Specifically, the distance between two XML Schemas S_i and S_j, belonging to $SchemaSet$, is computed by determining the euclidean distance between the corresponding points in $\Re^P$ and by normalizing this distance in such a way to obtain a value in the real interval $[0, 1]$, as required by clustering algorithms. This is obtained by means of the following formula:

$$ d(Q_i, Q_j) = \frac{\sqrt{\sum_{\nu=1}^{P} \left(q_\nu^i - q_\nu^j\right)^2}}{\sqrt{\sum_{\nu=1}^{P} \left(\xi\left(x_\nu\right)\right)^2}} $$

Here, the numerator represents the classical euclidean distance between two points; the denominator represents the maximum distance possibly existing between two points in the considered space and is exploited for normalizing the numerator[4].

Proposition 4. Let $SchemaSet = \{S_1, S_2, \ldots, S_n\}$ be a set of XML Schemas; let P be the total number of x-components relative to the Schemas of $SchemaSet$; finally, let $QSet = \{Q_1, Q_2, \ldots, Q_n\}$ be the set of points in $\Re^P$ associated with all Schemas of $SchemaSet$. The worst case time complexity for constructing the Dissimilarity Matrix is $O(n^2 \times P)$.

Proof. In order to construct the Dissimilarity Matrix, it is necessary to compute the distance for each of the $O(n^2)$ pairs of points in $QSet$.

The computation of this distance requires the computation of the sums at both the numerator (whose cost is $O(P)$) and the denominator (whose cost is, again, $O(P)$) of $d(Q_i, Q_j)$.

Therefore, the total cost of the matrix construction is $O(n^2) \times O(2P) = O(n^2 \times P)$. □

The previous reasonings show that, for constructing the Dissimilarity Matrix, two phases are necessary. The former aims at determining the points in the metric space corresponding to the involved XML Schemas; this activity costs $O(P^2 \times \log P)$ (see Corollary 1). The latter aims at computing the reciprocal distances among the previously defined points and costs $O(n^2 \times P)$ (see Proposition 4).

---

[4] Recall that $q_\nu^i = \xi(x_\nu) \cdot \psi(x_\nu, S_i, ID, VSSD, SSD, HWSD, OWSD)$ and that the maximum (resp., minimum) value of ψ is equal to 1 (resp., 0).

Table 2. The Dissimilarity Matrix computed for S_1, S_2, S_3, S_4 and S_5

-	S_1	S_2	S_3	S_4	S_5
S_1	0	0.44	0.78	0.77	0.74
S_2	0.44	0	0.80	0.79	0.76
S_3	0.78	0.80	0	0.20	0.42
S_4	0.77	0.79	0.20	0	0.38
S_5	0.74	0.76	0.42	0.38	0

3.4 Example (cnt'd)

Consider the set of XML Schemas $SchemaSet = \{S_1, S_2, S_3, S_4, S_5\}$ introduced in Section 3.2.

In order to show an example of the computation of the generic coordinate of a point, we illustrate the computation of the coordinate corresponding to the x-component $course_{[S_2]}$ for the point associated with S_1. In this case we have that:

- $\xi(course_{[S_2]}) = 1$, because $course_{[S_2]}$ is a complex element;
- $\psi(course_{[S_2]}, S_1, ID, VSSD, SSD, HWSD, OWSD) = \alpha_{VS}$ because S_1 includes $subject_{[S_1]}$ and $\langle subject_{[S_1]}, course_{[S_2]} \rangle \in VSSD$.

As a consequence, the final value of the coordinate corresponding to $course_{[S_2]}$ for the point associated with S_1 is $1 \cdot \alpha_{VS} = \alpha_{VS}$.

In the same way, all the coordinates of all involved Schemas can be computed.

After each point corresponding to an XML Schema of $SchemaSet$ has been determined, it is possible to compute the distance between each pair of points and, consequently, the Dissimilarity Matrix.

The Dissimilarity Matrix computed for $\alpha_I = 0.95$, $\alpha_{VS} = 0.90$, $\alpha_S = 0.80$, $\alpha_{HW} = 0.60$, $\alpha_{OW} = 0.60$ and $\gamma = 0.40$ is shown in Table 2[5]. This matrix indicates that the nearest (i.e., the most similar) pair of distinct XML Schemas is $\langle S_3, S_4 \rangle$; in fact, the distance between the points corresponding to them is only 0.20. This implies that most of the x-components belonging to S_3 and S_4 are related by some interschema property and, consequently, that, overall, S_3 and S_4 are very similar. On the contrary, the farthest (i.e., the most dissimilar) pair of XML Schemas is $\langle S_2, S_3 \rangle$ whose distance is 0.80. This indicates that many of the x-components of S_2 and S_3 are not related each other and, consequently, that, overall, the two Schemas represent quite different information.

3.5 Application of the Pre-existing Clustering Algorithms on the Constructed Dissimilarity Matrix

Once the Dissimilarity Matrix has been defined, it is possible to apply on it a large variety of clustering algorithms previously proposed in the literature. These

---

[5] A complete discussion on how these coefficients values have been selected can be found in Section 4.3.

differ for their time complexity, for their result accuracy, as well as for their behaviour. Therefore, it is clear that the choice of the clustering algorithm to be adopted in a certain domain strictly depends on its main features. In order to evaluate this fact we have considered three clustering algorithms, characterized by different features. For implementation purposes, we have chosen to apply three algorithms available in WEKA [42], one of the most popular Data Mining tools; specifically, we have chosen to apply K-Means, Expectation Maximization and Farthest First Traversal.

In this section we provide a brief overview of the behaviour of these algorithms when applied to our reference context.

K-Means [30]. When applied to our reference context, K-Means receives a parameter k and partitions the set of points of $\Re^P$ in k clusters.

The worst case time complexity of K-Means is $O(n \times k \times t)$, where n is the cardinality of *SchemaSet*, k is the desired number of clusters, and t is the number of iterations necessary for the algorithm to converge. Typically, k and t are much smaller than n; therefore, the worst case time complexity of K-Means can be considered linear against the cardinality of *SchemaSet*; for this reason K-Means is relatively scalable for clustering large sets of XML Schemas.

A difficulty in the application of K-Means to our context regards its sensitivity to noise and outliers: this implies that, if there exist some Schemas semantically very different from the others, K-Means could return not particularly satisfactory results. Another drawback of K-Means consists of its necessity to preventively know the best value for k; if this information is not available, a try-and-check approach should be adopted for determining it. Clearly, this would increase the time necessary to the algorithm for providing the final results.

Expectation Maximization [12,43]. Expectation Maximization (hereafter, *EM*) models involved objects as a collection of k Gaussians[6], where k is the number of clusters to be derived. For each involved object, *EM* computes a degree of membership to each cluster.

The implementation of *EM* is very similar to that of K-Means. As with K-Means, *EM* begins with an initial guess of the cluster centers (*Expectation* step) and iteratively refines them (*Maximization* step). It terminates when a parameter, measuring the quality of obtained clusters, no longer shows significant increases. *EM* is guaranteed to converge to a local maximum, that often coincides with the global one.

An important feature of this algorithm is its capability of modelling quite a rich set of cluster shapes. Moreover, it can be instructed to determine by itself the best number of clusters to be derived, even if the user can directly specify such an information, if he wants.

The quite refined statistical model underlying *EM* allows it to often obtain optimal results; for this reason *EM* is frequently adopted in a large variety of

---

[6] Although Gaussians are the generally used distributions in EM, other different distributions might be considered.

application contexts. Moreover, its capability of automatically determining the best number of clusters makes it particularly suited for our reference context.

Farthest First Traversal [23]. The basic idea of Farthest First Traversal (hereafter, FFT) is to get k points out of n, that are mutually "far" from each other; in our reference context, the points to cluster are the points of $\Re^P$ associated with XML Schemas.

FFT operates as follows: first it randomly selects a point Q_1 and puts it into the so-called "Traversed Set" TS. After this, it performs $k - 1$ iterations for constructing TS; during each iteration it inserts into TS the point Q_i having the maximum distance from TS; the distance of Q_i from TS is defined as $d(Q_i, TS) = min_{Q_j \in TS} d(Q_i, Q_j)$, where $d(Q_i, Q_j)$ could be any dissimilarity measure between two points (in our approach it is the dissimilarity measure defined in Section 3.3).

After TS has been constructed, each point $Q_i \in TS$ is chosen as the centroid of a cluster; then, for each point $Q_k \notin TS$, the algorithm computes its distance from the various centroids and puts Q_k in the cluster whose centroid has the minimum distance from it.

FFT requires the user to specify the number k of clusters to be constructed; moreover, the quality of its results might be influenced by the choice of the initial point Q_1 of TS. However, the worst case time complexity of this algorithm is $O(n \times k)$, where n is the cardinality of $SchemaSet$ and k is the number of clusters to be obtained. As a consequence, it is scalable and particularly suited in application contexts, like ours, where objects to be clustered could be very numerous.

3.6   Example (cnt'd)

Consider the Dissimilarity Matrix derived in Section 3.4 and shown in Table 2. The application of EM (i.e., the application of that clustering algorithm that does not require the number of desired clusters as input) returns two clusters, namely $C_1 = \{S_1, S_2\}$ and $C_2 = \{S_3, S_4, S_5\}$. The application of K-Means and FFT, when it is specified that the number of desired clusters is equal to 2, returns the same clusters C_1 and C_2 returned by EM. A further application of K-Means and FFT, with a number of desired clusters equal to 1 (resp., 3, 4 and 5) returns less accurate results and, consequently, confirms that the best number of clusters for this example is 2.

4   Experiments

4.1   Description of the Exploited Information Sources

In order to verify the validity of our approach we have performed various experiments. Specifically, we have considered 97 XML Schemas belonging to various application contexts, such as Biomedical Data, Project Management, Property Register, Industrial Companies, Universities, Airlines, Scientific Publications and Biological Data.

Table 3. Main features of the XML Schemas adopted in our experiments

Application context	Number of Schemas	Maximum depth of Schemas	Minimum, Average and Maximum Number of x-components	Minimum, Average and Maximum Number of complex elements
Biomedical Data	33	9	12 - 25 - 44	3 - 9 - 18
Project Management	9	6	35 - 40 - 46	5 - 6 - 9
Property Register	6	6	61 - 72 - 77	13 - 15 - 17
Industrial Companies	15	5	20 - 26 - 48	5 - 7 - 10
Universities	15	7	12 - 16 - 20	3 - 5 - 9
Airlines	2	4	12 - 13 - 13	4 - 4 - 4
Scientific Publications	2	6	17 - 18 - 18	8 - 9 - 9
Biological Data	15	9	230 - 322 - 658	33 - 55 - 221

These Schemas have been derived from specific Web sites or public sources. As an example, some XML Schemas relative to Biomedical Data have been derived from `http://www.biomediator.org`. Some of the Schemas relative to Project Management, Property Register and Industrial Companies have been derived from Italian Central Government Office information sources and are shown at the address `http://www.mat.unical.it/terracina/tests.html`. Some of the Schemas relative to Universities have been downloaded from the address `http://anhai.cs.uiuc.edu/archive/domains/courses.html`. Schemas relative to Airlines have been found in [35]. Schemas relative to Scientific Publications have been supplied by the authors of [27]. Finally, Schemas relative to Biological Data have been downloaded from specialized sites; among them we cite `http://smi-web.stanford.edu/projects/helix/pubs/ismb02/schemas/`. The main features of the XML Schemas that we have considered in our experiments are described in Table 3.

4.2 Description of the Adopted Measures

The accuracy measures of a clustering approach can be subdivided into: *(i) external measures*, that compare the results obtained by the approach into examination with the clusters defined by a domain expert and considered correct; *(ii) internal measures*, that evaluate the capability of the considered approach to produce homogeneous clusters.

External measures. In the following we introduce (and tailor to our reference context) some of the most popular external measures for the evaluation of clustering approaches [1].

Let *SchemaSet* be the set of XML Schemas which the clustering task must be performed on; we indicate with $ClSet^* = \{Cl_1^*, Cl_2^*, \ldots, Cl_l^*\}$ the set of correct classes defined by a domain expert, and with $ClSet = \{Cl_1, Cl_2, \ldots, Cl_k\}$ the set of clusters produced by the algorithm to evaluate. Accuracy measures we have considered are:

- *Precision* (hereafter, *Pre*). The Precision of a cluster Cl_j w.r.t. a class Cl_i^* is defined as $Pre(Cl_i^*, Cl_j) = \frac{|Cl_j \cap Cl_i^*|}{|Cl_j|}$. The total Precision of a clustering approach, when applied on *SchemaSet*, is defined as:

$$Pre = \sum_{i=1}^{|ClSet^*|} \left[\frac{|Cl_i^*|}{|SchemaSet|} \cdot \left(\max_{1 \leq j \leq |ClSet|} Pre(Cl_i^*, Cl_j) \right) \right]$$

- *Recall* (hereafter, *Rec*). The Recall of a cluster Cl_j w.r.t. a class Cl_i^* is defined as $Rec(Cl_i^*, Cl_j) = \frac{|Cl_j \cap Cl_i^*|}{|Cl_i^*|}$. The total Recall of a clustering approach, when applied on *SchemaSet*, is defined as:

$$Rec = \sum_{i=1}^{|ClSet^*|} \left[\frac{|Cl_i^*|}{|SchemaSet|} \cdot \left(\max_{1 \leq j \leq |ClSet|} Rec(Cl_i^*, Cl_j) \right) \right]$$

- *F-Measure*. F-Measure represents the harmonic mean between Precision and Recall; it is defined as $F\text{-}Measure(Cl_i^*, Cl_j) = 2 \cdot \frac{Pre(Cl_i^*, Cl_j) \cdot Rec(Cl_i^*, Cl_j)}{Pre(Cl_i^*, Cl_j) + Rec(Cl_i^*, Cl_j)}$. The total F-Measure of a clustering approach, when applied on *SchemaSet*, is defined as:

$$F\text{-}Measure = \sum_{i=1}^{|ClSet^*|} \left[\frac{|Cl_i^*|}{|SchemaSet|} \cdot \left(\max_{1 \leq j \leq |ClSet|} F\text{-}Measure(Cl_i^*, Cl_j) \right) \right]$$

- *Overall*. Overall measures the effort needed for adding false negatives and removing false positives from the set of clusters returned by the system to evaluate. It is defined as: $Overall(Cl_i^*, Cl_j) = Rec(Cl_i^*, Cl_j) \cdot \left(2 - \frac{1}{Pre(Cl_i^*, Cl_j)} \right)$. The total Overall of a clustering approach, when applied on *SchemaSet*, is defined as:

$$Overall = \sum_{i=1}^{|ClSet^*|} \left[\frac{|Cl_i^*|}{|SchemaSet|} \cdot \left(\max_{1 \leq j \leq |ClSet|} Overall(Cl_i^*, Cl_j) \right) \right]$$

- *Entropy*. Entropy provides a measure of the purity of clusters w.r.t. classes; it is defined as:

$$Entropy = \sum_{j=1}^{|ClSet|} \left[\frac{|Cl_j|}{|SchemaSet|} \cdot \sum_{i=1}^{|ClSet^*|} [-p_{ij} \ln(p_{ij})] \right]$$

where p_{ij} is the probability that an XML Schema of a cluster Cl_j belongs to the class Cl_i^*.

Values of Precision, Recall and F-Measure fall in the real interval $[0, 1]$, whereas values of Overall vary between $-\infty$ and 1. The higher the value of these measures is, the better the accuracy of the approach into examination will be. Values of Entropy belong to the real interval $[0, \ln(|ClSet^*|)]$; the lower Entropy is, the purer produced clusters will be.

Internal measures. Two interesting internal measures for evaluating clustering techniques are:

- *Uncoupling Degree*. This measure has been derived from the *coupling bound* measure introduced in [37]. Specifically, let Cl_i and Cl_j be two clusters and let τ be a number in the real interval $[0, 1]$; we define the set CU_{ij}^τ of the τ-uncoupled pairs between Cl_i and Cl_j as: $CU_{ij}^\tau = \{\langle S_a, S_b \rangle \mid S_a \in Cl_i, S_b \in Cl_j, d(S_a, S_b) \geq \tau\}$, where $d(S_a, S_b)$ represents the distance (i.e., the dissimilarity) between S_a and S_b; in our approach $d(S_a, S_b)$ is computed by means of the formula introduced in Section 3.3.

  The τ-Uncoupling Degree Unc_{ij}^τ between two clusters Cl_i and Cl_j is defined as the ratio between the τ-uncoupled pairs relative to Cl_i and Cl_j and the total number of possible pairs relative to Cl_i and Cl_j; in other words, $Unc_{ij}^\tau = \frac{|CU_{ij}^\tau|}{|Cl_i| \cdot |Cl_j|}$.

Finally, the *Uncoupling Degree* $\mathcal{U}^\tau$ is defined as $\mathcal{U}^\tau = \min_{\substack{1 \leq i,j \leq |ClSet| \\ i \neq j}} Unc_{ij}^\tau$. $\mathcal{U}^\tau$ belongs to the real interval $[0,1]$ and measures the capability of a clustering algorithm to return sufficiently separated clusters; given a value of τ, the higher $\mathcal{U}^\tau$ is, the higher the separation between clusters will be.

- *Cohesiveness Degree.* This measure has been derived from the *cohesiveness* parameter introduced in [37]. Specifically, given a cluster Cl_i and a real number $\tau \in [0,1]$, we define the set of τ-cohesive pairs as $CC_i^\tau = \{\langle S_a, S_b \rangle \mid S_a, S_b \in Cl_i, S_a \neq S_b, d(S_a, S_b) \leq \tau\}$.

  The τ-Cohesiveness Degree of a cluster Cl_i is defined as the ratio between the number of τ-cohesive pairs and the total number of pairs of XML Schemas in Cl_i; specifically, $Cohes_i^\tau = \frac{|CC_i^\tau|}{|Cl_i| \cdot (|Cl_i|-1)}$.

  Finally, the *Cohesiveness Degree* $\mathcal{C}^\tau$ is defined as $\mathcal{C}^\tau = \min_{1 \leq i \leq |ClSet|} Cohes_i^\tau$. $\mathcal{C}^\tau$ belongs to the real interval $[0,1]$ and measures the capability of an algorithm to produce cohesive clusters, i.e., clusters composed by very "similar" XML Schemas.

As pointed out in [37], a clustering algorithm should produce very cohesive and sufficiently uncoupled clusters; therefore, the higher the values of internal measures are, the better the performance of the algorithm will be.

4.3   Tuning of the Parameters Exploited by Our Approach

As pointed out in Section 3.3, our approach exploits some parameters; therefore, before carrying out any test, we had to experimentally find the values to be associated with them for guaranteeing the optimal (or, at least, a sub-optimal) value of accuracy measures. In order to perform such an evaluation, we have applied K-Means, *EM* and *FFT* on the Dissimilarity Matrixes constructed by our approach and we have considered various values of the parameters to tune; after this, we have computed Precision, Recall and Entropy on returned clusters.

In this activity an important issue concerned the number of clusters to be provided as input to K-Means and *FFT* (remember that *EM* is capable of automatically deriving this information). The number of clusters that we have specified in K-Means and *FFT* is 8; this number has been determined from the convergence of the following observations:

- The XML Schemas involved in our tests belonged to 8 different application domains; now, it is plausible that two Schemas belonging to different domains should belong to different clusters. However, it might happen that two or more clusters originate from the same domain and, consequently, that two Schemas belonging to the same domain actually belong to different clusters. As a consequence, the observation that the initial application domains were 8 might be not sufficient to conclude that the best number of clusters in our tests is 8.
- The execution of *EM* (that, as previously pointed out, is capable of automatically derive the best number of clusters) returned exactly 8 clusters for the involved Schema set.

The convergence of these two evidences allowed us to conclude that the best number of clusters to be provided as input to K-Means and FFT was exactly 8.

Since the number of possible combinations for parameter values was significant, we have subdivided our tuning activity in two phases: the former one aimed at determining *rough* optimal parameter values; the latter one aimed at performing an analysis for *refining* the previously obtained rough optimal values.

In the first phase we have subdivided the possible parameter values in four intervals[7], namely: *Low* (hereafter L), corresponding to the interval $[0, 0.4]$, *Medium* (hereafter M), corresponding to the interval $(0.4, 0.7]$, *High* (hereafter H), corresponding to the interval $(0.7, 0.9]$, and *Very High* (hereafter VH), corresponding to the interval $(0.9, 1]$. For each of these intervals we have considered the corresponding mean value as its representative (e.g., the representative value for M was 0.55). Observe that defined intervals have not the same length. This choice has been made for speeding up the second phase of our tuning activity. In fact, we estimated that, presumably, most of the values of the considered parameters would have been quite high, especially those involved in the function ψ; in fact, almost all considered parameters express the role of interschema properties in improving the quality of the clustering activity and, as informally shown in the Introduction (and as experimentally shown in this and in the next subsections), this role is quite important. As a consequence of this assumption, in order to reduce the effort to find the refined optimal values during the second phase, we considered smaller intervals for high values and longer intervals for low ones; this allowed us to restrict the range of variation of the most occurring intervals and, consequently, to focus our attention only on the most plausible parameter values. However, it is worth pointing out that this assumption does not limit the possibility that a parameter has a low value; it only implies that a longer time is necessary during the refinement phase for determining the exact value of this parameter.

After this, we have computed Precision, Recall and Entropy for all the possible combinations of values that could be assigned to the involved parameters within the set $\{L, M, H, VH\}$.

Table 4 shows the values of Precision, Recall and Entropy for some of the combinations that we have considered. At the end of these tests we have found that our approach shows the best results for $\alpha_I = VH$, $\alpha_{VS} = H$, $\alpha_S = H$, $\alpha_{HW} = M$, $\alpha_{OW} = M$, and $\gamma = L$, which correspond to the following rough values: $\alpha_I = 0.95$, $\alpha_{VS} = 0.80$, $\alpha_S = 0.80$, $\alpha_{HW} = 0.55$, $\alpha_{OW} = 0.55$, and $\gamma = 0.20$.

It is worth noticing that the "farther" from these optimal values the combinations are, the worse the values of Precision, Recall and Entropy are. The examination of Table 4 allows a further, interesting feature to be observed; in fact, it is possible to note that Precision increases when Recall increases, and vice versa. Such an interesting trend can be explained by the following reasoning. An increase of Precision implies that the predicted distribution of XML Schemas

---

[7] Recall that the values of all involved parameters can vary within the real interval $[0,1]$.

Table 4. Results obtained during the first phase of our tuning activity

α_I	α_{VS}	α_S	α_{HW}	α_{OW}	γ	K-Means			EM			FFT		
						Precision	Recall	Entropy	Precision	Recall	Entropy	Precision	Recall	Entropy
VH	VH	VH	VH	VH	VH	0.73	0.77	0.45	0.80	0.78	0.34	0.79	0.74	0.42
VH	VH	VH	H	H	H	0.76	0.83	0.41	0.84	0.84	0.31	0.83	0.79	0.38
VH	VH	VH	L	L	L	0.79	0.86	0.38	0.86	0.87	0.29	0.86	0.83	0.36
VH	VH	H	M	M	M	0.82	0.91	0.35	0.90	0.92	0.27	0.89	0.87	0.33
VH	H	H	M	L	M	0.81	0.90	0.36	0.89	0.91	0.27	0.88	0.86	0.33
VH	H	H	M	M	L	0.84	0.94	0.33	0.92	0.95	0.25	0.91	0.90	0.31
H	VH	VH	M	M	L	0.80	0.88	0.37	0.88	0.89	0.28	0.87	0.85	0.35
H	VH	VH	L	L	M	0.77	0.84	0.40	0.84	0.85	0.31	0.83	0.80	0.38
H	H	H	VH	VH	L	0.77	0.83	0.41	0.84	0.84	0.31	0.83	0.80	0.38
H	H	H	M	M	M	0.81	0.90	0.36	0.89	0.91	0.27	0.88	0.86	0.33
M	VH	VH	H	M	L	0.78	0.86	0.39	0.86	0.87	0.29	0.85	0.82	0.36
M	H	H	L	M	L	0.80	0.87	0.38	0.87	0.88	0.29	0.86	0.84	0.35
M	M	H	H	H	M	0.76	0.82	0.42	0.83	0.83	0.32	0.82	0.78	0.39
M	M	M	H	H	VH	0.71	0.75	0.46	0.78	0.76	0.35	0.77	0.72	0.44
L	M	M	M	L	L	0.76	0.82	0.42	0.83	0.83	0.32	0.82	0.78	0.39
L	L	L	H	H	VH	0.69	0.71	0.49	0.75	0.72	0.37	0.75	0.68	0.46
L	L	L	M	M	M	0.74	0.79	0.44	0.81	0.80	0.33	0.80	0.76	0.41
L	L	L	L	L	L	0.72	0.76	0.46	0.79	0.77	0.35	0.78	0.73	0.43

into the various clusters is more accurate and, consequently, that the fraction of true positives increases. However, since, in our tests, XML Schemas into consideration are fixed, an increase of true positives implies a decrease of the number of misclassified Schemas and, consequently, an improvement of Recall.

In order to make a further verification on the correctness of the optimal rough parameter values selected by the previous test and to verify the generality of our clustering approach we have performed a further test aiming at applying *k-fold cross validation* [21] on Schemas into consideration. This technique was originally introduced in statistics; afterwards, it has been extended to estimate the accuracy of machine learning and data mining techniques: for instance, it has been widely applied to determine the accuracy of a classifier. In order to apply k-fold cross validation, the set of input Schemas must be partitioned into k mutually exclusive subsets $F_1, F_2, \ldots, F_k$ called *folds*; the various folds should approximately have the same cardinality.

In our application context, k-fold cross validation has been implemented as follows. First, we randomly partitioned input Schemas into 8 folds such that 7 of them contained 12 Schemas and the last one comprised 13 Schemas. After this, we have performed an iterative procedure; during the ith iteration ($i = 1..8$) we have exploited all folds except F_i for training parameter values and we have used F_i for testing obtained results. Both training and testing were based on the computation of Precision, Recall and Entropy.

For each computation of accuracy measures, we first applied EM, because it does not require the number of desired clusters to be specified. After this, we verified if the number of clusters returned by EM was also optimal for K-Means and FFT; this last verification was performed by means of a try-and-check procedure (i.e., we considered various values for the number of desired clusters and selected that value capable of guaranteing the best performances). At the end of this activity, we have found that, in all our tests, the number of clusters identified by EM was always optimal.

As far as the training sub-task of k-fold cross validation is concerned, the best parameter combinations were: $\{\alpha_I = VH, \alpha_{VS} = H, \alpha_S = H, \alpha_{HW} = $

Table 5. Results obtained during the second phase of our tuning activity

α_I	α_{VS}	α_S	α_{HW}	α_{OW}	γ	K-MEANS			EM			FFT		
						Precision	Recall	Entropy	Precision	Recall	Entropy	Precision	Recall	Entropy
0.95	0.80	0.80	0.55	0.55	0.20	0.840	0.941	0.330	0.921	0.952	0.251	0.910	0.903	0.310
1,00	0.90	0.90	0.68	0.68	0.40	0.839	0.937	0.335	0.917	0.949	0.252	0.907	0.897	0.315
1,00	0.90	0.90	0.60	0.60	0.30	0.844	0.949	0.317	0.929	0.954	0.246	0.919	0.909	0.297
1,00	0.90	0.90	0.42	0.45	0.40	0.849	0.957	0.305	0.937	0.959	0.242	0.927	0.917	0.285
1,00	0.90	0.85	0.68	0.68	0.20	0.844	0.948	0.318	0.928	0.954	0.246	0.918	0.908	0.298
1,00	0.85	0.85	0.50	0.50	0.20	0.845	0.950	0.315	0.930	0.955	0.245	0.920	0.910	0.295
0.98	0.90	0.90	0.50	0.50	0.10	0.845	0.951	0.314	0.931	0.955	0.245	0.921	0.911	0.294
0.98	0.90	0.90	0.42	0.42	0.20	0.843	0.947	0.320	0.927	0.953	0.247	0.917	0.907	0.300
0.98	0.85	0.85	0.68	0.70	0.20	0.848	0.955	0.308	0.935	0.958	0.243	0.925	0.915	0.288
0.98	0.85	0.85	0.50	0.50	0.20	0.844	0.947	0.320	0.927	0.954	0.247	0.917	0.907	0.300
0.95	0.90	0.90	0.50	0.52	0.10	0.843	0.946	0.321	0.926	0.953	0.247	0.916	0.906	0.301
0.95	0.90	0.80	0.60	0.60	0.40	0.851	0.963	0.307	0.944	0.963	0.241	0.938	0.925	0.281
0.95	0.85	0.85	0.42	0.50	0.10	0.837	0.935	0.338	0.915	0.947	0.253	0.905	0.895	0.318
0.95	0.80	0.85	0.60	0.60	0.20	0.844	0.949	0.317	0.929	0.954	0.246	0.919	0.909	0.297
0.95	0.80	0.80	0.60	0.58	0.40	0.846	0.953	0.311	0.933	0.956	0.244	0.923	0.913	0.291
0.92	0.80	0.80	0.50	0.50	0.10	0.833	0.927	0.350	0.907	0.943	0.257	0.897	0.887	0.330
0.92	0.72	0.72	0.60	0.60	0.40	0.838	0.936	0.336	0.916	0.948	0.252	0.906	0.896	0.316
0.92	0.72	0.72	0.50	0.50	0.20	0.829	0.919	0.362	0.899	0.939	0.261	0.889	0.879	0.342
0.92	0.72	0.72	0.42	0.40	0.10	0.823	0.907	0.380	0.887	0.933	0.267	0.877	0.867	0.360

$M, \alpha_{OW} = M, \gamma = L\}$ for $i = 1, 3, 4, 7$ and 8; $\{\alpha_I = VH, \alpha_{VS} = H, \alpha_S = H, \alpha_{HW} = M, \alpha_{OW} = L, \gamma = M\}$ for $i = 2$ and 6; $\{\alpha_I = VH, \alpha_{VS} = VH, \alpha_S = H, \alpha_{HW} = M, \alpha_{OW} = M, \gamma = M\}$ for $i = 5$. For each iteration, the testing sub-task confirmed the correctness of trained values. This allowed us to draw two important conclusions:

- the results about the optimal rough parameter values obtained by the previous method (i.e., that the best rough parameter values where $\{\alpha_I = VH, \alpha_{VS} = H, \alpha_S = H, \alpha_{HW} = M, \alpha_{OW} = M, \gamma = L\}$) are confirmed by the current test;
- our clustering approach is general, i.e., it does not suffer from overlearning problems.

In the second phase of this experiment, we tried to refine the rough configuration of parameter values obtained during the first phase. Specifically, we considered several values to be assigned to each parameter within the optimal interval found for it during the first phase. The results of this analysis, for some of the considered configurations, are presented in Table 5. From the analysis of this table, we may observe that the best performances (i.e., the best values of Precision, Recall and Entropy) are obtained for $\alpha_I = 0.95$, $\alpha_{VS} = 0.90$, $\alpha_S = 0.80$, $\alpha_{HW} = 0.60$, $\alpha_{OW} = 0.60$ and $\gamma = 0.40$.

As for this second phase, we have not performed k-fold cross validation since, in spite of its great time expensiveness, in the first phase it totally confirmed the results of the other parameter tuning method (that is, also, the method adopted in the second phase).

The results we obtained for α_I, α_{VS}, α_S, α_{HW}, α_{OW} and γ allow us to conclude that, in our application context, synonymies are more important than overlappings and hyponymies; these results confirm the idea, generally accepted in the literature, that synonymies are more important than hyponymies and overlappings for characterizing concept semantics. However, the quite high values of α_{HW} and α_{OW} show that also these last kinds of properties play a sufficiently important role in characterizing the semantics of a concept. Analogously, the results we have obtained for γ confirm our reasoning, expressed in Section 3.3, when we say that complex elements are more characterizing than simple elements and attributes for determining the semantics of a concept, even if, in any case, these last play an important role.

4.4 Evaluation of the Impact of Our Approach for Dissimilarity Matrix Computation on the Clustering Quality

The quality of results produced by any clustering algorithm strongly depends on the Dissimilarity Matrix received in input, since it summarizes the relationships existing among the objects into examination. Clearly, a sophisticated approach for the calculation of the Dissimilarity Matrix causes an increase of the computational cost, on one hand, but allows an improvement of the accuracy of obtained results, on the other hand.

Since our approach for the computation of the Dissimilarity Matrix is quite complex, we have planned to quantify the improvement it produces on the result accuracy w.r.t. an approach that takes into account the semantics of the involved Schemas in a simpler way. The "simplified" definition of the semantic distance existing between two XML Schemas, exploited in this test (called d_S in the following), considers only the fraction of the dissimilarity properties existing between them. Specifically, d_S is defined as:

$$d_S(S_i, S_j) = 1 - \frac{|sim(S_i)| + |sim(S_j)|}{|XCompSet(S_i)| + |XCompSet(S_j)|}$$

where $sim(S_i)$, (resp., $sim(S_j)$) indicates the set of x-components of S_i (resp., S_j) involved in at least one synonymy with an x-component of S_j (resp., S_i).

It is worth pointing out that this dissimilarity measure is really used in the literature; moreover, we observe that it is not a metrics; for this reason, in this test, we have adopted FFT as clustering algorithm, since it does not necessarily need a metric space.

In this test we have performed two analyses, devoted to consider external and internal measures, respectively.

Analysis of external measures. In a first series of experiments we have compared the values of external measures, obtained by applying our approach and the "simplified" one. Table 6 shows the obtained results; from its examination we deduce that our approach allows a substantial improvement on the quality of results; specifically, if compared with the "simplified" one, Precision increases of 20%, Recall improves of 13%, F-Measures increases of 16%, Overall improves of 46% and Entropy decreases of 17%.

Analysis of internal measures. The computation of internal measures depends on the parameter τ, specifying when two XML Schemas can be considered uncoupled or cohesive (see Section 4.2). In our analysis we have considered various values of τ and, for each of them, we have computed the Uncoupling and the Cohesiveness Degrees, obtained by exploiting our approach and the "simplified"

Table 6. Comparison of the accuracy of our approach w.r.t. the accuracy of the "simplified" one

Measure	Precision	Recall	F-Measure	Overall	Entropy
Our Approach	0.94	0.93	0.93	0.86	0.28
"Simplified" Approach	0.78	0.82	0.80	0.59	0.34

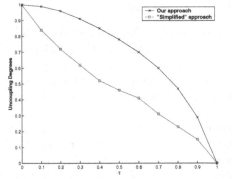 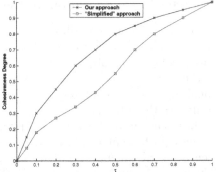

Fig. 6. Variation of Uncoupling Degree against τ, obtained by exploiting our approach and the "simplified" one

Fig. 7. Variation of Cohesiveness Degree against τ, obtained by exploiting our approach and the "simplified" one

one. Figures 6 and 7 show the corresponding results. Also in this case the improvement we have obtained is significant; in fact, the maximum increase of the Uncoupling Degree (resp., the Cohesiveness Degree) determined by exploiting our approach is obtained for $\tau = 0.40$ (resp., $\tau = 0.50$) and is equal to 0.33 (resp., 0.27).

4.5   Analysis of the Robustness of Our Approach

As pointed out in Section 3.3, our approach is based on the interschema properties stored in IPD. In order to measure its robustness against errors in IPD, we have carried out some variations in the correct dictionary and, for each of them, we have computed the values of external measures returned by it. This analysis is important because, if the number of involved XML Schemas is high, it is compulsory to (semi-)automatically compute IPD; clearly, (semi-)automatic techniques are more error-prone than manual ones.

The variations we have performed in the correct dictionary are: *(a)* the removal of 10% of correct properties; *(b)* the removal of 20% of correct properties; *(c)* the removal of 30% of correct properties; *(d)* the removal of 50% of correct properties; *(e)* the insertion of 10% of wrong properties; *(f)* the insertion of 20% of wrong properties; *(g)* the insertion of 30% of wrong properties; *(h)* the insertion of 50% of wrong properties. In this experiment we have exploited both K-Means and *EM* and *FFT* for performing clustering activity.

Table 7. Variations of the values of external measures in presence of errors in IPD

Case	K-Means			EM			FFT		
	Precision	Recall	Entropy	Precision	Recall	Entropy	Precision	Recall	Entropy
No error	0.85	0.96	0.31	0.94	0.96	0.24	0.94	0.93	0.28
(a) -10%	0.85	0.88	0.34	0.94	0.88	0.26	0.94	0.84	0.31
(b) -20%	0.85	0.80	0.37	0.94	0.80	0.29	0.93	0.77	0.34
(c) -30%	0.84	0.73	0.40	0.94	0.73	0.31	0.93	0.70	0.37
(d) -50%	0.84	0.67	0.44	0.93	0.67	0.34	0.93	0.64	0.40
(e) +10%	0.78	0.96	0.34	0.86	0.96	0.27	0.86	0.92	0.31
(f) +20%	0.71	0.96	0.38	0.79	0.96	0.30	0.78	0.92	0.35
(g) +30%	0.65	0.95	0.42	0.72	0.95	0.33	0.71	0.92	0.39
(h) +50%	0.59	0.95	0.47	0.65	0.95	0.37	0.65	0.91	0.43

Table 7 illustrates obtained results. From its analysis we can observe that our approach is quite robust against errors present in IPD; however, at the same time, it shows a good sensitivity against these errors since, if the correct properties that are removed or the wrong properties that are added are excessive, the result accuracy significantly decreases.

4.6   Evaluation of the Impact of Hyponimies and Overlappings on the Quality of Results

In this section we analyze the impact of hyponimies and overlappings on the quality of clusters derived by our system. In fact, most of the approaches previously proposed in the literature consider only synonymies and do not take hyponymies and overlappings into account (see, below, Section 6). In order to quantify the importance of these last kinds of properties, we carried out the following operations:

- We ran our prototype on the input Schemas reported in Table 3 by setting coefficients α_I, α_{VS}, α_S, α_{HW}, α_{OW} and γ to the values that guarantee the best performances, i.e. we set $\alpha_I = 0.95$, $\alpha_{VS} = 0.90$, $\alpha_S = 0.80$, $\alpha_{HW} = 0.60$, $\alpha_{OW} = 0.60$ and $\gamma = 0.40$; we call *Configuration A* this scenario. This task generated a set $CLSet_A$ of clusters.
- We ran our prototype on the input Schemas reported in Table 3 by setting $\alpha_{HW} = 0$ and $\alpha_{OW} = 0$; in this way, we forced our approach to disregard hyponymies and overlappings stored in IPD; this implies that the computation of the distance function $d(Q_i, Q_j)$ is only affected by synonymies. In this case, the value of α_I, α_{VS}, α_S and γ exploited in *Configuration A* might be inadequate; in other words, the hypothesis that $\alpha_{HW} = 0$ and $\alpha_{OW} = 0$ requires to appropriately re-tune the values of α_I, α_{VS}, α_S and γ.

   As a consequence of the previous reasoning, we have re-tuned α_I, α_{VS}, α_S and γ for $\alpha_{HW} = 0$ and $\alpha_{OW} = 0$; this task has been performed by applying the same methodology described in Section 4.3. Specifically: *(i)* we have considered various intervals for α_I, α_{VS}, α_S and γ (namely L, M, H and VH); *(ii)* we have applied K-Means, EM and FFT for producing a set of clusters; *(iii)* we have computed Precision, Recall and Entropy for all possible combinations of these intervals; *(iv)* we have selected those intervals guaranteeing the highest accuracy; *(v)* we have performed a refinement task

Table 8. Accuracy of our approach in *Configuration A* and *Configuration B*

	K-MEANS			EM			FFT		
Configuration	Precision	Recall	Entropy	Precision	Recall	Entropy	Precision	Recall	Entropy
Configuration A	0.85	0.96	0.31	0.94	0.96	0.24	0.94	0.93	0.28
Configuration B	0.77	0.82	0.39	0.84	0.85	0.32	0.81	0.82	0.34

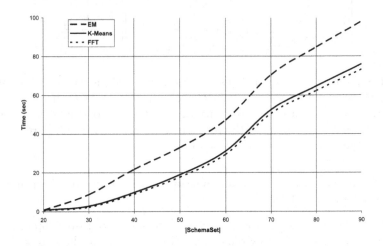

Fig. 8. Response Time against the cardinality of *SchemaSet*

for finding the best values (among those admissible in the selected intervals) for α_I, α_{VS}, α_S and γ.

At the end of these tests we have found that, under the condition that $\alpha_{HW} = 0$ and $\alpha_{OW} = 0$, our approach shows the best performance for $\alpha_I = 0.98$, $\alpha_{VS} = 0.90$, $\alpha_S = 0.85$ and $\gamma = 0.40$; we call *Configuration B* this scenario and $CLSet_B$ the set of obtained clusters.

- We compared $CLSet_A$ and $CLSet_B$ with the set of classes $CLSet^*$ provided by human experts (see Section 4.2). This comparison allowed Precision, Recall and Entropy, associated with *Configurations A* and *B*, to be determined.

The results of this experiment are reported in Table 8. From the analysis of this table we observe that the results associated with *Configuration A* are always better than those obtained with *Configuration B*. Such a trend can be justified as follows: if we ignore the contribution of hyponymies and overlappings, two concepts linked by this kind of properties are considered completely distinct; this influences the position, in the vectorial space, of the points associated with the corresponding Schemas (specifically, their distance is overestimated), which negatively influences the performance of any clustering algorithm.

4.7   Response Time

We have conducted an experimental study on our test Schemas to compute the increase of the Response Time caused by an increase of the cardinality of

SchemaSet (i.e., the number of XML Schemas to be clustered). In this experiment we have adopted all the three clustering techniques considered in this paper, i.e., K-Means, *EM* and *FFT*. All tests have been performed on a machine with a Pentium IV 2.6 GHz CPU and 1 Gb of RAM.

In Figure 8 we plot the average Response Time of our approach as a function of the cardinality of *SchemaSet*. From the analysis of this figure we can observe that the increase of the Response Time is "softer" than that we could expect from the theoretical, worst case, analysis. In our opinion this is a very interesting result because it shows that our approach is really adequate in those contexts characterized by numerous data sources to be clustered.

Furthermore, we can note that *EM* is more time consuming than K-Means or *FFT*. This behaviour, along with the results presented in the previous sections, confirm the theoretical results about these algorithms (see [21,42]), specifying that *EM* is generally more time consuming, but also more precise, than K-Means and *FFT*.

5 Applications

Data source clustering has a large variety of applications; among them we cite the extraction of relevant information from semi-structured data sources [8], the change detection in semi-structured information sources [6], the DTD induction from a set of XML documents [33], and the query optimization in XML sources [28].

In this section we provide a brief overview of five applications that, in our opinion, are well suited and tailored when data sources to be clustered are XML documents.

5.1 User-Guided Organization of Web Sites

This application is based on the assumption that information stored in a Web site has both an objective and a subjective component; in fact, the same site can be perceived under different points of view by different visitors (think, for example, to the site of Ferrari visited by a car collector, a supporter and a stockholder). This observation makes it particularly interesting an approach that, given a user, clusters the Web sites he visits on the basis of his perception of them (think, for example, to the possibility to supply a personalized access to e-commerce, e-government or e-learning providers).

Let u be a user; the categorization of the Web sites of his interest can be obtained by: *(i)* associating an intelligent agent with each visited site; this agent registers in a Site Profile P_i (stored as an XML document) the content of the site S_i as it is perceived by u (see [19] for details about the behaviour of this agent); *(ii)* organizing the Site Profiles thus obtained into a Cluster Hierarchy.

This last activity requires the following problems to be solved:

– The number of basic clusters (i.e., the clusters at the bottom of the Hierarchy) and, more in general, the number of sites considered for a user cannot

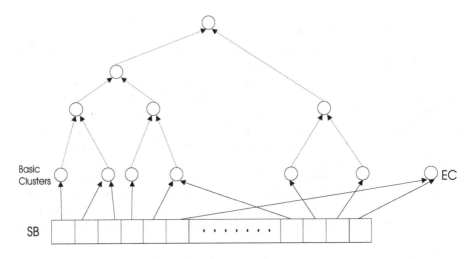

Fig. 9. Structure of the proposed Cluster Hierarchy

grow indefinitely. Thus, some mechanism for limiting this number must be defined.

- The perception a user has of a site can change over time (think, for example, to a Ferrari supporter that becomes a car collector); if this happens, it could be necessary to move the corresponding Site Profile from a basic cluster to another one appearing to be closer to the new perception. In this sense, the Hierarchy must be dynamic and requires a continuous checking. However, making a redo operation at each new access does not lead to a feasible approach: some less naive strategy, guaranteing, at each time, an acceptable correctness of site classification, is necessary.
- It may happen that a new site cannot be classified into any correct basic cluster.

Clearly enough, in order to construct the Cluster Hierarchy in such a way that user interests are properly modelled, the semantics of the involved Site Profiles must be carefully taken into account. In this perspective, interschema properties, possibly existing among concepts represented in the involved Site Profiles, play a relevant role.

We describe, now, an approach for both constructing and maintaining the Cluster Hierarchy that can solve the problems outlined above. It exploits a support buffer SB, storing a certain number of Site Profiles; SB implements also an index on the basic clusters of the Hierarchy in such a way that each Site Profile of SB points to the basic cluster it belongs to. There is an Extra Cluster EC that collects all currently unclassified Site Profiles. The whole structure is depicted in Figure 9.

The construction and the maintenance of the Cluster Hierarchy requires the following three activities to be performed:

- A new Site Profile P_i must be inserted in the Hierarchy. If SB is not full, P_i is stored therein. If SB is full, a Site Profile P_j is selected (according to the Least Recently Used strategy) to be removed. After its removal, a counter C_R is increased, P_i is inserted in SB and an attempt to classify P_i into one of the existing basic clusters is performed; if this is not possible, P_i is classified into EC.
- A periodic check must be performed on all Site Profiles of SB to verify if some of them appear to be no longer correctly clustered. Let P_i be one of these profiles. P_i must be moved from the current cluster to that having the highest similarity with it, or to EC, in case no cluster appears to be sufficiently similar. In any case, a counter C_M is increased.
- A periodic check must be carried out to verify the Hierarchy consistency. A good measure of the Hierarchy inconsistency degree is given by the value $C_R + C_M$, since it counts how many times a Site Profile is removed from some cluster without updating the Cluster Hierarchy. If $C_R + C_M$ is greater than a certain threshold, representing the maximum tolerated inconsistency degree, then C_R and C_M are set to 0, the current Cluster Hierarchy is deleted and a new one is constructed by applying, on the Site Profiles of SB, the algorithm described in Section 3. After this operation EC is emptied.

It is worth pointing out that, in all these activities, it is necessary the computation of a distance measure between XML Schemas (the Site Profiles) which takes their relative semantics into account. This is exactly what is done by the distance function d introduced in Section 3.3.

5.2   E-Service Providers-Guided Organization of Users

This application is the dual of the previous one. In this case there is a Provider and many users accessing its services; the application aims at constructing a Cluster Hierarchy classifying users according to their perception of the Provider's services.

The Provider associates an intelligent agent with each user, monitoring his behaviour and registering, in a User Profile (organized as an XML source), the services provided by it that appear of interest for the user. An agent performing this task is described in [41].

The Cluster Hierarchy is constructed and maintained by means of the methodology described in the previous section; the only difference is that SB stores User Profiles and not Site Profiles and that clusters represent groups of users having the same interests.

5.3   Customized E-Service Portals

A Cluster Hierarchy can be exploited for implementing a challenging application in the context of e-service Portals. These generally provide a user with a set of categories helping him to choose the sites of his interest.

The Cluster Hierarchy could be exploited for constructing a Portal front-end, adapting itself to user preferences; in this way a different, personalized, Portal organization is presented to each user.

The customized front-end is dynamically built on the basis of the Cluster Hierarchy associated with the user contacting the Portal.

This application needs an agent, called *u-agent*, for each user, and an agent, called *p-agent*, for the Portal. Each site handled by the Portal should have an associated XML Schema.

The application behaves as follows: let u be a user contacting the Portal; the u-agent associated with u applies the approach illustrated in Section 5.1 for constructing and maintaining a Cluster Hierarchy representing a user-guided categorization of information of interest for u.

When u contacts the Portal, his u-agent and the Portal's p-agent start a negotiation. Specifically, the u-agent sends its Cluster Hierarchy to the p-agent that tries to classify its sites into the basic clusters of the Hierarchy. It could happen that some Portal sites cannot be classified in any basic cluster of the Hierarchy; these sites are collected in a dummy basic cluster that is inserted as a child node of the root.

At this point, Portal sites are categorized according to the Cluster Hierarchy of u, representing his profile; therefore, their customized organization is completed and a Portal front-end reflecting this organization can be presented to u; this front-end is organized in such a way that u is provided with a Hierarchy of site categories, reflecting the structure of his Cluster Hierarchy, except for the presence of the dummy category.

5.4   Integration of Our System with LDAP Protocol and Other Directory Services

Our system can be fruitfully integrated with LDAP protocol [26] and, more in general, with other directory services. LDAP (Lightweight Directory Access Protocol) is an open industry standard supporting the search of information concerning people, computers, network devices and applications. LDAP organizes available information in hierarchies of directories. In order to handle directory information, LDAP adopts an XML-based language called DSML (Directory Service Markup Language); this language has been conceived for bridging the gap between classical and XML-based applications operating on directory services. LDAP relies on a client-server model. Each user is directly assisted by either an LDAP server or an LDAP-collaborating application; if an LDAP server cannot satisfy a client request it specifies the URL of another LDAP server storing required information; this behaviour is known as *referral mechanism*.

A first fruitful integration of our system with LDAP might be as follows. In LDAP, a user typically submits an XPath query that is mapped onto an LDAP query [26]. This could be processed by means of traditional techniques; as an example, a DSML directory could be represented by means of a set of linked tables [28]; in this case the evaluation of an LDAP query would require a certain number of joins among inferred tables. This would negatively influence query processing activity: in fact, the execution of a join is computationally expensive and, in several cases, the number of joins to be performed might be very high [28,39]. Our system might provide a contribution to solve this problem;

in fact, by exploiting it, DSML directories might be grouped in clusters and, for each cluster, a representative Schema might be constructed. At this point, queries could be processed against cluster representative Schemas; this would significatively reduce the number of joins to be executed.

A further problem about LDAP querying consists in the high distribution of LDAP directories [26]. As a consequence, in order to process an LDAP query, it is necessary to contact several LDAP servers and exchange a large amount of messages among them. This would lead to an increase of query response time (because a query is routed through several servers) and data load (because LDAP servers exchange a large amount of messages). As in the previous case, we can alleviate these problems by grouping available directories into homogeneous clusters and by evaluating a query against cluster representatives.

5.5   XML Indexing

Our approach can be fruitfully applied for supporting XML document indexing (see [4] for a comprehensive survey). Roughly speaking, an index is a data structure that provides a quick access to the information stored in a database. Indexes are usually exploited for speeding up querying activities.

Due to the intrinsic tree-based structure of XML documents, XML indexing is quite a difficult task; in fact, XML indexes must be capable of storing information about both the position of elements in a document and the paths connecting the root of the corresponding tree to the various nodes [4,24,40]. As a consequence, XML indexes are often complex and quite large data structures; for instance, [13] observes that indexed data might be even larger than the corresponding documents. In this case indexes might not fit in main memory and this would cause unacceptable long delays in query answering.

Our approach might provide a contribution in this setting; in fact, it might be exploited for grouping input Schemas into homogeneous clusters and for building a representative Schema for each cluster. In this case indexes might be constructed on representative Schemas instead of on original Schemas.

This idea shares some similarities with some, well known, indexing techniques. As an example, [4] observes that *not all paths* in an XML document are equally interesting and relevant and proposes to construct *partial indexes* containing only a small subset of the most common paths; as shown in [5], partial indexes can ensure a good accuracy. Our approach follows this philosophy; in fact, a representative Schema summarizes the main features of a collection of Schemas and, clearly, contains only the most common paths.

As a consequence, our approach would reduce the space required for storing indexes and would speed up query processing activity even if it would produce approximate answers to user queries. Therefore, it could be an effective solution in those contexts in which the exigency of quickly returning (possibly approximate) query answers outweights the need of exact results.

One of these scenarios is *on-line decision support systems*; in this case users and analysts explore large XML data sets by means of declarative interfaces (often based on XQuery) and use appropriate tools for visualizing query answers and for detecting interesting patterns in retrieved data; the success of this application strongly depends on the capability of producing timely (even if approximate) feedbacks to users.

6   Related Work

In this section we compare our approach with other related ones already presented in the literature.

Approach of [36]. In [36] an approach for clustering DTDs is proposed. It operates as follows: first it applies any clustering algorithm for grouping elements of the involved DTDs in a set of clusters. After this, it creates one array for each DTD, having one component for each cluster; the ith component of the array indicates how many elements of the corresponding DTD belong to the ith cluster. Finally, it applies any clustering algorithm on the set of constructed arrays.

There are some similarities between our approach and that described in [36]. Specifically: *(i)* both of them construct a "vector"-based representation of the involved Schemas that, next, is provided in input to a clustering algorithm; *(ii)* both of them have been specifically conceived for XML.

The main differences between the two approaches are the following: *(i)* in [36] the computation of the similarity degree between two DTDs privileges their *structural* properties (i.e., the hierarchical organization of the corresponding elements); on the contrary, our approach considers interschema properties, that define a *semantic* information; *(ii)* the clustering activity performed during the first phase allows the approach described in [36] to carry out a preliminary reduction of the number of involved elements; this feature is not present in our approach; however, errors possibly occurring during this initial clustering activity could negatively influence the final results.

XClust. In [27] the system *XClust*, defining a DTD clustering technique as a part of a more complex DTD integration approach, is proposed. In *XClust* each DTD is modelled by means of a tree; this representation allows the definition of a *similarity measure* for each pair of elements belonging to different DTDs; these measures are, then, exploited for computing the *similarity degree* of two DTDs. Once the similarity degree associated with each pair of available DTDs has been computed, a hierarchical clustering algorithm is applied.

The main similarities between our approach and *XClust* are the following: *(i)* both of them have been specifically conceived for XML; *(ii)* both of them operate on the intensional component of involved information sources.

As for differences between the two approaches we observe that: *(i)* *XClust* considers only synonymies and does not take hyponymies and overlappings into account; *(ii)* *XClust* aims mainly at constructing a global DTD from a set of input ones; the clustering activity, in *XClust*, is used for producing the global DTD; on the contrary, the clustering activity is the main purpose of our system.

Approach of [22]. In [22] an approach for clustering structured information sources present in the Web is proposed. It assumes the existence, for each application domain, of a *hidden model* containing a finite vocabulary of attributes; this assumption allows sources to be clustered by means of a specific algorithm called MD (*Model Differentiation*).

The main similarities between our approach and that described in [22] are the following: *(i)* both of them define a suitable mechanism for representing involved sources; *(ii)* both of them exploit semantic information; specifically, our approach uses interschema properties whereas the approach of [22] considers the hidden model.

The main differences between the two approaches are the following: *(i)* the approach presented in [22] requires a deep analysis of the extensional component of involved information sources; this analysis produces very satisfactory results but requires a significant pre-processing phase for constructing, among others, the hidden model; *(ii)* the approach proposed in [22] has been specifically conceived for analyzing structured information sources present in the Web; on the contrary, our approach is specialized for XML Schemas.

Approach of [33]. In [33] an approach for clustering XML documents is described. It models available documents by means of *ordered trees* and exploits a dynamic programming algorithm for defining a similarity measure for them. Finally, it uses a hierarchical clustering algorithm to group documents into homogeneous classes.

There exist some similarities between our approach and that described in [33]. Specifically: *(i)* both of them propose a suitable model for representing involved information sources; in our case this model has a "vectorial" nature whereas, in the approach of [33], it is based on trees; *(ii)* both of them are *flexible*, in the sense that they allow the exploitation of any clustering algorithm.

As for the main differences between the two approaches, we observe that: *(i)* for computing the similarity degree among involved sources, the approach described in [33] considers structural information whereas our approach exploits the semantic one; *(ii)* our approach focuses on XML Schemas whereas the approach of [33] has been conceived to operate on XML documents.

Approach of [9]. In [9] an approach for clustering XML documents is proposed. It represents available documents by means of ordered trees and measures their similarity by means of a dynamic programming algorithm; after this, it constructs a labelled graph G, whose nodes represent XML documents and whose arcs denote the corresponding similarity degrees; finally, it applies the Prim algorithm for partitioning the set of nodes of G and associates a cluster with each partition.

There are some similarities between our approach and that presented in [9]; in fact, *(i)* both of them have been specifically conceived for XML; *(ii)* both of them define a suitable mechanism for representing information sources; this is "vector"-based in our approach and tree-based in the approach of [9].

The main differences existing between the two approaches are the following: *(i)* in order to compute document similarity, the approach described in [9] exploits the structural information of involved sources whereas our approach considers the semantic one; *(ii)* the approach illustrated in [9] operates on the extensional component of the information sources into consideration; on the contrary, our approach works on the intensional one.

Approach of [7]. [7] presents an approach for clustering XML documents on the basis of their structural similarities. This approach represents each document by means of a tree and applies *tree matching* algorithms for identifying the structural similarities existing among available trees. In this way, it is possible to partition available documents into homogeneous classes and, then, to define, for each class, a tree (called *XML cluster representative*), summarizing the main characteristics of its documents. This partitioning is, finally, refined by applying a suitable hierarchical clustering algorithm called XRep.

There exist some similarities between our approach and that described in [7]. Specifically: *(i)* both of them propose a suitable formalism for representing involved information sources; in our approach this formalism has a "vectorial" nature whereas, in the approach of [7], it is based on trees; *(ii)* both of them operate on XML sources.

The main differences between the two approaches are the following: *(i)* for computing similarities existing between two XML documents, the approach of [7] exploits structural information, whereas our approach uses the semantic one; *(ii)* the approach of [7] is quite sophisticated; as a consequence, it produces very refined results but requires quite a complex pre-processing phase; on the contrary, our approach is lighter, even if the results it obtains are satisfactory; *(iii)* the approach of [7] is extensional whereas our own is intensional.

Approach of [28]. In [28] an approach for clustering XML documents according to their structural similarities is proposed. This approach works as follows: for each XML document $\mathcal{D}$, it constructs a suitable directed graph $sg(\mathcal{D})$ called *structural graph*. It also defines a notion of distance between structural graphs; specifically, given two structural graphs $sg(\mathcal{D}_1)$ and $sg(\mathcal{D}_2)$, their distance is computed as the ratio between the number of common edges between $sg(\mathcal{D}_1)$ and $sg(\mathcal{D}_2)$ and the maximum between the number of edges of $sg(\mathcal{D}_1)$ and that of $sg(\mathcal{D}_2)$. This notion of distance is quite interesting; in fact, it is capable of capturing structural similarities between two documents that are usually neglected by simpler approaches, like the Jaccard Coefficient and the Cosine Similarity Coefficient; in addition, its computation is quicker than that of other metrics, like those based on tree edit distance. The defined distance between structural graphs is exploited for clustering input XML documents; clustering activity is performed by means of *S-GRACE*, a hierarchical clustering algorithm derived by *ROCK* [20].

We can recognize some similarities between our approach and that of [28]. Specifically, both of them: *(i)* allow a fast and scalable clustering of XML data sources; *(ii)* define a formalism for both representing XML data sources and assessing their similarity; this formalism is "vector"-based in our approach and graph-based in the approach of [28]; *(iii)* require a limited amount of memory for their execution; in fact, structural graphs (required by the approach of [28]) and intensional information (required by our approach) are, generally, small enough to be stored in main memory.

As for the main differences between them, we observe that: *(i)* the approach of [28] is extensional whereas our own is intensional; *(ii)* for the computation of data source similarity, the approach of [28] exploits structural information whereas our own uses interschema properties, i.e., semantic information; *(iii)* for performing the clustering task, the approach of [28] exploits an ad-hoc algorithm whereas our own allows a large variety of, both classical and new, clustering algorithms to be adopted.

As a final remark, we argue that some differences between the approach of [28] and our own (e.g., extensional/intensional, structure-based/semantics-based) make them complementary and capable of taking various facets of the same reality into account. As a consequence, it could be possible to define a system that executes both of them on the same XML sources and combines the results obtained by them in such a way to produce a final, more accurate, result.

Approach of [16]. In [16] an approach for clustering XML documents, taking their similarities into account, is described. This approach represents each XML document as a suitable sequence of real numbers (*time series*). The evaluation of the similarity degree existing between two XML documents D_1 and D_2 is, then, performed by comparing the time series T_1 and T_2 associated with D_1 and D_2; such a comparison is performed by computing the *Discrete Fourier Transform* (DFT) of T_1 and T_2.

We can highlight some similarities between our approach and that of [16]. In fact, *(i)* both of them "linearize" the structure of an XML source; specifically, the approach of [16] represents it as a numerical sequence, whereas our approach adopts a "vector"-based representation; *(ii)* both of them are specific for XML sources.

As for the main differences, we can observe that: *(i)* the approach of [16] returns very accurate results but needs a deep analysis of the structural properties of an XML document; *(ii)* it does not consider semantic similarities among the concepts of involved sources; on the contrary, in our approach, this information plays an important role; *(iii)* the approach of [16] is extensional whereas ours is intensional.

Approach of [44]. In [44] a framework exploiting matrix algebra for clustering XML documents is presented. Specifically, let $\mathcal{C}$ be a collection of XML documents; let $\mathcal{D}_i$ be a document of $\mathcal{C}$; let n_i be the number of tags of $\mathcal{D}_i$; finally, let m be the number of distinct XML elements in the documents of $\mathcal{C}$. $\mathcal{D}_i$ can be represented as a $n_i \times m$ matrix M_i such that $M_i[l, k]$ indicates how much the tag t_l of $\mathcal{D}_i$ can be represented by the element e_k. After the matrixes corresponding to the XML documents of $\mathcal{C}$ have been determined, a similarity coefficient is computed for each pair of them; these coefficients are exploited by a clustering technique for producing the final clusters.

We can recognize some similarities between our approach and that of [44]. Specifically, both of them: *(i)* consider a "vector"-based framework for representing XML sources, and *(ii)* have been specifically conceived for managing XML sources.

As for the main differences between them, we observe that: *(i)* the approach of [44] considers only synonymies whereas our approach handles a wide range of interschema properties; *(ii)* the approach of [44] is quite sophisticated and precise, since it computes various statistics on the terms occurring in an XML source (e.g., the frequency of a term in a document); this allows accurate results to be obtained but requires a significant computational effort.

Approach of [10]. In [10] an approach for clustering XML documents is proposed. This approach represents each document as a tree; the distance between two documents D_i and D_j is computed as the *edit distance* between the corresponding trees T_i and T_j. Initially, the approach creates a cluster for each tree and computes a matrix M whose generic element $M[i,j]$ denotes the distance between T_i and T_j. After this, it iteratively selects the most similar clusters and merges them; this process is repeated until to a stop condition is satisfied. Finally, for each obtained cluster, a *representative element*, i.e., a document capable of capturing the structural specificities of the documents belonging to it, is constructed.

The main similarities between our approach and that of [10] are the following: *(i)* both of them have been specifically conceived for handling XML sources; *(ii)* both of them define a methodology for computing the distance between two XML sources; distance computation relies on interschema properties in our approach, and on a dynamic programming algorithm, capable of determining the edit distance between two trees, in the approach of [10].

As for the main differences between the two approaches, we can observe that: *(i)* the approach of [10] is extensional whereas our own is intensional; *(ii)* the approach of [10] is quite sophisticated, since it performs complex operations, like tree merging or tree pruning; as a consequence, it can obtain accurate results; however, since exploited algorithms work on the extensional component of involved XML data sources, they could suffer from scalability problems when the size of input data sources becomes large.

Approach of [29]. In [29] an approach for clustering XML documents referring to the same "piece of reality" is proposed. This approach first represents an XML document D as an unordered and labelled tree T_D; then, it maps T_D into a "high-dimensional" array A_D (i.e., an array that could be mapped into a high-dimensional Euclidean space); after this, it applies tools based on Principal Component Analysis [25] for reducing the dimensionality of input arrays; finally, it applies K-Means on the set of "reduced arrays" for constructing the final clusters.

As for the main similarities between our approach and that of [29] we can observe that: *(i)* both of them use a "vector"-based model for representing XML sources; *(ii)* in both of them an XML source is represented by means of a *weighted array* whose entries range in the real interval $[0,1]$.

As for the main differences between them we observe that: *(i)* the approach of [29] tries to reduce the dimensionality of involved arrays; this feature is not present in our approach; *(ii)* the approach of [29] has been conceived for clustering XML documents whereas our approach operates on XML Schemas;

(iii) the algorithms underlying the approach of [29] are quite sophisticated; as a consequence, they might return very accurate results; however, in many real cases, they might be prohibitively time-expensive; on the contrary, our approach is based on the analysis of the intensional component of an XML data source and, therefore, is quite "light".

In our opinion the approach of [29] and our own might be integrated. Specifically, given a large collection of XML documents, possibly associated with different XML Schemas, our approach could be applied for determining a set of classes $C_1, C_2, \ldots, C_k$, each containing a set of similar XML Schemas. After this, the approach of [29] could be applied for clustering the documents of each class.

Approach of [45]. In [45] an approach for clustering a set $\mathcal{D} = \{D_1, D_2, \ldots, D_n\}$ of XML documents is proposed. This approach is based on the concept of *e-path*; an e-path is a set of nested elements labelled with the same tag; an e-path might be present in more than one document of $\mathcal{D}$. The approach constructs a matrix M whose generic element $M[i,j]$ is set equal to 1 if and only if the document D_i contains the e-path p_j. The distance between two documents D_i and D_k is computed by applying the XOR bitwise operator to the ith and the kth rows of M. This distance is exploited by the approach for performing the clustering activity.

We can recognize some similarities between our approach and that of [45]. Specifically, both of them: *(i)* use a "vector"-based model for representing a collection of XML sources; *(ii)* apply a fast methodology for computing the distance between two XML sources; in fact, our approach is polynomial against the number of x-components of the involved Schemas whereas the number of steps performed by the approach of [45] is proportional to the number of all available e-paths existing in $\mathcal{D}$.

As for the main differences between them we can observe that: *(i)* our approach operates on XML Schemas whereas the approach of [45] manages XML documents; *(ii)* in the approach of [45] the coefficients exploited for representing an XML document are 0 or 1; on the contrary, our approach uses a discrete set of values belonging to the real interval $[0, 1]$; *(iii)* the computation of the Dissimilarity Matrix relies on e-paths in the approach of [45], whereas it is based on x-components in our approach.

7   Conclusions

In this paper we have presented an approach that exploits interschema properties for clustering semantically heterogeneous XML Schemas. We have seen that our approach takes the semantics of involved Schemas into account and can be easily integrated with most of the clustering techniques already proposed in the literature.

After a technical description of our approach, we have shown various experimental results that we have obtained by applying it to a large number of semantically heterogeneous XML Schemas. Then, we have illustrated some applications that can highly benefit of it. Finally, we have presented a comparison between our approach and other related ones previously proposed in the literature.

In our opinion the approach presented in this paper could be improved in several directions. Specifically, we plan to further refine the technique for the computation of the Dissimilarity Matrix by taking other interschema properties into account. In addition, we would like to exploit our approach as the core of new methodologies for producing fast and approximate answers to XML queries, for constructing user communities in which involved members share their knowledge or cooperate for solving a problem and, finally, for better handling task assignments in an organization.

Acknowledgments

The authors thank Giuseppe Meduri for his contribution to the implementation of the proposed approach.

References

1. Beil, F., Ester, M., Xu, X.: Frequent term-based text clustering. In: Proc. of the International Conference on Knowledge Discovery and Data Mining (KDD'02), Edmonton, Alberta, Canada, pp. 436–442. ACM Press, New York (2002)
2. Bergamaschi, S., Castano, S., Vincini, M.: Semantic integration of semistructured and structured data sources. SIGMOD Record 28(1), 54–59 (1999)
3. Castano, S., De Antonellis, V., De Capitani di Vimercati, S.: Global viewing of heterogeneous data sources. IEEE Transactions on Data and Knowledge Engineering 13(2), 277–297 (2001)
4. Catania, B., Maddalena, A., Vakali, A.: XML document indexes: A classification. IEEE Internet Computing 9(5), 64–71 (2005)
5. Chung, C., Min, J., Shim, K.: APEX: an adaptive path index for XML data. In: Proc. of the ACM International Conference on Management of Data (SIGMOD '02), Madison, Wisconsin, USA, pp. 121–132. ACM Press, New York (2002)
6. Cobena, G., Abiteboul, S., Marian, A.: Detecting changes in XML documents. In: Proc. of the IEEE International Conference on Data Engineering (ICDE '02), San Jose, California, USA, pp. 41–52. IEEE Computer Society Press, Los Alamitos (2002)
7. Costa, G., Manco, G., Ortale, R., Tagarelli, A.: A tree-based approach to clustering XML documents by structure. In: Boulicaut, J.-F., Esposito, F., Giannotti, F., Pedreschi, D. (eds.) PKDD 2004. LNCS (LNAI), vol. 3202, pp. 137–148. Springer, Heidelberg (2004)
8. Crescenzi, V., Mecca, G., Merialdo, P.: RoadRunner: Towards automatic data extraction from large Web sites. In: Proc. of the International Conference on Very Large Data Bases (VLDB'01), pp. 109–118. Morgan Kaufmann, San Francisco (2001)
9. Dalamagas, T., Cheng, T., Winkel, K., Sellis, T.K.: A methodology for clustering XML documents by structure. Information Systems 31(3), 187–228 (2006)
10. De Francesca, F., Gordano, G., Ortale, R., Tagarelli, A.: Distance-based clustering of XML documents. In: Proc. of the International Workshop on Mining Graphs, Trees and Sequences (MGTS '03), pp. 75–78, Cavtat-Dubrovnik, Croatia (2003)

11. De Meo, P., Quattrone, G., Terracina, G., Ursino, D.: Extraction of synonymies, hyponymies, overlappings and homonymies from XML Schemas at various "severity" levels. In: Proc. of the International Database Engineering and Applications Symposium (IDEAS 2004), Coimbra, Portugal, pp. 389–394. IEEE Computer Society, Los Alamitos (2004)
12. Dempster, A., Laird, N., Rubin, D.: Maximum likelihood from incomplete data via the EM algorithm. Journal of the Royal Statistical Society Series B 30(1), 1–38 (1977)
13. Deschler, K.W., Rundensteiner, E.A.: MASS: a multi-axis storage structure for large XML documents. In: Proc. of ACM International Conference on Information and Knowledge Management (CIKM 2003), New Orleans, Louisiana, USA, pp. 520–523. ACM Press, New York (2003)
14. Dhamankar, R., Lee, Y., Doan, A., Halevy, A., Domingos, P.: iMAP: Discovering complex semantic matches between database schemas. In: Proc. of the ACM International Conference on Management of Data (SIGMOD 2004), Paris, France, pp. 383–394. ACM Press, New York (2004)
15. Fankhauser, P., Kracker, M., Neuhold, E.J.: Semantic vs. structural resemblance of classes. ACM SIGMOD RECORD 20(4), 59–63 (1991)
16. Flesca, S., Manco, G., Masciari, E., Pontieri, L., Pugliese, A.: Fast detection of XML structural similarity. IEEE Transactions on Knowledge Data Engineering 17(2), 160–175 (2005)
17. Gal, A., Anaby-Tavor, A., Trombetta, A., Montesi, D.: A framework for modeling and evaluating automatic semantic reconciliation. The International Journal on Very Large Databases 14(1), 50–67 (2005)
18. Galil, Z.: Efficient algorithms for finding maximum matching in graphs. ACM Computing Surveys 18, 23–38 (1986)
19. Garruzzo, S., Modafferi, S., Rosaci, D., Ursino, D.: X-Compass: an XML agent for supporting user navigation on the Web. In: Andreasen, T., Motro, A., Christiansen, H., Larsen, H.L. (eds.) FQAS 2002. LNCS (LNAI), vol. 2522, pp. 197–211. Springer, Heidelberg (2002)
20. Guha, S., Rastogi, R., Shim, K.: ROCK: A robust clustering algorithm for categorical attributes. Information Systems 25(5), 345–366 (2000)
21. Han, J., Kamber, M.: Data Mining: Concepts and Techniques. Morgan Kaufmann, San Francisco (2001)
22. He, B., Tao, T., Chang, K.C.-C.: Organizing structured Web sources by query schemas: a clustering approach. In: Proc. of the ACM International Conference on Information and Knowledge Management (CIKM 2004), Washington, Columbia, USA, pp. 22–31. ACM Press, New York (2004)
23. Hochbaum, D.S., Shmoys, D.B.: A best possible heuristic for the k-center problem. International Journal on Digital Libraries 10(2), 180–184 (1985)
24. Jiang, H., Lu, H., Wang, W., Chin, B.: XR-Tree: Indexing XML Data for Efficient Structural Joins. In: Proc. of the International Conference on Data Engineering (ICDE 2003), Bangalore, India, pp. 253–263. IEEE Computer Society, Los Alamitos (2003)
25. Jolliffe, I.T.: Principal Component Analysis, 2nd edn. Springer, Heidelberg (2002)
26. Koutsonikola, V.A., Vakali, A.: LDAP: Framework, practices, and trends. IEEE Internet Computing 8(5), 66–72 (2004)
27. Lee, M.L., Yang, L.H., Hsu, W., Yang, X.: XClust: clustering XML schemas for effective integration. In: Proc. of the ACM International Conference on Information and Knowledge Management (CIKM 2002), McLean, Virginia, USA, pp. 292–299. ACM Press, New York (2002)

28. Lian, W., Cheung, D.W., Mamoulis, N., Yiu, S.: An efficient and scalable algorithm for clustering XML documents by structure. IEEE Transactions on Knowledge and Data Engineering 16(1), 82–96 (2004)

29. Liu, J., Wang, J.T.L., Hsu, W., Herbert, K.G.: XML clustering by principal component analysis. In: Proc. of the IEEE International Conference on Tools with Artificial Intelligence (ICTAI 2004), Boca Raton, Florida, USA, pp. 658–662. IEEE Computer Society, Los Alamitos (2004)

30. MacQueen, J.B.: Some methods for classification and analysis of multivariate observations. In: Proc. of the International Symposium on Mathematics, Statistics and Probability, Berkeley, California, USA, pp. 281–297. University of California Press (1967)

31. Madhavan, J., Bernstein, P.A., Rahm, E.: Generic schema matching with Cupid. In: Proc. of the International Conference on Very Large Data Bases (VLDB 2001), Roma, Italy, pp. 49–58. Morgan Kaufmann, San Francisco (2001)

32. Miller, A.G.: WordNet: A lexical database for English. Communications of the ACM 38(11), 39–41 (1995)

33. Nierman, A., Jagadish, H.V.: Evaluating structural similarity in XML documents. In: Proc. of the International Workshop on the Web and Databases (WebDB 2002), pp. 61–66, Madison, Wisconsin, USA (2002)

34. Palopoli, L., Saccà, D., Terracina, G., Ursino, D.: Uniform techniques for deriving similarities of objects and subschemes in heterogeneous databases. IEEE Transactions on Knowledge and Data Engineering 15(2), 271–294 (2003)

35. Passi, K., Lane, L., Madria, S.K., Sakamuri, B.C., Mohania, M.K., Bhowmick, S.S.: A model for XML Schema integration. In: Bauknecht, K., Tjoa, A.M., Quirchmayr, G. (eds.) EC-Web 2002. LNCS, vol. 2455, pp. 193–202. Springer, Heidelberg (2002)

36. Qian, W., Zhang, L., Liang, Y., Qian, H., Jin, W.: A two-level method for clustering DTDs. In: Lu, H., Zhou, A. (eds.) WAIM 2000. LNCS, vol. 1846, pp. 41–52. Springer, Heidelberg (2000)

37. Qian, Y., Zhang, K.: A customizable hybrid approach to data clustering. In: Matsui, M., Zuccherato, R.J. (eds.) SAC 2003. LNCS, vol. 3006, pp. 485–489. Springer, Heidelberg (2004)

38. Rahm, E., Bernstein, P.A.: A survey of approaches to automatic schema matching. VLDB Journal 10(4), 334–350 (2001)

39. Shanmugasundaram, J., Tufte, K., He, G., Zhang, C., DeWitt, D., Naughton, J.: Relational databases for querying XML documents: limitations and opportunities. In: VLDB'99. Proc. of Very Large DataBase Conference, Edinburgh, Scotland, UK, pp. 302–314. Morgan Kaufmann, San Francisco (1999)

40. Tatarinov, I., Viglas, S.D., Beyer, K., Shanmugasundaram, J., Shekita, E., Zhang, C.: Storing and querying ordered xml using a relational database system. In: SIGMOD '02. Proc. of the ACM International Conference on Management of Data, Madison, Wisconsin, USA, pp. 204–215. ACM Press, New York (2002)

41. Terziyan, V., Vitko, O.: Intelligent information management in mobile electronic commerce. Artificial Intelligence News. Journal of Russian Association of Artificial Intelligence 5 (2002)

42. Witten, I.H., Frank, E.: Data Mining: Practical machine learning tools with Java implementations. Morgan Kaufmann, San Francisco, California, USA (2000)

43. Xu, L., Jordan, M.I.: On convergence properties of the EM algorithm for gaussian mixtures. Neural Computation 8(1), 129–151 (1996)

44. Yang, J., Cheung, W.K., Chen, X.: Integrating element and term semantics for similarity-based XML document clustering. In: WI'05. Proc. of the IEEE/WIC/ACM International Conference on Web Intelligence, Compiegne-Cedex, France, pp. 222–228. IEEE Computer Society Press, Los Alamitos (2005)
45. Yoon, J.P., Raghavan, V., Chakilam, V.: BitCube: A three-dimensional bitmap indexing for XML documents. In: SSDBM 2001. Proc. of the International Conference on Scientific and Statistical Database Management, Fairfax, Virginia, USA, pp. 158–167. IEEE Computer Society, Los Alamitos (2001)

A Formal Framework for
Adaptive Access Control Models

Stefanie Rinderle[1] and Manfred Reichert[2]

[1] Department Databases and Information Systems, University of Ulm, Germany
stefanie.rinderle@uni-ulm.de
[2] Information Systems Group, University of Twente, The Netherlands
m.u.reichert@cs.utwente.nl

Abstract. For several reasons enterprises are frequently subject to organizational change. Respective adaptations may concern business processes, but also other components of an enterprise architecture. In particular, changes of organizational structures often become necessary. The information about organizational entities and their relationships is maintained in organizational models. Therefore the quick and correct adaptation of these models is fundamental to adequately cope with organizational changes. However, model changes alone are not sufficient to guarantee consistency. Since organizational models also provide the basis for defining access rules (e.g., actor assignments in workflow management systems or access rules in document-centered applications) this information has to be adapted accordingly (e.g., to avoid dangling references or non-resolvable actor assignments). Current approaches do not adequately address this problem, which often leads to security gaps and delayed change implementation.In this paper we introduce a formal framework for the controlled evolution of organizational models and related access rules. Firstly, we introduce a set of operators with well-defined semantics for defining and changing organizational models. Secondly, we show how to define access rules based on such models. In this context we also define a notion of correctness for access rules. Thirdly, we present a formal framework for the (semi-automated) adaptation of access rules when the underlying organizational model is changed by exploiting the semantics of the applied changes. Altogether the presented approach provides an important contribution for realizing adaptive access control frameworks.

1 Introduction

Enterprise information systems comprise a variety of application and system components. Important tasks to be accomplished include the support of business processes, the management of enterprise documents, and the integration of enterprise applications. For the implementation of respective system services different middleware exists, including workflow management technology, document management systems, and tools for enterprise application integration [1,2,3].

S. Spaccapietra et al. (Eds.): Journal on Data Semantics IX, LNCS 4601, pp. 82–112, 2007.

1.1   Problem Description

Controlled access to its application services as well as to the application objects managed by them (e.g., business processes, documents, resources, or application systems) constitutes an important task for any information system (IS) [4,5,6,7,8]. This results in a large number of *access rules* covering different system aspects and user privileges [9]. Usually, these access rules have to be frequently adapted due to changes of organizational structures [10,11,12]. Such changes become necessary, for instance, when an organizational unit is split into two sub-units, two existing units are joined to a new one, a group of users is reassigned to a new organizational unit, or simply an employee leaves the organization.[1] As a consequence, access rules whose definition refers to organizational entities may have to be modified as well. We denote the ability of an enterprise IS to adapt access rules after organizational model changes as *adaptive access control*.

Typically, information about organizational entities (e.g., organizational units, roles, and users) and the relations between them (e.g., assignment of a user to a role, hierarchical relations between organizational units) is kept in an *organizational model*. Based on such a model, access rights and user privileges (e.g., actor assignments in workflow systems or access rules in document-centered applications) can be defined (cf. Fig. 1). Consequently, when organizational changes occur, both the organizational model and related access rules have to be adapted in a correct and consistent manner. The focus of this paper is on the correct handling of the evolution of organizational models and related access rules.

Another problem arises from the fact that the (middleware) components used to build the application services of information systems often maintain their own organizational model and security component; i.e., the information about organizational entities and their relations as well as the access rules based on them may be scattered over different system components. On the one hand this has led to functional redundancy, on the other hand (heterogeneous) information about organizational structures is kept redundantly in different security components. The latter very often results in inconsistencies, high costs for system maintainability, and inflexibility when dealing with organizational change. In this paper, however, we abstain from issues related to this heterogeneity problem.

The correct evolution of an organizational model is only one side of the coin when dealing with organizational changes; the other one is to correctly and efficiently adapt the access rules whose definition is based on this organizational model. Note that in large environments hundreds up to thousands of access rules may exist, each of them capturing different privileges of the IS. This, in turn, makes it a hard job for the system administrator to quickly and correctly adapt access rules to model changes. Current approaches do not sufficiently deal with this issue. They neither exploit the semantics of the applied model changes nor do they provide automated support for adaptating access rules and for migrating them to the changed organizational model. In practice, this often leads to problems like non-resolvable actor assignments, unauthorized access

---

[1] For respective results from one of our case studies in the clinical domain see [10].

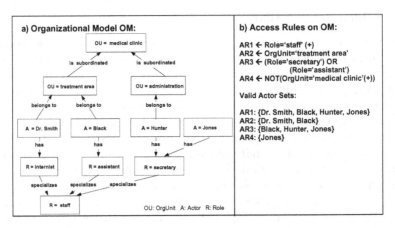

Fig. 1. Organizational Model and Related Access Rules (simplified)

to documents, or inconsistent user worklists. Assume, for example, that two organizational units are joined to make the enterprise more efficient (cf. Fig. 3). If this change is performed in an uncontrolled manner, orphaned (dangling) references may result; i.e., access rules referring to org. entities which are no longer present in the new organizational model. Even more critical might be cases where changes of an organizational model lead to access rules for which no actor qualifies any more. In process–aware information systems [13], for example, such non-resolvable actor assignments lead to tasks which cannot be processed and therefore have to be forwarded to the system administrator. As a consequence, business process execution may be delayed and security gaps may arise.

To deal with these challenges we need an enterprise security service which manages the organizational model as well as its evolution in a consistent and correct manner. Furthermore, model changes have to be efficiently propagated to access rules without causing inconsistencies or security gaps. Finally, we have to consider *passive* access rules, which are checked when a certain privilege is applied (e.g., at the moment a user wants to access a document), as well as *active* access rules used to determine a set of potential users before accessing an object or task (e.g., to create work items for user worklists in workflow systems).

Altogether these tasks are non-trivial. Both organizational models and access rules may have complex structure, and we have to analyze and understand the interdependencies between changes of an organizational model and necessary adaptations of related access rules. This necessitates a framework with precise and formal semantics for reasoning about model and rule changes.

1.2   Contribution

In this paper, we present a formal framework for the controlled evolution of organizational models and related access rules. Firstly, we introduce a meta model and a set of operators with well-defined semantics for defining and changing organizational models. Secondly, we show how to define access rules based on such models. We provide a precise semantics for access rules and introduce a notion of correctness for them. These are important pre-conditions for reasoning about rule changes. Thirdly, we present a formal framework for the (semi-automated) adaptation of access rules when changing the related organizational model. For selected organizational changes we show how they can be realized in our formal framework, how their effects on access rules look like, and how these access rules can be migrated to the new version of the organizational model. Thereby we make use of the semantics of model changes and we introduce formally sound migration concepts. Altogether the presented approach provides an important contribution for realizing adaptive enterprise access control frameworks.

In [14] we have already introduced first results on adaptive access control (i.e., a criterion for correctness of access rules and exemplary strategies for avoiding dangling references in such rules after model changes). This paper extends this work in several directions: On the one hand, we elaborate these previous results (e.g., by considering more complex access rules and model changes, or by providing more details on architectural issues). On the other hand, as completely new results, the effects of organizational changes on actor sets are evaluated. For example, we deal with the challenging question when actor sets become empty after model changes. The remainder of this paper is organized as follows: Section 2 introduces our framework for defining and changing organizational models. Section 3 shows how to define access rules based on this framework, and Section 4 illustrates how to adapt access rules to model changes. Architectural and implementation issues are sketched in Section 5. Section 6 discusses related work and Section 7 concludes with a summary and an outlook on future work.

2 Framework for Creating and Evolving Organizational Models

In order to be able to analyze changes of organizational models as well as their impact on related access rules we need a formalization of organizational structures; i.e., a formal description of organizational entities and the relations between them. Based on such a formalization it should be possible to specify changes and their operational semantics. For this purpose, first of all, we introduce a meta model for defining organizational structures, which is comparable to the meta models current access control models are based on (e.g., [6,15,16]). In this paper we restrict our considerations to the basic entity types *organizational unit*, *role* and *actor* (cf. Fig. 2), and to the particular relation types existing between respective entities (e.g., actor A_1 belongs to organizational unit O_1, actor A_1 has role R_1, role R_1 specializes role R_0, etc.). In the overall framework, we are currently realizing in the ADEPT2 project [17], we additionally consider entity types like *position*, *group*, and *capability* (see [18] for details). However, in this paper we omit these entity types in order to better focus on core issues related to the evolution of organizational models and related access rules.

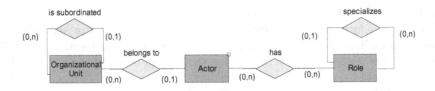

Fig. 2. Organizational Meta Model (in ER Notation)

Regarding the meta model OMM used in this paper (cf. Fig. 2) we specify the set of valid entity types *EntityTypes* and the set of valid relation types *RelationTypes* as follows:

- *EntityTypes* := {OrgUnit, Actor, Role}
- *RelationTypes* := {(OrgUnit, OrgUnit, is subordinated), (Role, Role, specializes), (Actor, OrgUnit, belongs to), (Actor, Role, has)}

We further denote

- $\mathcal{E} := \mathcal{E}_{Id} := \{(\text{entId}, \text{entType}) \mid \text{entId} \in \text{Id}, \text{entType} \in \text{EntityTypes}\}$ as the set of all entities definable over a set of identifiers Id and
- $\mathcal{R}_{\mathcal{E}} := \{(\text{e}_1, \text{e}_2, \text{relType}) \mid \text{e}_1 = (\text{eId}_1, \text{eType}_1), \text{e}_2 = (\text{eId}_2, \text{eType}_2) \in \mathcal{E},$ $(\text{eType}_1, \text{eType}_2, \text{relType}) \in \text{RelationTypes}\}$ as the set of all tuples that can be used to define relations over $\mathcal{E}$

Actors are users (or resources) who need privileges to work on certain tasks (e.g., workflow activities) or to access certain data objects (e.g., business documents). Generally, access rules are not directly linked to actors, but to the more abstract concept of a *role*. Roles group privileges and are assigned to actors based on their capabilities and competences. Furthermore, an actor can play different roles: A physician in a hospital, for example, may possess the two roles *ward doctor* and *radiologist*. Actors with same role are being considered as interchangeable. Roles can be hierarchically organized, i.e., a role may have one or more specialized sub-roles. Thereby a sub-role inherits all privileges of its super–role and may extend this set by additional privileges. Finally, each actor can be assigned to an *organizational unit*. Like roles, organizational units can be hierarchically structured; i.e., a particular unit may have one or more subordinated units (e.g., a hospital may have an intensive care unit and an emergency laboratory as subordinated units). Based on this meta model we can define the notion of *organizational model* (cf. Def. 1). For the sake of readability, we do not consider the cardinalities associated with the relation types of our meta model.

Definition 1 (Organizational Model). *For the organizational meta model OMM let $\mathcal{E}$ be the set of all entities over a given set of identifiers and let $\mathcal{R}_{\mathcal{E}}$ be the set of all relations over $\mathcal{E}$ (see above). Then:*
An organizational model OM is defined as a tuple (Entities, Relations) with Entities $\subseteq \mathcal{E}$ and Relations $\subseteq \mathcal{R}_{\mathcal{E}}$ such that

- *all entity identifiers are used in a unique way*
- *there are no cyclic dependencies between roles (relation* specializes*) or between organizational units (relation* is subordinated*), formally:*
  - $\forall$ *(role, Role)* $\in$ *Entities: (role, Role)* $\notin$ *Spec(OM, (role, Role))* *with*
    $Spec(OM, el) := \bigcup_{el':(el',el,specializes) \in Relations} (\{(el', Role)\} \cup Spec(OM, el'))$
  - $\forall$ *(ou, OrgUnit)* $\in$ *Entities: (ou, OrgUnit)* $\notin$ *Sub(OM, (ou, OrgUnit))* *with*
    $Sub(OM, el) := \bigcup_{el':(el',el,issubordinated) \in Relations} (\{(el', OrgUnit)\} \cup Sub(OM, el'))$

The set of all org. models definable on basis of OMM is denoted as $\mathcal{OM}$.

As it can be seen from Def. 1 we define a notion of *correctness* imposed on organizational models. It is based on different correctness constraints in order to exclude undesired effects when creating and changing such models. For example, a unique usage of entity identifiers is claimed. Another constraint refers to the exclusion of cyclic dependencies between roles (relation specializes) as well as cyclic dependencies between organizational units (relation belongs to) due to their unclear semantics. The definition of further correctness constraints depends on the particular application scenario and is omitted in this paper.

In order to be able to express all relevant kinds of changes on an organizational model *OM* our framework provides a complete set of basic change operations; e.g., for creating or deleting organizational entities and the relations between them. For each change operation we define formal pre– and post–conditions, which preserve the correctness properties of *OM* when applying the operation(s) to this model (assuming that *OM* has been a correct model before). In addition to these basic change operations we provide frequently used, high–level operations in order· to facilitate change definition and to capture more semantics about model changes. Examples for such high-level operations include the join of two entities (e.g., fusion of two organizational units; cf. Fig. 3) or the split of an existing entity into two new entities (e.g., a role; cf. Fig. 3).

Definition 2 (Change Framework for Organizational Models). *Let* $\mathcal{E}$ *be the set of all entities over a set of identifiers and let* $\mathcal{R}_\mathcal{E}$ *be the set of all relations over* $\mathcal{E}$. *Let further OM = (Entities, Relations) be a (correct) organizational model which can be transformed into another (correct) organizational model OM'* *:= (Entities', Relations') by applying change (transaction)* $\Delta = op_1, ..., op_n$. *The notion* $\Delta = op_1, ..., op_n$ *describes the sequential application of basic (cf. Tab. 1) or high-level (cf. Tab. 2) change operations* $op_1, ... op_n$ *to OM. This sequence of change operations is encapsulated within change (transaction)* Δ.

For example, a new relation (of type *relType*) between two entities *e1* and *e2* of an organizational model *OM = (Entities, Relations)* can be created by applying the basic change operation CreateRelation(OM, e1, e2, relType) to *OM*. The pre–conditions associated with this operation ensure that both entities *e1* and *e2* are present in *OM* and that *(e1, e2, relType)* constitutes a valid relation not yet present in *OM*. The post–condition of this operation, in turn, describes the effects resulting from the application of this operation to *OM*. In our example, relation *(e1, e2, relType)* is added to the set *Relations* whereas set *Entities* remains unchanged.

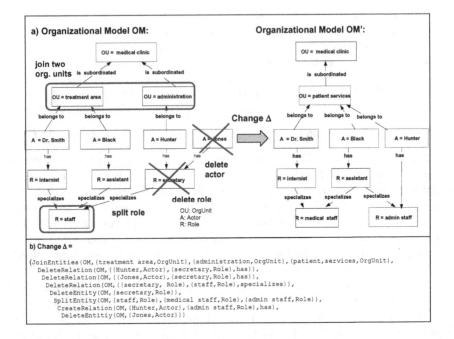

Fig. 3. Structural Change of the Organizational Model *OM* from Fig. 1

Table 2 contains high–level change operations which can be realized by ap-plying a sequence of basic change operations. The purpose of these high–level operations is to better assist users in defining complex, but common changes. In this paper we consider the operations for reassigning existing relations, for join-ing two entities (e.g., two organizational units), and for splitting entities (e.g., roles). An example for joining two organizational units `treatment area` and `administration` to the new unit `patient services` is depicted in Fig. 3.

3   Framework for Defining (Correct) Access Rules

How do changes of an organizational model *OM* affect the access rules based on it? In order to find a correct and precise answer to this challenging question, first of all, we must be able to formally define access rules as well as their semantics. Based on this formalization it should be possible to determine which access rules (on *OM*) are affected by a model change Δ, how the effects of Δ on these rules look like, and which rule adaptations become necessary.

Let *OM* = (*Entities, Relations*) be an organizational model. Based on the entities and relations defined by *OM* we can specify rules for controlling the access to processes, documents, or other objects. Since the structuring as well as the semantics of these access rules is fundamental for the (semi-) automated derivation of rule adaptations after model changes, we consider this issue in more detail. We distinguish between elementary and complex access rules.

Table 1. Basic Change Operations on Organizational Models

CreateEntity:$\mathcal{OM} \times Identifier \times EntityType \mapsto \mathcal{OM}$ with CreateEntitiy(OM, eId, entType) = OM'
Preconditions: • (eId, entType) $\not\in$ Entities
Postconditions: • Entities' = Entities $\cup$ {(eId, entType)}
• Relations' = Relations
DeleteEntity: $\mathcal{OM} \times \mathcal{E} \mapsto \mathcal{OM}$ with DeleteEntity(OM, e) = OM'
Preconditions: • e $\in$ Entities
• $\not\exists$ rel = (e1, e2, relType) $\in$ Relations with e1 = e $\vee$ e2 = e
Postconditions: • Entities' = Entities \ {e}
• Relations' = Relations
CreateRelation: $\mathcal{OM} \times \mathcal{E} \times \mathcal{E} \times RelType \mapsto \mathcal{OM}$ with CreateRelation(OM, e1, e2, relType) = OM')
Preconditions: • e1 := (eId1, eType1), e2 := (eId2, eType2) $\in$ Entities
• (e1, e2, relType) $\in \mathcal{R}$
• (e1, e2, relType) $\not\in$ Relations
Postconditions: • Entities' = Entities
• Relations' = Relations $\cup$ {(e1, e2, relType)}
• for eType1=eType2 = Role $\wedge$ relType = specializes: e1 $\not\in$ Spec(OM, e2)$^{\ominus}$
• for eType1=eType2 = OrgUnit $\wedge$ relType = is subordinated: e1 $\not\in$ Sub(OM, e2)
DeleteRelation: $\mathcal{OM} \times \mathcal{R_E} \mapsto \mathcal{OM}$ with DeleteRelation(OM, relation) = OM'
Preconditions: • relation $\in$ Relations
Postconditions: • Entities' = Entities
• Relations' = Relations \ {relation}

$^{\ominus}$ For a formal definition of *Spec* and *Sub* see Definition 1

An *elementary access rule* (cf. Def. 3) consists of a simple expression that qualifies a set of entities from OM (i.e., a subset of *Entities*) for this rule. The elementary access rule `Actor = 'Hunter'`, for example, expresses that exactly one entity, namely the actor with name 'Hunter', qualifies for this rule and therefore owns the privileges associated with it. As a second example consider the elementary access rule `OrgUnit = 'medical clinic'`. For this access rule we denote the organizational unit `medical clinic` as the *qualifying entity*. Furthermore, all actors belonging to this unit own the privileges associated with this rule.

For entities that can be hierarchically organized (i.e., for organizational units and roles in our meta model) we further support the definition of *transitive* elementary access rules. As an example consider the elementary access rule `OrgUnit = medical clinic(+)`. For this transitive rule (indicated by the '+') the set of qualifying entities comprises the organizational unit `medical clinic` itself and all of its directly or indirectly subordinated units (i.e., the *transitive closure* with respect to the 'is subordinated' relation). All actors belonging to one of these qualifying units own the privileges associated with this elementary rule.

Similar considerations can be made regarding the 'specializes' relation between entities of type `Role`.

Definition 3 (Elementary Access Rule). *Let OM = (Entities, Relations) be an organizational model based on OMM. Then an elementary access rule* EAR *on OM is defined as follows:*

EAR $\equiv$ EAR1 | EAR2 | EAR3 *with*

EAR1 $\longleftarrow$ (EntityType = el), EAR2 $\longleftarrow$ (OrgUnit = el(+)), EAR3 $\longleftarrow$ (Role = el(+))

Table 2. High-Level Change Operations on Organizational Models

`ReAssignRelaton:` $\mathcal{OM} \times \mathcal{R}_\mathcal{E} \times \mathcal{E} \times \mathcal{E} \mapsto \mathcal{OM}$ with `ReAssignRelation(OM, r, e, eNew)` = OM'	
Preconditions:	• r = (e1, e2, relType) ∈ Relations
	• e = e1 ∨ e = e2
	• eNew := (eIdNew, eTypeNew) ∈ Entities
	• e = e1:=(eId1, eType1) $\Longrightarrow$ eTypeNew = eType1
	• e = e2:=(eId2, eType2) $\Longrightarrow$ eTypeNew = eType2
	• e = e1:=(eId1, eType1) $\Longrightarrow$ (eNew, e2, relType) $\notin$ Relations
	• e = e2:=(eId2, eType2) $\Longrightarrow$ (e1, eNEw, relType) $\notin$ Relations
Postconditions:	• e = e1 $\Longrightarrow$ Relations' = Relations ∪ {(eNew, e2, relType} \ {(e1, e2, relType}
	• e = e2 $\Longrightarrow$ Relations' = Relations ∪ {(e1, eNew, relType} \ {(e1, e2, relType}
	• for e = e1 ∧ eType1 = eType2 = eTypeNew = Role ∧ relType = `specializes`: eNew $\notin$ pred*(OM, e1)
	• for e = e2 ∧ eType1 = eType2 = eTypeNew = Role ∧ relType = `specializes`: e2 $\notin$ pred*(OM, eNew)
	• for e = e1 ∧ eType1 = eType2 = eTypeNew = OrgUnit ∧ relType = `is subordinated`: eNew $\notin$ pred*(OM, e1)
	• for e = e2 ∧ eType1 = eType2 = eTypeNew = OrgUnit ∧ relType = `is subordinated`: e2 $\notin$ pred*(OM, eNew)
`JoinEntities:` $\mathcal{OM} \times \mathcal{E} \times \mathcal{E} \times Identifiers \mapsto \mathcal{OM}$ with `JoinEntities(OM, e1, e2, nId)` = OM'	
Preconditions:	• e1= (eId1, eType), e2 = (eId2, eType) ∈ Entities
	• (nId, eType) $\notin$ Entities
	• eType ≠ `Actor`
Basic Change Operations:	• CreateEntity(OM, (nId, eType)), eNew := (nId, eType)
	• ∀ (e, e1, relType) ∈ Relations: ReassignRelation(OM, (e, e1, relType), e1, eNew)
	• ∀ (e, e2, relType) ∈ Relations: ReassignRelation(OM, (e, e2, relType), e2, eNew)
	• ∀ (e1, e, relType) ∈ Relations: ReassignRelation(OM, (e1, e, relType), e1, eNew)
	• ∀ (e, e2, relType) ∈ Relations: ReassignRelation(OM, (e, e1, relType), e2, eNew)
	• DeleteEntity(OM, e1)
	• DeleteEntity(OM, e2)
`SplitEntity:` $\mathcal{OM} \times \mathcal{E} \times \mathcal{E} \times \mathcal{E} \mapsto \mathcal{OM}$ with `SplitEntity(OM, eOld, e1, e2)` = OM'	
Preconditions:	• (eIdOld, eType) := eOld ∈ Entities
	• (e1Id, eType) := e1, (e2Id, eType) := e2 $\notin$ Entities
	• eType ≠ `Actor`
Basic Change Operations:	• CreateEntity(OM, e1)
	• CreateEntity(OM, e2)
	• All actors belonging to the splitted org. unit or possessing the role to be splitted have to be assigned to one of the new entities or to both of them
	• Default behavior[x] for sub-roles: If the entity to split is of type `Role` reassign its sub-roles to both new resulting roles after split.
	• Default behavior for super-roles: If the entity to split is of type `Role` and has a super-role reassign both resulting roles after split to this super-role.
	• Default behavior for subordinated org. units: If the entity to split is of type `OrgUnit` reassign its subordinated org. units to exactly one of the new org. units (user decision).
	• Default behavior for superordinated org. units: If the entity to split is of type `OrgUnit` and has a superordinated org. unit assign both new org. units to this superordinated unit.
	• DeleteEntity(OM, eOld)

The post conditions of the high-level changes result from the aggregation of the post conditions of the applied basic change operations.
[x] The user may override the default behavior any time.

The set of entities qualifying for one of the elementary access rules **EAR1, EAR2** *or* **EAR3** *can be determined as follows:*

- EAR1 ⟵ (EntityType = el)

$$QualEntities(OM, \texttt{EAR1}) = \begin{cases} \{(el, EntityType)\} & : & (el, EntityType) \in Entities \\ \emptyset & : & otherwise \end{cases}$$

- EAR2 ⟵ (OrgUnit = el(+))

$$QualEntities(OM, \texttt{EAR2}) = \begin{cases} \{(el, \texttt{OrgUnit})\} \cup Sub(OM, el) & : & (el, \texttt{OrgUnit}) \in Entities \\ \emptyset & : & otherwise \end{cases}$$

with

$$Sub(OM, el) := \bigcup_{el' : (el', el, \texttt{issubordinated}) \in Relations} (\{(el', \texttt{OrgUnit})\} \cup Sub(OM, el'))$$

- EAR3 ⟵ (Role = el(+))

$$QualEntities(OM, \texttt{EAR3}) = \begin{cases} \{(el, \texttt{Role})\} \cup Spec(OM, el) & : & (el, \texttt{Role}) \in Entities \\ \emptyset & : & otherwise \end{cases}$$

with

$$Spec(OM, el) := \bigcup_{el' : (el', el, \texttt{specializes}) \in Relations} (\{(el', \texttt{Role})\} \cup Spec(OM, el'))$$

In general, the semantics of an access rule (defined on OM) is determined by the set of actors from OM qualifying for this rule (*valid actor set*). Definition 4 presents the valid actor sets for elementary access rules.

Definition 4 (Valid Actor Set for Elementary Access Rules). *Let $OM = (Entities, Relations)$ be an organizational model. Let $Act(OM) := \{(a, \texttt{Actor}) | (a, \texttt{Actor}) \in Entities\}$ be the set of all actors defined by OM, and let EAR be an elementary access rule on OM. Then: Valid actor set VAS(OM, EAR) denotes the set of all actors (from OM) who qualify for EAR, i.e., who own the privileges associated with rule EAR. Formally:*

- AR ⟵ (EntityType = el) ⟹

$$VAS(OM, \texttt{AR}) = \begin{cases} \{(el, \texttt{Actor}) | (el, \texttt{Actor}) \in Act(OM)\} & if EntityType = \texttt{Actor} \\ \{(a, \texttt{Actor}) | (a, \texttt{Actor}) \in Act(OM) \wedge \\ \quad \exists (a, el, \texttt{belongsto}) \in Relations)\} & if EntityType = \texttt{OrgUnit} \\ \{(a, \texttt{Actor}) | (a, \texttt{Actor}) \in Act(OM) \wedge \\ \quad \exists (a, el, \texttt{has}) \in Relations)\} & if EntityType = \texttt{Role} \end{cases}$$

- AR ⟵ (EntityType = el(+)) ⟹

$$VAS(OM, \texttt{AR}) = \begin{cases} \{(a, \texttt{Actor}) | (a, \texttt{Actor}) \in Act(OM) \wedge \\ \quad \exists el' \in QualEntities(OM, \texttt{AR}) : \\ \quad \exists (a, el', \texttt{belongsto}) \in Relations)\} & if EntityType = \texttt{OrgUnit} \\ \{(a, \texttt{Actor}) | (a, \texttt{Actor}) \in Act(OM) \wedge \\ \quad \exists el' \in QualEntities(OM, \texttt{AR}) : \\ \quad \exists (a, el', \texttt{has}) \in Relations)\} & if EntityType = \texttt{Role} \end{cases}$$

In order to enable the definition of more *complex access rules* we allow for the composition of existing rules (cf. Def. 5). For this purpose the following operators can be used: *negation*, *conjunction* and *disjunction*. Def. 5 also sets out a precise semantics for complex access rules based on their valid actor sets.

Definition 5 ((Complex) Access Rule). *Let $OM = (Entities, Relations)$ be an organizational model based on OMM. Then an access rule AR on OM is defined as follows:*

AR ≡ EAR | NEAR | CAR | DAR *with*

- EAR *is an elementary access rule (cf. Def. 3)*

- NEAR ⟵ (NOT (EAR)) *where* EAR *is an elementary access rule*
  $VAS(OM, \texttt{NEAR}) = Act(OM) \setminus VAS(OM, \texttt{EAR})$

- DAR ⟵ (AR1 OR AR2) *with* AR1 *and* AR2 *are access rules*
  VAS(OM, AR) = VAS(AR1) ∪ VAS(AR2)

- CAR ⟵ (AR1 AND AR2) *with* AR1 *and* AR2 *are access rules*
  VAS(OM, AR) = VAS(AR1) ∩ VAS(AR2)

Consider the organizational model OM depicted in Fig. 1a). An example for a complex access rule on OM is the expression AR ⟵ (OrgUnit = medical clinic(+) AND Role = assistant) with valid actor set VAS(AR) = {Dr. Smith, Black, Hunter, Jones} ∩ {Black} = {Black}.

Finally, we provide a criterion which allows us to decide when an access rule AR is *valid* with respect to a given organizational model OM. We call an access rule valid if the following two conditions hold:

(1) AR does not contain *dangling references*, i.e., it does not refer to entities which are not present in OM. Formally:

$$DanglingRef(OM, \text{AR}) = \begin{cases} \text{False } if \forall \text{ EAR } in \text{ AR} : QualEntities(OM, \text{EAR}) \neq \emptyset \\ \text{True } otherwise \end{cases}$$

where the notion EAR ∈ AR describes all elementary access rules EAR contained in access rule AR.

(2) AR is resolvable, i.e., the set of valid actors VAS(OM, AR) does not become empty. We consider this second constraint as an important property of any access control module in order to ensure that objects remain accessible or tasks remain doable. Formally:

$$Resolv(OM, \text{AR}) = \begin{cases} \text{True } \; if \; VAS(\text{OM}, \text{AR}) \neq \emptyset \\ \text{False } otherwise \end{cases}$$

Note that dangling references or non-resolvable access rules might occur when organizational models are changed in an uncontrolled manner (cf. Fig. 4).

Definition 6 (Valid Access Rule). *Let OM = (Entities, Relations) be an organizational model and let* AR *be an access rule on OM. Then* AR *is valid regarding OM if and only if there are no dangling references within the elementary access rules contained in* AR *and* AR *is resolvable over the set Entities. Formally:*
$Valid(OM, \text{AR}) = \text{True} \iff (DanglingRef(OM, \text{AR}) = \text{False} \land Resolv(OM, \text{AR}) = \text{True})$

As an example consider the change scenario depicted in Fig. 4 where organizational model OM is transformed into another organizational model OM' by applying change Δ (for a formal definition of this change see Fig. 3 b)). Access rule AR1 ⟵ Role='staff(+)' defined on OM would contain a dangling reference when migrating this rule to the new organizational model OM'. The same holds for access rules AR2 and AR3. Access rule AR4 ⟵ NOT(OrgUnit='medical clinic'(+)) is resolvable on OM (VAS(OM',AR4) = {Jones}), but no longer resolvable on OM'. These simple examples demonstrate that uncontrolled changes of an organizational model can lead to security gaps or access errors later on if not treated in an adequate way. In the following section we introduce a formalism for adaptive access control rules in order to avoid such problems.

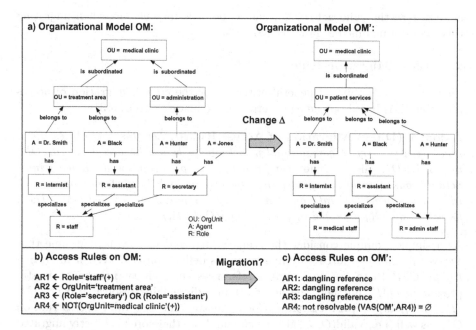

Fig. 4. Changing the Organizational Model OM from Fig. 1 and the Resulting Problem of Migrating Access Rules

4   Impact of Organizational Changes on Access Rules

In this section we introduce our formal framework for realizing adaptive access control models. When transforming an organizational model OM into another model OM' one must be able to decide which access rules defined on OM can be *directly migrated* to OM', i.e., which rules can be re–linked to the new model version without need for adaptation. Intuitively, this is the case for access rules which are also valid on OM' (cf. Def. 6). Otherwise, we have to adapt access rules that are no longer valid in order to keep the total set of access rules on the new model version OM' consistent. Due to the potentially large number of access rules to be managed we want to assist users as much as possible in accomplishing this task. In particular, we aim at the (semi-) automated migration and transformation of access rules in order to adapt them to changes of the organizational model if possible. Finding meaningful access rule adaptations is based on exploiting the semantics of the applied change operation(s). With 'semi-automated' we mean that the system shall assist the user in an adequate way, i.e., by explaining the potential conflicts arising after org. model changes (e.g., dangling references) and by making suggestions about potential rule transformations.

In Section 4.1 we provide a general criterion for the correct migration of access rules when changing the organizational model these rules are based on. Section 4.2 deals with the problem of dangling references. In Section 4.3 we analyze how the valid actor set of an access rule may change when migrating this rule to a modified organizational model.

4.1 Basic Migration Rule

First of all, we provide a general criterion for the correct migration of access rules, which is based on the considerations we made in Section 3:

Axiom 1 (Direct Migration of Access Rules). *Let OM = (Entities, Relations) be a (correct) organizational model and* AR *be a valid access rule on OM, i.e., Valid(OM,* AR*) =* True. *Let further* $\Delta = op_1, ..., op_n$ *be a change (transaction) consisting of a sequence of basic and/or high–level change operations, which transforms OM into another (correct) organizational model OM'. Then:* AR *can be directly migrated to OM' if Valid(OM',* AR*) =* True.

As a simple example consider the scenario depicted in Fig. 4a). Assume that access rule AR5 ⟵ Role = 'internist' is defined on *OM*. When migrating AR5 to *OM'* there are no dangling references since entity **internist** is still present in *OM'*. Further, the actor set of AR5 remains resolvable over *OM'* (VAS(OM',AR5) = {Dr. Smith}). Consequently, AR5 is a valid access rule on *OM'* as well (i.e., Valid(*OM'*, AR) = True) and can therefore be directly migrated to *OM'* according to Axiom 1.

4.2 Static Aspect – Dangling References

We analyze the problem of dangling references when migrating access rules to a changed organizational model. For the sake of readability, first of all, we consider the application of one single change operation. Following this, we deal with multi-operation changes and their effects on access rules.

Application of Single Change Operations Δ_{op}. We consider a change consisting of one single, basic or high–level change operation $\Delta_{op} := \Delta = op$ applied to an organizational model *OM*. We analyze the effects of this model change on related access rules, particularly regarding the occurence of dangling references.

As a first important result we can conclude that direct migration of an access rule from *OM* to *OM'* (without additional checks) is always possible in connection with change operation CreateEntity(OM, ...)(cf. Proposition 1).

Proposition 1 (Direct Migration of Access Rules). *Let OM be a (correct) org. model and let* AR *be a valid access rule on OM, i.e., Valid(OM,* AR*) =* True. *Let further Δ_{op} be a change operation which transforms OM into another (correct) org. model OM'. Then:* AR *can be directly migrated (re-linked) to OM' (i.e., Valid(OM',* AR *) =* True*) if Δ_{op} =* CreateEntity(OM, ...).

When creating a new entity and solely adding this entity to *OM* we can always guarantee that an arbitrary access rule valid on *OM* will remain valid on the new model version OM' as well: No dangling references occur and the change is invariant regarding the set of valid actors (of any access rule).

If an access rule AR cannot be directly transferred to the changed org. model OM' there may be two reasons for that. Either there are dangling references (e.g., after deleting an entity from OM to which AR refers) or the set of valid actors becomes empty for AR on OM'. In this section we cope with the first problem. Proposition 2 states for which basic change operations we can guarantee that there will be no dangling references within existing rules after a change.

Proposition 2 (No Dangling References). *Let OM be a (correct) organizational model and let* AR *be a valid access rule on OM, i.e., Valid(OM,* AR) = True. *Let further Δ_{op} be a change operation which transforms OM into another (correct) organizational model OM'. Then: DanglingRef(OM',* AR) = False *if* $\Delta_{op} \in$ {CreateEntity(OM,...), CreateRelation(OM,...), DeleteRelation(OM,...), ReAssignRelation(OM,...)}.

The application of all other basic and high–level change operations $\Delta_{op} \in$ {DeleteEntity, JoinEntities, SplitEntity} to an org. model OM may result in dangling references for access rules defined on OM. The challenging question is whether we can adapt respective access rules in a syntactically and semantically correct manner in order to migrate them to the new org. model OM; i.e., no dangling reference must occur after the rule transformation and the derived rule should still be compliant with its original objective.

We have a more detailed look at the two change operations JoinEntities and SplitEntity from Table 2 in order to deal with these questions. When applying one of these high–level change operations to an organizational model, obviously, dangling references within access rules might occur. Adaptation Policy 1 indicates which rule adaptations can be automatically derived in such a case. Particularly, Adaptation Policy 1 makes use of the semantics of these high-level change operations. For example, if two entities $e1$ and $e2$ are joined to a new entity $e3$, resulting dangling references to $e1$ or $e2$ within access rules could be substituted by references to $e3$. At this point it is important to mention that all derived rule adaptations solely constitute suggestions, i.e., users may apply another strategy if more favorable.

Rule Adaptation Policy 1 (Avoiding Dangling References). *Let OM = (Entities, Relations) be a (correct) org. model and let* AR *be a valid access rule on OM. Let further $\Delta_{op} \in$ {JoinEntities(OM, ...), SplitEntity(OM, ...)} be a high-level change operation which transforms OM into another (correct) org. model OM'. Then: When applying adaptation rule δ_{AR} (see below) to* AR *this rule can be transformed into an access rule* AR' *on OM' which does not contain dangling references and which is semantically "close" to* AR. *For respective Δ_{op} the adaptation rule δ_{AR} turns out as follows:*

– Δ_{op} = JoinEntities(OM, e1, e2, newE) $\Longrightarrow \delta_{AR}$:
  ∀ [N]EAR *in* AR *with*
    [N]EAR:= [NOT](EntityType = e1) ∨ [N]EAR:= [NOT](EntityType = e2)
    replace [N]EAR *by* [N]EAR' ≡ [NOT](EntityType = newE) ∧

$\forall$ [N]EAR *in* AR *with*
  [N]EAR:=[NOT](EntityType=e1(+)) $\lor$ [N]EAR:= [NOT](EntityType=e2(+))
    replace [N]EAR *by* [N]EAR' $\equiv$ [NOT](EntityType = newE(+))
- $\Delta_{op} =$ SplitEntity(OM, e, e1, e2) $\Longrightarrow \delta_{AR}$:
  $\forall$ [N]EAR *in* AR *with* [N]EAR:= [NOT](EntityType = e)
    replace [N]EAR *by*
        [N]EAR $\equiv$ [NOT](EntityType = e1 OR EntityType = e2) $\land$
  $\forall$ [N]EAR *in* AR *with* [N]EAR:= [NOT](EntityType = e(+))
    replace [N]EAR *by*
        [N]EAR $\equiv$ [NOT](EntityType = e1(+) OR EntityType = e2(+))

We illustrate these rule adaptations policies by means of examples. Figure 5a shows the join of two organizational units OU1 and OU2 resulting in a new organizational unit OUNew. Access rules AR1 and AR2 on OM refer to one or both of the joined organizational units (cf. Figure 5b). According to Adaptation Policy 1 these access rules could then be adapted by substituting the "old" reference to OU1(+) OR OU2(+) in AR1 by a reference to OUNew(+) and the "old" reference to OU1(+) in AR2 by a reference to OUNew (+) (analogously for AR3).

Note that the described adaptation policies may also affect the valid actor sets of access rules when migrating them to the changed organizational model OM'. For example, for access rule AR2 its valid actor set on OM' becomes bigger: VAS(OM, AR2) = {A1, A2} and VAS(OM',AR2) = {A1, A2, A3}. Generally, changes of the valid actor set are more critical if it becomes smaller or even an empty set. Regarding our example from Figure 5, for instance, this would be exactly the case for access rule AR3 when migrating it to OM' in the described way. We come back to this problem in Proposition 3 (cf. Section 4.3).

Figure 6 shows how access rules can be adapted when applying a split operation (here splitting organizational unit OU2 into two new organizational units OU2_1 and OU2_2). According to Adaptation Policy 1 the given access rule containing a reference to the splitted organizational unit OU2 could be adapted by

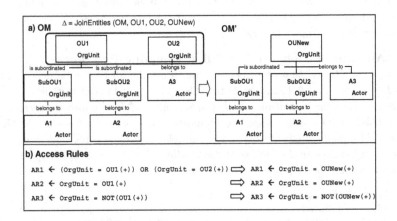

Fig. 5. Automatic Adaptation of Access Rules when Applying a Join Operation

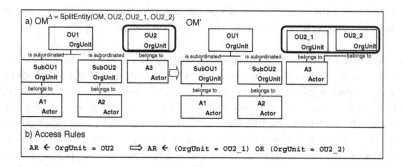

Fig. 6. Automatic Adaptation of Access Rules when Applying a Split Operation

replacing this reference with the expression (OU2_1 OR OU2_2). Again it has to be pointed out that this only constitutes a suggestion by the system.

In addition to split and join operations the deletion of entities may lead to dangling references. In certain cases no automatic strategy for adapting a particular access rule can be provided; the system then only reports the problem to the user and asks him for an adequate solution strategy. However, there exist many situations in which automatic rule adaptations become possible, and thus users can be assisted in transforming rules in a way such that they become valid on the new model version OM' as well. In particular, this possibility exists in connection with the migration of complex access rules (cf. Def. 5). As an example take access rule (AR $\longleftarrow$ Role = R1 $\vee$ Role = R2). Assume that role R2 is deleted from the used org. model. This model change causes a dangling reference in AR. A meaningful suggestion for automatically adapting rule AR would then be to delete expression (EAR $\longleftarrow$ Role = R2) from AR. This would result in the simplified rule (AR $\longleftarrow$ Role = R1), which does not contain dangling references. Furthermore, we could exploit the semantics of hierarchical relations in order to come up with some adaptation suggestions for affected access rules. Assume, for example, that role r, which is a specialization of another role r_{super}, is deleted. Assume further that there exists an access rule AR $\longleftarrow$ "... Role = r ..." affected by this change. Then it could be a reasonable strategy to suggest adapted rule AR' $\longleftarrow$ "... Role = r_{super} ..." instead of AR (e.g., if it is not longer necessary to have a more specialized nurse working on a specific ward, patient care can be performed by a regular nurse as well). The same strategy may be applied in the contrary direction if super-role r is deleted and the associated references within affected access rules are adapted to reference more specific role r_{sub}. Justification is that actors having role r_{sub} possess all capabilities assigned to role r and therefore are able to substitute actors having role r. Similar considerations hold for hierarchical relations between organizational units.

Note that for join, split, and delete operations access rule transformations do not always become necessary. If an access rule does not refer to any entity joined, deleted, or splitted, the rule can stay unaltered after the respective model transformation. Finally, in addition to the described rule transformations in our current implementation we apply a number of other rule optimizations when migrating rules to a new version of the organizational model. The treatment of these optimizations, however, is outside the scope of this paper.

Application of Complex Changes $\Delta = op_1, ..., op_n$. We now consider the application of a sequence of change operations to an organizational model OM; i.e., the application of a change (transaction) $\Delta = op_1, ..., op_n$ to OM (resulting in OM') and its effects on related access rules. Again, when considering an access rule AR on OM, dangling references within AR may result after migration to OM'. As an example consider Fig. 4 where the migration of access rules AR1, AR2, and AR3 to OM' results in dangling references when applying change Δ to OM. In order to deal with this problem, we have to analyze the effects of each applied change operation op_i (i = 1, ..., n) on access rules defined on OM. Regarding a particular access rule this analysis is accomplished in the order these operations were applied to OM. For those change operations op_i which cause dangling references and for which there exists an adaptation policy (cf. Adaptation Policy 1) we can adapt the affected access rules accordingly.

For change Δ from Fig. 4 and Fig. 3, respectively, we check for the effects of operations op_1 = JoinEntities(OM, ...), op_2 = DeleteRelation(OM, ...), and so on (for a complete definition of Δ see Fig. 3b). Consider, for example, access rule AR2 ⟵ OrgUnit='treatment area' in Fig. 4b. The application of op_1 = JoinEntities(OM, ...) already results in a dangling reference for AR2. Therefore AR2 is modified to (AR2 ⟵ OrgUnit = 'patient services') by applying Adaptation Policy 1 for the join operation. According to Proposition 2 the following three change operations related to Δ (and being of type DeleteRelation(OM, ...)) do not cause dangling references when migrating access rules to OM'. For the applied DeleteEntity(OM, ...) operation there may be dangling references, but not for access rule AR2. The next SplitEntity(OM, ...) operation does not affect AR2 and the following CreateRelation(OM, ...) operation is uncritical regarding dangling references. Finally, the last DeleteEntity(OM, ...) operation could cause dangling references, but again not for access rule AR2. Altogether, AR2 can migrate to OM' by adapting it to (AR2 ⟵ OrgUnit = 'patient services'). According to Adaptation Policy 1 we can ensure that AR2 does not contain dangling references based on OM'.

4.3 Dynamic Aspect – Valid Actor Set

Even if the problem of dangling references is satisfactorily solved we still may be confronted with non–resolvable access rules when changing an org. model. This may cause runtime errors or at least runtime delays (e.g., if activities cannot immediately be worked on since there is no qualifying actor any more). It may also impose security problems (e.g., if then the non-resolvable activity is offered to the system or process administrator as it is the case in several existing systems).

General Considerations. Let OM be an org. model which is transformed into another org. model OM' by change Δ. Furthermore, let AR be an access rule on

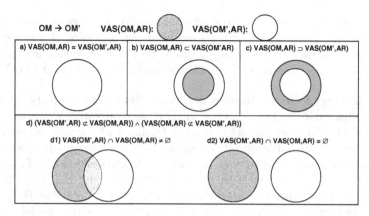

Fig. 7. Changing Organizational Models and Migrating Access Rules

OM. First of all, we illustrate at an abstract level how the valid actor set of an access rule AR based on OM may change when migrating this rule to the new model version OM'. Figure 7 depicts possible relations between the valid actor set of AR on OM VAS(OM,AR) and the valid actor set of AR on OM' VAS(OM',AR):

In Fig. 7a the migration of AR from OM to OM' does not influence the valid actor set, i.e., the set of valid actors remains the same. In this case, first of all, AR is still resolvable over OM' and does not require any adaptation of work lists or lists of qualified actors afterwards.

Figure 7b shows the case where the valid actor set is expanded when migrating AR to OM'. In practice this may require, for example, an update of user worklists by additionally inserting the associated work items into the worklists of newly qualified actors from the difference set VAS(OM', AR) \ VAS(OM, AR). By contrast, the valid actor set may be also reduced due to a model change as depicted in Fig. 7c. Consequently, for all actors no longer qualified for accessing the associated object or task (i.e., VAS(OM, AR) \ VAS(OM', AR)) the associated access privileges have to be adapted accordingly. Note that for the case depicted in Fig. 7c, it is possible that the valid actor set of AR on OM' becomes empty, i.e., AR may be no longer resolvable on OM'.

The scenario depicted in Figure 7d, where VAS(OM, AR) is not a subset of VAS(OM', AR) (or vice versa) can be further divided into two sub-cases d1 and d2. For case d1 there are still actors contained in both valid actor sets, i.e., the intersection of VAS(OM, AR) and VAS(OM', AR) is non–empty. For this case, we firstly have to withdraw the privileges associated with AR for all actors contained in VAS(OM, AR) \ VAS(OM', AR). Second, we have to newly assign these privileges to the actors contained in VAS(OM', AR) \ VAS(OM, AR). Finally, if VAS(OM, AR) and VAS(OM', AR) are disjoint as depicted in case d2 the privileges associated with AR have to be removed for all actors from VAS(OM, AR) and be added for all actors from VAS(OM', AR).

Knowing which of this cases applies in a given change scenario is helpful in order to conduct the necessary adaptations of qualified actor lists or work lists when migrating an access rule to the changed organizational model. In the following, first of all, we study the effects on valid actor sets of both elementary and complex access rules when a single change operation Δ_{op} is applied to OM. This is followed by a discussion of complex changes where a sequence of operations $op_1, ..., op_n$ is applied within one change transaction Δ to OM.

Impact of Org. Model Changes on Actor Sets When Applying Single Change Operations. Let Δ_{op} be a single change operation which transforms org. model OM into org. model OM'. Let further AR be a valid access rule on OM. According to Proposition 2 the application of a change operation $\Delta_{op} \in$ {CreateRelation(...) DeleteRelation(...) ReAssignRelation(...)} does not lead to dangling references in AR afterwards. However, Δ_{op} may affect the valid actor set of AR when migrating this access rule to OM', i.e. VAS(OM', AR) $\neq$ VAS(OM, AR) (cf. Fig. 7). Assume, for example, that in the org. model from Fig. 1 the relation indicating that actor Black belongs to treatment area (i.e., relation ((Black, Actor), (treatment area, OrgUnit), belongs to)) is reassigned to (Black, Actor), (administration, OrgUnit), belongs to). Then the valid actor set for access rule (AR2 ⟵ OrgUnit='treatment area') is then reduced from {Dr. Smith, Black} to {Dr. Smith}.

We first analyze the effects of Δ_{op} on the valid actor sets of elementary access rules EAR and negated elementary access rules NEAR. For the sake of readability we do not consider all scenarios from Fig. 7, but focus on the most "critical" cases; i.e., changes of the oganizational model due to which the valid actor set of [N]EAR is reduced (or even becomes empty) when migrating this access rule from OM to OM'. These cases are summarized in Table 3. The first column of this table shows the change operation (and its parameters) and the third column the (negated) elementary access rule(s) to be considered. Note that we may examine more than one access rule for a given change operation. Further, the effects of a change operation on the valid actor set of an access rule is depicted in the second column. As can be seen, in most cases the actor set will reduced when applying the change operation and migrating the access rule to the new organizational model. Regarding operation ReassignRelation we also give examples where new actors may be also added to the valid actor set.

The following figures illustrate some interesting situations from Table 3. Firstly we consider the creation of a new relation between two entities of the organizational model as depicted in Fig. 8. In this example, for both negated access rules NEAR1 and NEAR2 their valid actor set based on OM will be reduced when migrating the rule to OM'. In particular, due to change Δ_2 for NEAR2 the valid actor set becomes empty afterwards. Analogously, the application of change operation DeleteRelation(OM, ...) may lead to reduced actor sets. As an example consider the change scenario from Fig. 9. When deleting the relation ((a2, Actor), (r1, Role), has) from OM, for instance, for access rules EAR ⟵ (Role = 'r1') or EAR ⟵ (ROLE='r5'(+) the valid actor set will be reduced afterwards. The same applies to access rule EAR ⟵ (ROLE=r3(+)) after deleting relation (((r1, Role), (r2, Role), specializes).

As discussed in Section 4.2, when applying change operations joinEntities or splitEntity, dangling references within certain access rules may emerge

Table 3. Reduction of Valid Actor Set After Application of Change Operation Δ

Assume in the following that organizational model OM is transformed into organizational model OM'
by applying change operation Δ. Let further AR be an access rule defined on the basis of OM.

Change Operation Δ	VAS(OM',[N]EAR) = VAS(OM, [N]EAR) \ δ ($\cup$ ϵ)	$\forall$ [N]EAR $\in$ AR $\Longrightarrow$
CreateRelation(OM, (a,Actor),(r,Role),has)	δ = {(a, Actor)}	NEAR $\longleftarrow$ NOT(Role=r1[(+)]) with (r, Role) $\in$ QualEntities(OM,Role=r1[(+)])
CreateRelation(OM, (a,Actor),(o,OrgUnit),belongsTo)	δ = {(a, Actor)}	NEAR $\longleftarrow$ NOT(OrgUnit=o1[(+)]) with (o, OrgUnit) $\in$ QualEntities(OM,OrgUnit=o1[(+)])
CreateRelation(OM, (r1,Role),(r2,Role),specializes)	δ = VAS(OM,EAR') with EAR' $\longleftarrow$ Role=r1	NEAR $\longleftarrow$ NOT(Role=r3[(+)]) with (r1,Role), (r2,Role) $\in$ QualEntities(OM',Role=r3[(+)])
CreateRelation(OM, (o1,OrgUnit),(o2,OrgUnit), is subordinated)	δ = VAS(OM,EAR') with EAR' $\longleftarrow$ OrgUnit=o1	NEAR $\longleftarrow$ NOT(OrgUnit=o3[(+)]) with(o1,OrgUnit), (o2,OrgUnit) $\in$ QualEntities(OM',OrgUnit=o3[(+)])
DeleteRelation(OM, (a Actor),(r,Role),has)	δ = {(a, Actor)}	EAR $\longleftarrow$ Role = r1[(+)] with (r, Role) $\in$ QualEntities(OM,Role=r1[(+)])
DeleteRelation(OM,(a,Actor), (o,OrgUnit),belongsTo)	δ = {(a, Actor)}	EAR $\longleftarrow$ OrgUnit=o1[(+)] with (o, OrgUnit) $\in$ QualEntities(OM,OrgUnit=o1[(+)])
DeleteRelation(OM, (r1,Role),(r2,Role),specializes)	δ = VAS(OM,EAR') with EAR' $\longleftarrow$ Role=r1	EAR $\longleftarrow$ Role=r3[(+)] with (r1,Role), (r2,Role) $\in$ QualEntities(OM',Role=r3[(+)])
DeleteRelation(OM, (o1,OrgUnit),(o2,OrgUnit), is subordinated)	δ = VAS(OM,EAR') with EAR' $\longleftarrow$ OrgUnit=o1	EAR $\longleftarrow$ OrgUnit=o3[(+)] with (o1,OrgUnit), (o2,OrgUnit) $\in$ QualEntities(OM',OrgUnit=o3[(+)])
ReassignRelation(OM, ((a,Actor),(r,Role),has), (r,Role),(rN,Role))	δ = {(a,Actor)}	EAR $\longleftarrow$ Role=r1[(+)] with (r,Role) $\in$ QualEntities(OM,Role=r1[(+)])
	δ = {(a,Actor)}	NEAR $\longleftarrow$ NOT(Role=r1[(+)]) with (rN, Role) $\in$ QualEntities(OM,Role=r1[(+)])
ReassignRelation(OM, ((a,Actor),(o,OrgUnit),belongsTo), (o,OrgUnit),(oN,OrgUnit))	δ = {(a,Actor)}	EAR $\longleftarrow$ OrgUnit=o1[(+)] with (o,OrgUnit) $\in$ QualEntities(OM,OrgUnit=o1[(+)])
	δ = {(a,Actor)}	NEAR $\longleftarrow$ NOT(Role=o1[(+)]) with (oN,OrgUnit) $\in$ QualEntities(OM,OrgUnit=o1[(+)])
ReassignRelation(OM, ((r1,Role),(r2,Role),specializes), (r1,Role),(rN,Role))	δ = VAS(OM,EAR') with EAR' $\longleftarrow$ Role=r1(+)	EAR $\longleftarrow$ Role=r'[(+)] with (r2, Role) $\in$ QualEntities(OM,Role=r'[(+)])
	δ = VAS(OM,EAR') with EAR' $\longleftarrow$ Role=r1(+)	NEAR $\longleftarrow$ Role=r'[(+)] with (r2, Role) $\in$ QualEntities(OM,Role=r'[(+)]):
	δ = VAS(OM,EAR') with EAR' $\longleftarrow$ Role=r1(+)	NEAR $\longleftarrow$ Role=r'[(+)] with (rN, Role) $\in$ QualEntities(OM,Role=r'[(+)])
ReassignRelation(OM, ((r1,Role),(r2,Role),specializes), (r2,Role),(rN,Role))	δ = VAS(OM,EAR')) with EAR' $\longleftarrow$ Role=r1(+) ϵ = VAS(OM,EAR'') with EAR'' $\longleftarrow$ Role = rN(+)	EAR $\longleftarrow$ Role=r'[(+)] with (r2, Role) $\in$ QualEntities(OM,Role=r'[(+)])
	ϵ = VAS(OM,NEAR'') with NEAR' $\longleftarrow$ NOT(Role=r1(+)) δ = VAS(OM,NEAR'') with NEAR'' $\longleftarrow$ NOT(Role = rN(+))	NEAR $\longleftarrow$ NOT(Role=r'[(+)]) with (r2, Role) $\in$ QualEntities(OM,Role=r'[(+)])
ReassignRelation(OM, ((o1,OrgUnit),(o2,OrgUnit),is subordinated), (o1,OrgUnit),(oN,OrgUnit))	δ = VAS(OM,EAR') with EAR' $\longleftarrow$ OrgUnit=o1(+)	EAR $\longleftarrow$ OrgUnit=o'[(+)] with (o2,OrgUnit) $\in$ QualEntities(OM,OrgUnit=o'[(+)])
	δ = VAS(OM,EAR') with EAR' $\longleftarrow$ OrgUnit=o1(+)	NEAR $\longleftarrow$ NOT(OrgUnit=o'[(+)]) with (o2,OrgUnit) $\in$ QualEntities(OM,OrgUnit=o'[(+)])
	δ = VAS(OM,EAR') with EAR' $\longleftarrow$ OrgUnit=OrgUnit=o1(+)	NEAR $\longleftarrow$ NOT(OrgUnit=o'[(+)]) with (oN,OrgUnit) $\in$ QualEntities(OM,OrgUnit=o'[(+)])
ReassignRelation(OM, ((o1,OrgUnit),(o2,OrgUnit),is subordinated), (o2,OrgUnit),(oN,OrgUnit))	δ = VAS(OM,EAR') with EAR' $\longleftarrow$ OrgUnit=o1(+) ϵ = VAS(OM,EAR'') with EAR'' $\longleftarrow$ OrgUnit = oN(+)	EAR $\longleftarrow$ OrgUnit=o'[(+)] with (o2,OrgUnit) $\in$ QualEntities(OM,OrgUnit=o'[(+)])
	ϵ = VAS(OM,NEAR')) with NEAR' $\longleftarrow$ NOT(OrgUnit=o1(+)) δ = VAS(OM,NEAR'')) with NEAR'' $\longleftarrow$ NOT(OrgUnit = oN(+))	NEAR $\longleftarrow$ OrgUnit=o'[(+)] with (o2, OrgUnit) $\in$ QualEntities(OM,OrgUnit=o'[(+)])

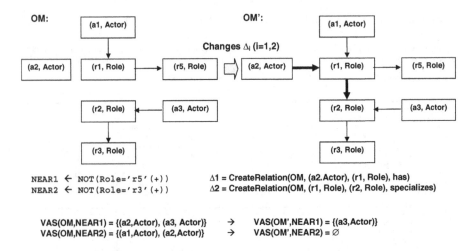

NEAR1 ← NOT(Role='r5'(+))   Δ1 = CreateRelation(OM, (a2.Actor), (r1, Role), has)
NEAR2 ← NOT(Role='r3'(+))   Δ2 = CreateRelation(OM, (r1, Role), (r2, Role), specializes)

VAS(OM,NEAR1) = {(a2,Actor), (a3, Actor)}   →   VAS(OM',NEAR1) = {(a3,Actor)}
VAS(OM,NEAR2) = {(a1,Actor), (a2,Actor)}   →   VAS(OM',NEAR2) = ∅

Fig. 8. Reduction of Valid Actors Sets After Creating Relations

(cf. Figures 5 and 6). Therefore we have provided rules (cf. Adaptation Policy 1) which enable the system to suggest automatic adaptations of the affected access rules to the user. However, after applying these adaptation rules the actor sets of the adapted and migrated access rules may be affected as well. In detail: For operation joinEntities it has to be checked how the actor sets of affected access rules have changed after the applicastion of adaptation rule δ (cf. Adaptation Policy 1). In particular, for negated access rules, the actor set may become smaller (and therefore even empty) afterwards. For operation splitEntity the application of adaptation rule δ does not affect the actor sets of access rules. Therefore no checks become necessary afterwards.

Proposition 3 (Actor Set After Joining Entities and Adaptation of Access Rules). *Let a (correct) organizational model OM be transformed into another (correct) organizational model OM' by applying change operation* $\Delta =$ JoinEntities(OM, ...). *Let further AR be an access rule defined on OM which is transformed into access rule AR' (by applying adaptation rules* δ_{AR}*; cf. Adaptation Policy 1) and then migrated to OM'. Then:*

- $\forall$ EAR ← (OrgUnit=o1) ∨ (OrgUnit=o2)) ∧ $\forall$ NEAR ← NOT((OrgUnit=o1) ∨ (OrgUnit=o2)) $\implies$
  VAS(OM',[N] EAR) = VAS(OM,[N] EAR)
- $\forall$ EAR ← OrgUnit=o1 $\implies$
  VAS(OM',EAR) = VAS(OM,EAR) ∪ VAS(OM,EAR') with EAR' ← OrgUnit=o2
- $\forall$ NEAR ← NOT(OrgUnit=o1) $\implies$
  VAS(OM',NEAR) = VAS(OM,NEAR) \ VAS(OM,EAR') with EAR' ← OrgUnit=o2
- $\forall$ EAR ← OrgUnit=o2 $\implies$
  VAS(OM',EAR) = VAS(OM,EAR) ∪ VAS(OM,EAR') with EAR' ← OrgUnit=o1
- $\forall$ NEAR ← NOT(OrgUnit=o2) $\implies$
  VAS(OM',NEAR) = VAS(OM,NEAR) \ VAS(OM,EAR') with EAR' ← OrgUnit=o1

Consider, for example, access rule AR3 as depicted in Fig. 3. Before migration the valid actor set of this rule turns out as VAS(OM,AR3) = {A3}. According to the adaptation policies provided by Rule Adaptation Policy 1, AR3 is adapted to

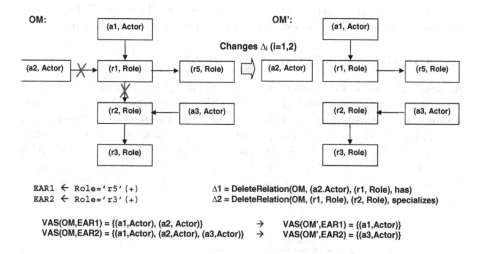

Fig. 9. Reduction of Valid Actors Sets After Deleting Relations

$AR3 \longleftarrow$ NOT(OUNew). This adaptation affects the valid actor set as follows:
$VAS(OM',AR3) = VAS(OM,AR3) \setminus VAS(OM,EAR')$ with $EAR' \longleftarrow$ (OrgUnit=OU2)
which results in $VAS(OM',AR3) = \{A3\} \setminus \{A3\} = \emptyset$ (cf. Proposition 3). Such critical
effects should be at least reported to the user.

Impact of Org. Model Changes on Actor Sets When Applying Complex Change Operations. Finally, we sketch potential effects on the valid actor set of access rules when migrating them from an org. model OM to a changed org. model OM' after application of a (complex) change $\Delta = op_1, ..., op_n$. When considering Fig. 7, it becomes clear that the application of each change operation op_i ($i = 1, ..., n$) may result in a change of the valid actor set. In particular, some of the changes may add actors to the valid actor set whereas others remove elements from it. Therefore a general statement on how the actor set changes is difficult. Similar to the considerations about dangling references resulting after the application of a complex (i.e., multi-operation) change, the effects of each change operation op_i (in the order of their application) on the valid actor set can be determined. Doing so finally results in the new actor set of an access rule based on OM. However, we have to consider the efforts for this approach. In order to decrease the computing time for the resulting actor set, the analysis and adaptation for dangling references and the determination of the actor set changes can be done in one go. We will address the issue of possible optimization methods in future work.

5 Architectural and Implementation Issues

In this section we sketch architectural and implementation issues which arise when realizing the described framework. Section 5.1 summarizes the architecture of the implemented adaptive enterprise security service. In Section 5.2 we discuss its concrete usage in the context of process-aware information systems.

5.1 Overview of the Enterprise Security Service

As proof-of-concept we realized an advanced *enterprise security service* (ESS) which implements the described framework. We have chosen a service–oriented design in order to support the reuse of the security component in different context and by different system components (e.g., workflow systems or document management tools). Fig. 10 depicts the overall architecture of the ESS (simplified illustration). The developed ESS comprises both tools and programming interfaces for creating, evolving and managing organizational models as well as the access rules based on them.

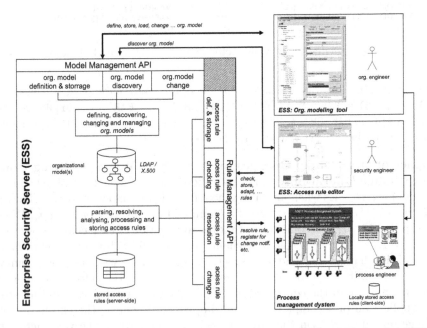

Fig. 10. (Simplified) architecture of the adaptive Enterprise Security Service (ESS)

For creating and adapting org. models the ESS offers a standard editor (cf. Fig. 10). Among other things this tool utilizes the change operations presented in this paper. All changes are logged and are traceable. Different org. models in different versions can be maintained. For editing elementary as well as complex access rules another tool is provided (cf. Fig. 10). Rules can be only released if they are syntactically and semantically correct, which requires cross-checks with the related org. model. The rule editor is realized as plug-in and can therefore be easily integrated in different client applications (for further details see [18]). Implementation is based on Java and SVG (Scalable Vector Graphics).

As mentioned the ESS offers powerful programming interfaces. The model management API provides the basis for defining and storing new org. models, for adapting existing ones to environmental changes, and for discovering information about org. models. Based on this interface, adapted client components for editing, displaying and analyzing org. models can be realized. Furthermore, the ESS offers a complete interface for the management of access rules. This interface allows to define, check and store new access rules (based on a referred organizational model) and to maintain these rules by the ESS.

In general, we do not require clients of the ESS to store and maintain their access rules within the ESS; this is only an optional feature. After having defined an access rule, it may be also maintained by the client system itself (e.g., a workflow system). In this case, the rule is represented as "query string" following the syntax of our rule definition language. This string can be resolved at runtime by sending it to the ESS (e.g., when an activity in a workflow becomes activated), which then parses and processes the access rule string, finally returning the set of actors who qualify for it. For access rules already stored in the ESS these steps can be partially omitted, resulting in higher system performance and better response rates. In this case the client simply invokes a generic procedure with the respective context information via the ESS interface.

The realized ESS extends the features of existing access control components by offering more advanced change facilities. Adaptations of the org. model are based on the operational framework described in Section 2. The ability to concomitantly adapt access rules is of particular importance. It uses the rule adaptation framework introduced in Section 4. Further, we offer different migration and adaptation policies for access rules depending on whether they are directly maintained by the ESS or by the client application. Access rules stored within the ESS can be immediately processed in order to decide whether there is a need for adaptation and - if yes - how it should look like. Further the ESS determines for which rules actor sets have changed. Based on this information users or clients can be notified in order to accept the suggested rule adaptations or to accommodate them.

Rules outside ESS control cannot be immediately migrated. This, in turn, might lead to non-resolvable access rules which require lazy migration techniques and advanced exception handling mechanisms. By using the provided API, however, clients can register for change notification events. When a model change occurs the ESS notifies registered clients, which then can check the validity of their access rules against the newly released version of the org. model. Finally, if a non-resolvable access rule is sent to the ESS, an exception is thrown providing the client with the information about necessary rule adaptations. Due to lack of space we omit further details and a more precise presentation of the interaction patterns between clients (buildtime and runtime) and the ESS. Current implementation of the ESS is based on Java and relational database management technology. Integration with LDAP (Lightweight Directory Access Protocol) services [19] is one important requirement for the future.

Clients can be components of information systems or supporting technology (e.g., workflow systems). Different clients may share one org. model (e.g., to achieve consistency across multiple systems) or may maintain their own model if favorable. In any case the information about org. entities and access rules can be separated from the business logic implemented by the client programs. Note that this provides the basis for the controlled evolution of org. models and related access rules, and also constitutes a significant improvement when compared to the proprietary, heterogeneous security components we can find in current information systems. We strongly believe that a component like ESS is very useful for dealing with org. change in a secure and intelligent manner, and for providing better maintainability and traceability in this context.

5.2   Managing Actor Assignments and Worklists in Process-Aware Information Systems

To illustrate our results we apply them to important elements of process-aware information systems (PAIS) - activity actor assignments, user worklists, and their adaptation due to org. changes. More precisely we sketch how changes of an org. model have to be handled within a workflow system and how the different system components interact with each other to cope with model changes. Usually, a PAIS maintains different process templates each of them representing a particular business process. Each of these process templates captures different aspects of a business process like process activities, control and data flow between activities, and actor assignments. The latter are of particular interest in the context of the present work. They represent the access rules needed by the PAIS to decide which users may work on instances of the respective activity. As an example, consider the two actor assignment rules R1: (OrgUnit = OU_2 and Role = Role_2) and R2: Role = Role_1 as depicted in Fig. 11. When an activity instance becomes activated at runtime the PAIS determines all actors qualifying for this activity, creates corresponding work items, and adds them to the worklists of these users.

At buildtime the PAIS must support the definition of actor assignments based on an org. model and their correlation with process activities. For this the PAIS either can utilize the standard modeling tools offered by the ESS or realize own buildtime clients based on ESS interfaces. Within the ADEPT project, for example, we have utilized the tools and plug-ins mentioned above. Access rules can be assigned to activities or to other privileges relevant for the PAIS. Both org. models and access rules are stored within the ESS.

Consider the scenario depicted in Fig. 11. When a change occurs within the organization, an authorized user can adapt the org. model accordingly. In the example from Fig. 11, for instance, the two org. units OU_2 and OU_3 are joined and the "has-role" relation between Actor_1 and Role_1 is deleted. This results in a new version of the respective model, which then triggers the adaptation and migration of related access rules. In the given example, for instance, at the process template level the two actor assignment rules R1: (OrgUnit = OU_2 and Role = Role_2) and R2: Role = Role_1 may have to be adapted. If these rules are directly maintained by the ESS, this service analyses them for necessary

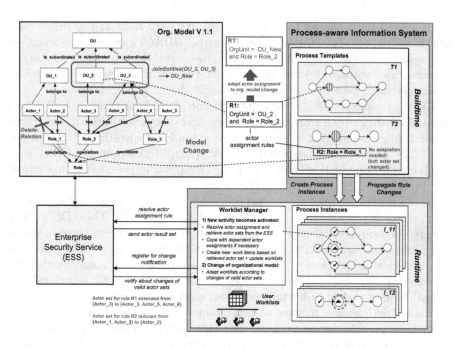

Fig. 11. Adapting actor assignment rules and worklists in process-aware IS

adaptations. As a result the ESS suggests the process engineer to adapt rule R1 to rule R1' (cf. Fig. 11), but to remain rule R2 unchanged.

As discussed in Section 4 the adaptation of access rules (actor assignments) is only one side of the coin. We also have to analyze the effects of the performed model and rule changes to valid actor sets. This is of particular importance for PAIS in order to avoid outdated or inconsistent worklists. As an example take the adaptation applied for rule R1 in Fig. 11. Obviously, this extends the valid actor set of this rule from {Actor_3} to {Actor_3, Actor_5, Actor_6}. For currently activated activity instances based on this rule this should imply the creation of new work items for Actor_5 and Actor_6. As another example consider rule R2. Though this rule must not be adapted due to the model change (see above) its valid actor set is reduced from {Actor_1, Actor_2} to {Actor_2}. Therefore, respective work items currently assigned to Actor_1 on basis of R2 should be removed from the worklist of this actor. In our approach, the worklist manager of the PAIS accomplishes such on-the-fly worklist updates based on the interfaces offered by the ESS. Due to lack of space we omit further details. However, we are aware of the fact that the efficient update of user worklists is a big challenge in the given context, particularly when thinking of scenarios with ten thousands of work items.

6 Related Work

The provision of an adequate access control framework is indispensable for any IS. In the literature numerous approaches have been presented dealing with challenging issues related to access control (e.g., [12,20,21,22]). Most of these approaches apply *Role–Based Access Control (RBAC)* models for defining and managing user privileges [6,23,20,24], e.g., to control the access to business documents and database objects, or to resolve the set of actors that qualify for a newly activated task in a *workflow system* [25,4,8,21,26,22].

Usually, corresponding models provide core RBAC features as well as role hierarchies. Regarding workflow–based applications, in addition, dynamic constraints (e.g., separation of duties) were extensively investigated in the past [4,8,27,28]. Practical issues related to RBAC (e.g., NIST's proposed RBAC standard, integration of RBAC with enterprise IT infrastructures, RBAC in commercial products) are summarized in [24].

In the workflow literature several proposals have been made aiming at adaptive process management (e.g., [29,30,31,32,33,34,35,36,37]). The ADEPT technology, for example, enables controlled changes at the process type as well as the process instance level (for details see [38,39,40]). Thereby, correctness and consistency constraints of a workflow are preserved when dynamically changing its structure, its state, or its attributes during runtime. In [22] an extension to RBAC is proposed in order to accomplish such process changes is a safe way; i.e. to restrict changes to selected user groups or processes if required. Though all these approaches stress the need for adaptive information systems and define different notions of correctness (for an overview see [30]), so far, focus has been on process changes (control and data flow).

There are only few approaches [12,41,42,43] which address the problem of organizational change. In [12,41,42] eight categories of structural changes on organizational models are identified. Examples include the splitting of organizational units, the creation of new organizational entities, and the reassignment of an actor to a new organizational unit. In principle, all these cases can be captured by our change framework as well. As opposed to [12], however, we additionally follow a rigorous formal approach in order to be able to derive the effects of organizational changes on related access rules as well. Corresponding issues are factored out in [12]. The approach introduced in [43] deals with the evolution of access rules in workflow systems. However, only very simple scenarios are described without any formal foundation. Furthermore, the compact definition of access rules is aggravated by the lack of adequate abstraction mechanisms (e.g., hierarchical structures).

Issues related to the modeling of organizational structures have been considered by different groups [11,21,18]. Most of them suggest a particular meta model for capturing org. entities and the relationships between them. Model changes and the adaptation of access rules, however, have not been studied by these approaches in sufficient detail. Particularly, no formal considerations exist and no proof-of-concept prototypes have been provided.

In [44] important issues related to changes of processes and org. structures are discussed. In this work the authors also motivate the need for the controlled change of organizational models. In particular, they discuss different kinds of adaptations that have to be supported by respective components (e.g., to extend, reduce, replace, and re-link model elements). However, no concrete solution approach is provided (like, for example, formal change operators with well–defined semantics or mechanisms for adapting access rules after model changes).

7 Summary and Outlook

The integrated and controlled evolution of organizational models as well as access rules will be key ingredients of next generation enterprise security services, ultimately resulting in adaptive and highly flexible access control frameworks. Together with our previous work on business process evolution and dynamic process change [38,45,40,39] the presented concepts contribute to a powerful platform enabling the realization of flexible and adaptive information systems.

In this paper, we have designed a comprehensive framework for defining and changing organizational models, for specifying access rules in a consistent manner, and for correctly adapting these access rules when model changes occur. We have discussed important challenges and requirements in this context as well as limitations of current approaches. Based on this we have introduced a comprehensive framework for the evolution of organizational models and the adaptation of related access rules. The very important aspect of our work is its formal foundation. We have provided precise definitions and formal propositions which are fundamental for the correct handling of model changes, for reasoning about the effects of such changes on access rules, and for adapting access rule if necessary. The treatment of both elementary and composed access rules as well as the consideration of runtime issues (e.g., effects of model changes on rule actor sets) add to the completeness of our approach. Finally, we have discussed important architectural issues and sketched a proof-of-concept implementation demonstrating the feasibility of the presented concepts.

The implemented security service has been coupled with the ADEPT2 process management system in order to enable the (dynamic) adaptation of actor assignments, user worklists, etc. when changes of the organizational model happen. For the sake of readability, in this paper we have restricted our consideration to a rather simple role-based access control model which applies basic entities (org. unit, role, and actor) and the relations between them (incl. role hierarchies). However, the enterprise security service realized by us within the ADEPT2 project is based on a more expressive meta model (incl. organizational entities like position, capability or project group).

There are many other challenging issues that can be linked to the evolution of org. models and related access rules. Firstly, we should consider semantical constraints as well. Uncontrolled changes of an org. model, for example, may violate semantical constraints like *separation of duty (SoD)* or *mutual exclusion* [27,28,46,47]. Among other things, this may result in security gaps. Secondly, we believe that changes of the org. model must be closely linked to other components of an IS. For example, actor assignments in workflow-based applications may have to be adapted on-the-fly in order to cope with org. changes. This, in turn, may require change propagation to hundreds up to thousands of in-progress process instances as well as to related user worklists. Doing this in a correct and efficient manner is a non-trivial problem that will be investigated by us in more detail in future. Thirdly, it is interesting to investigate how access rules can be improved, for example, based on previous adaptations (*access rule life cycle management*). First work in this field on the mining of access rules from workflow log data has been published in [48]. Finally, changes may not only concern the process model or the org. model but other components of the information systems as well. As an example take resource models or data models, which may be also subject of change. Thew more we extract the specification of these different aspects from application code the better will be the basis for setting up flexible adaptation mechanisms.

References

1. v.d. Aalst, W., van Hee, K.: Workflow Management. MIT Press, Cambridge (2002)
2. Sutton, M.: Document Management for the Enterprise: Principles, Techniques and Applications. John Wiley, Chichester (1996)
3. Linthicum, D.: Enterpise Application Integration. Addison-Wesley, Reading (1999)
4. Bertino, E., Ferrari, E., Alturi, V.: The specification and enforcement of authorization constraints in wfms. ACM Trans. on Inf. and Sys. Sec. 2, 65–104 (1999)
5. Sandhu, S.: Authentication, access control and audit. ACM Computings Surveys 28, 241–243 (1996)
6. Ferraiolo, D., Kuhn, D., Chandramouli, R.: Role–Based Access Control. Artech House (2003)
7. Sandhu, R.S., Coyne, E.J., Feinstein, H.L., Youman, C.E.: Role-based access control models. IEEE Computer 29, 38–47 (1996)
8. Wainer, J., Barthelmess, P., Kumar, A.: W–RBAC – a workflow security model incorporating controlled overriding of constraints. International Journal of Collaborative Information Systems 12, 455–485 (2003)
9. El Kalam, A., El Baida, R., Balbiani, P., Benferhat, S., Cuppens, F., Saurel, C., Deswarte, Y., Miege, A., Trouessin, G.: Organization-based access control. In: Proc. 4th IEEE Int. Workshop on Policies for Distributed Systems and Networks, IEEE Computer Society Press, Los Alamitos (2003)
10. Konyen, I.: Organizational structures and business processes in hospitals. Master's thesis, University of Ulm, Computer Science Faculty (in German) (1996)
11. Jablonski, S., Schlundt, M., Wedekind, H.: A generic component for the computer–based use of organizational models (in german). Informatik Forschung und Entwicklung 16, 23–34 (2001)
12. Klarmann, J.: A comprehensive support for changes in organizational models of workflow management systems. In: ISM 2001. Proc. 4th Int'l Conf. on Inf Systems Modeling, pp. 375–387 (2001)
13. Dumas, M., ter Hofstede, A.W.A. (eds.): Process Aware Information Systems. Wiley Publishing, Chichester (2005)
14. Rinderle, S., Reichert, M.: On the controlled evolution of access rules in cooperative information systems. In: Meersman, R., Tari, Z. (eds.) On the Move to Meaningful Internet Systems 2005: CoopIS, DOA, and ODBASE. LNCS, vol. 3760, pp. 238–255. Springer, Heidelberg (2005)
15. Ferraiolo, D., Sandhu, R., Gavrila, S., Kuhn, D., Chandramouli, R.: Proposed NIST standard for role-based acces control. ACM ToISS 4, 224–274 (2001)

16. Tolone, W., Ahn, G., Pai, T.: Access control in collaborative systems. ACM Computings Surveys 37, 29–41 (2005)
17. Reichert, M., Rinderle, S., Kreher, U., Dadam, P.: Adaptive process management with adept2. In: ICDE 2005. Proc. 21st Int'l Conf. on Data Engineering, Tokyo, pp. 1113–1114 (2005)
18. Berroth, M.: Design of a component for organizational models. Master's thesis, University of Ulm, Computer Science Faculty (in German) (2005)
19. Howes, T., Smith, M., Good, G.: Understanding and Deploying LDAP Directory Services. New Riders (2001)
20. Bertino, E.: Data security. DKE 25, 199–216 (1998)
21. Zur Muehlen, M.: Resource modeling in workflow applications. In: Proc. of the 1999 Workflow Management Conference (Muenster), pp. 137–153 (1999)
22. Weber, B., Reichert, M., Wild, W., Rinderle, S.: Balancing flexibility and security in adaptive process management systems. In: Meersman, R., Tari, Z. (eds.) On the Move to Meaningful Internet Systems 2005: CoopIS, DOA, and ODBASE. LNCS, vol. 3760, pp. 59–76. Springer, Heidelberg (2005)
23. NIST: Proposed Standard for Role-Based Access Control (2004), http://csrc.nist.gov/rbac/rbacSTDACM.pdf
24. Ferraiolo, D., Kuhn, D.: Role based access control. In: 15th National Computer Security Conference (1992)
25. Botha, R., Eloff, J.: A framework for access control in workflow systems. Information Management and Computer Security 9, 126–133 (2001)
26. Pfeiffer, V.: A framework for evaluating access control concepts in workflow management systems. Master's thesis, University of Ulm, Computer Science Faculty (in German) (2005)
27. Giuri, L., Iglio, P.: A formal model for role-based access control with constraints. In: Proc. Computer Security Foundations Workshop, pp. 136–145 (1996)
28. Kuhn, D.: Mutual exclusion of roles as a means of implementing separation of duty in role-based access control systems. In: Proc. 2nd ACM Workshop on Role-based Access Control, pp. 23–30. ACM Press, New York (1997)
29. v.d. Aalst, W.: Exterminating the dynamic change bug: A concrete approach to support worfklow change. Information Systems Frontiers 3, 297–317 (2001)
30. Rinderle, S., Reichert, M., Dadam, P.: Correctness criteria for dynamic changes in workflow systems – a survey. Data and Knowledge Engineering, Special Issue on Advances in Business Process Management 50, 9–34 (2004)
31. Agostini, A., De Michelis, G.: Improving flexibility of workflow management systems. In: BPM 2000. Proc. Int'l Conf. on Business Process Management, pp. 218–234 (2000)
32. Joeris, G., Herzog, O.: Managing evolving workflow specifications. In: CoopIS 1998. Proc. Int'l Conf. on Cooperative Information Systems, New York City, pp. 310–321 (1998)
33. Weske, M.: Workflow management systems: Formal foundation, conceptual design, implementation aspects. University of Münster, Germany, Habilitation Thesis (2000)
34. Sadiq, S., Marjanovic, O., Orlowska, M.: Managing change and time in dynamic workflow processes. IJCIS 9, 93–116 (2000)
35. Fent, A., Reiter, H., Freitag, B.: Design for change: Evolving workflow specifications in ULTRAflow. In: Pidduck, A.B., Mylopoulos, J., Woo, C.C., Ozsu, M.T. (eds.) CAiSE 2002. LNCS, vol. 2348, pp. 516–534. Springer, Heidelberg (2002)

36. Kochut, K., Arnold, J., Sheth, A., Miller, J., Kraemer, E., Arpinar, B., Cardoso, J.: IntelliGEN: A distributed workflow system for discovering protein-protein interactions. Distributed and Parallel Databases 13, 43–72 (2003)
37. Edmond, D., ter Hofstede, A.: A reflective infrastructure for workflow adaptability. Data and Knowledge Engineering 34, 271–304 (2000)
38. Reichert, M., Dadam, P.: ADEPT$_{flex}$ - supporting dynamic changes of workflows without losing control. JIIS 10, 93–129 (1998)
39. Rinderle, S., Reichert, M., Dadam, P.: Flexible support of team processes by adaptive workflow systems. Distributed and Parallel Databases 16, 91–116 (2004)
40. Rinderle, S., Weber, B., Reichert, M., Wild, W.: Integrating process learning and process evolution - a semantics based approach. In: van der Aalst, W.M.P., Benatallah, B., Casati, F., Curbera, F. (eds.) BPM 2005. LNCS, vol. 3649, Springer, Heidelberg (2005)
41. Klarmann, J.: A comprehensive support for changes in organizational models of workflow management systems. In: ISM 2001. Proc. Int'l Conf. on Information Systems Modeling, Hradec nad Moravici, Czech Republic (2001)
42. Domingos, D., Rito–Silva, A., Veiga, P.: Authorization and access control in adaptive workflows. In: Snekkenes, E., Gollmann, D. (eds.) ESORICS 2003. LNCS, vol. 2808, pp. 23–28. Springer, Heidelberg (2003)
43. v.d. Aalst, W., Jablonski, S.: Dealing with workflow change: Identification of issues an solutions. In: Snekkenes, E., Gollmann, D. (eds.) ESORICS 2003. LNCS, vol. 2808, pp. 267–276. Springer, Heidelberg (2003)
44. Klarmann, J.: Using conceptual graphs for organization modeling in workflow management systems. In: WM 2001. Proc. Conf. Professionelles Wissensmanagement, pp. 19–23 (2001)
45. Rinderle, S., Reichert, M., Dadam, P.: Disjoint and overlapping process changes: Challenges, solutions, applications. In: Meersman, R., Tari, Z. (eds.) On the Move to Meaningful Internet Systems 2004: CoopIS, DOA, and ODBASE. LNCS, vol. 3290, pp. 101–120. Springer, Heidelberg (2004)
46. Simon, R., Zurko, M.: Separation of duty in role based environments. In: Proc. Computer Security Foundations Workshop X (1997)
47. Botha, R., Eloff, J.: Separation of duties for access control enforcement in workflow environments. IBM Systems Journal 40(3) (2001)
48. Ly, T., Rinderle, S., Dadam, P., Reichert, M.: Mining staff assignment rules from event-based data. In: Castellanos, M., Weijters, T. (eds.) BPI 2005. First International Workshop on Business Process Intelligence, Nancy, France, pp. 177–190 (2005)

Putting Things in Context:
A Topological Approach to Mapping Contexts to Ontologies

Aviv Segev and Avigdor Gal

Technion - Israel Institute of Technology
Haifa 32000
Israel
asegev@tx.technion.ac.il, avigal@ie.technion.ac.il

Abstract. Ontologies and contexts are complementary disciplines for modeling views. In the area of information integration, ontologies may be viewed as the outcome of a manual effort to model a domain, while contexts are system generated models. In this work, we provide a formal mathematical framework that delineates the relationship between contexts and ontologies. We then use the model to handle the uncertainty associated with automatic context extraction from existing documents by providing a ranking method, which ranks ontology concepts according to their suitability to a given context. Throughout this work we motivate our research using QUALEG, a European IST project that aims at providing local governments with an effective tool for bi-directional communication with citizens. We empirically evaluate our model using two real-world data sets, coming from Reuters and news RSS. Our empirical analysis shows that the input needed to accurately define a concept by a context is small, and the classification of documents to concepts is accurate.

Keywords: Ontology, Context, Topology mapping.

1 Introduction

Ontologies and contexts are both used to model views, which are different perspectives of a domain. Some consider ontologies as shared models of a domain and contexts as local views of a domain. In the area of information integration, an orthogonal classification exists, in which ontologies are considered a result of a manual effort of modeling a domain, while contexts are system generated models [35]. As an example, consider an organizational scenario in which an organization (such as a local government) is modeled with a global ontology. A task of document classification, in which new documents are classified upon arrival to relevant departments, can be modeled as an integration of contexts (automatically generated from documents) into an existing ontology. A simple example of a context in this setting would be a set of words, extracted from the document.

Such an approach was recently adopted in QUALEG, a European Commission project aimed at increasing citizen participation in the democratic process.[1] In

---

[1] http://www.qualeg.eupm.net/

S. Spaccapietra et al. (Eds.): Journal on Data Semantics IX, LNCS 4601, pp. 113–140, 2007.

QUALEG, contexts are used to classify the input from citizens and map them to services provided by the local governments. In particular, QUALEG was designed to handle routing of emails to departments, opinion analysis on topics at the forefront of public debates, and identification of new topics on the public agenda.

The two classifications (*i.e.*, global *vs.* local and manual *vs.* automatic) of contexts and ontologies are not necessarily at odds. In the example given above, documents may be email messages from citizens, expressing a local view of a domain to be matched against a global view of government services. The former is automatically generated to allow rapid response to citizens, while the latter is a result of a carefully and manually crafted modeling of a domain. The classification of manual *vs.* automatic modeling of a domain has been the center of attention in the area of data integration in the past few years.

In this work, we aim at formalizing the inter-relationships between an ontology, a manually generated domain model, and contexts, partial and automatically generated local views. We provide a formal mathematical framework that delineates the relationships between contexts and ontologies. Following the motivation given above, we discuss the uncertainty associated with automatic context extraction from existing documents and provide a ranking model, which ranks ontology concepts according to their suitability to a given context.

Throughout this paper, we motivate our work with examples from the eGovernment domain. However, due to the absence of large scale data sets for this domain, we support our model with an empirical analysis using real-world news syndication traces.

Our contributions are as follows:

- We present a framework for combining contexts and ontologies using topological structures.
- We provide a model for ranking ontology concepts relative to a context that deals with the uncertainty inherent in the context extraction and classification.
- Using real world scenario, taken from email messages from citizens in a local government, we demonstrate three tasks that involve mapping contexts to ontologies, namely email routing, opinion analysis, and public agenda identification. Analyzing traces from Reuters and news RSS data, we analyze several aspects of our model, such as the context size required to define a concept and the accuracy of the classification of documents.

The rest of the paper is organized as follows. We first discuss related work in Section 2. Next, in Section 3 we propose a model for combining contexts and ontologies. In Section 4 we present a ranking model to map contexts to ontologies. Section 5 displays the results and analysis of the model implementation. Finally, Section 6 includes concluding remarks and suggestions for future work.

2   Related Work

This section describes related work in three different research areas, namely context representation and extraction, ontology, and topology.

2.1 Context Representation and Extraction

The context model we use is based on the definition of context as first class objects formulated by McCarthy [25]. McCarthy defines a relation $ist(\mathcal{C}, P)$, asserting that a proposition P is true in a context $\mathcal{C}$. We use this relation in Section 4.1 when discussing context extraction.

It has been proposed to use a multilevel semantic network to represent knowledge within several levels of contexts [42]. The zero level of representation is a semantic network that includes knowledge about basic domain objects and their relations. The first level of representation uses a semantic network to represent contexts and their relationships. The second level presents relationships of metacontexts, the next level describes metametacontext, and so forth. The top level includes knowledge that is considered to be true in all contexts. In this work we do not explicitly limit the number of levels in the sematic network. However, due to the limited capabilities of context extraction tools nowadays (see below), we define context as sets of sets of descriptors at zero level only and the mapping between contexts and ontology concepts is represented at level 1. Generally speaking, our model requires $n + 1$ levels of abstraction, where n represents the abstraction levels needed to represent contexts and their relationships.

A previous work on contexts [39] uses metadata for semantic reconciliation. They define the semantic domain of an attribute as the set of attributes used to define its semantics. Work by [16] uses contexts that are organized as a meet semi-lattice and associated operations like the greatest lower bound for semantic similarity are defined. The context of comparison and the type of abstractions used to relate the two objects form the basis of a semantic taxonomy. They define ontology as the specification of a representational vocabulary for a shared domain of discourse. Both these approaches use ontological concepts for creating contextual descriptions and serve best when creating new ontologies. In this work, we do not focus on ontology generation, which can be performed in any one of various methods, including those mentioned above. In the eGovernment application that we use as a motivation for this work, the existence of an ontology to which contexts should be mapped is assumed.

The creation of taxonomies from metadata (in XML/RDF) containing descriptions of learning resources was undertaken in [32]. Following the application of basic text normalization techniques, an index was built, which can be observed as a graph with learning resources as nodes connected by arcs labeled by the index words common to their metadata files. A cluster mining algorithm is applied to this graph and then the controlled vocabulary is selected statistically. A manual effort is necessary to organize the resulting clusters into hierarchies. When dealing with medium-sized corpora (a few hundred thousand words), the terminological network is too vast for manual analysis, and it is necessary to use data analysis tools for processing. Therefore, Assadi [1] employed a clustering tool that utilizes specialized data analysis functions and clustered the terms in a terminological network to reduce its complexity. These clusters are then manually processed by a domain expert to either edit them or reject them.

Several distance metrics were proposed in the literature and can be applied to measure the quality of context extraction. Prior work presented methods based on information retrieval techniques [43] for extracting contextual descriptions from data and evaluating the quality of the process. In Section 5.2 we compare our experiments with text classification using the Latent Semantic Indexing (LSI) approach presented in the work of [14] and [21]. The approach associates word-based vectors to topics in a taxonomy. The underlying idea of LSI is that the aggregate of all the word contexts in which a given word does and does not appear provides a set of mutual constraints that largely determines the similarity of meaning of words and sets of words.

Methods which included techniques for analyzing quality of information included Motro and Rakov [30] who proposed a standard for specifying the quality of databases based on the concepts of soundness and completeness. The method allowed the quality of answers to arbitrary queries to be calculated from overall quality specifications of the database. Another approach [28] is based on estimating loss of information in navigating ontological terms. The measures for loss of information were based on metrics such as precision and recall on extensional information. These measures are used to select results having the desired quality of information and we shall use them in our empirical evaluation as well.

To demonstrate our method, we propose in Section 4.1 the use of a fully automatic context recognition algorithm that uses the Internet as a knowledge base and as a basis for clustering [35]. Both the contexts and the ontology concepts are defined as topological sets, for which set distance presents itself as a natural choice for a distance measure.

2.2   Ontology

Ontologies have been defined and used in various research areas, including philosophy (where it was coined), artificial intelligence, information sciences, knowledge representation, object modeling, and most recently, eCommerce applications. In his seminal work, Bunge defines Ontology as a world of systems and provides a basic formalism for ontologies [4]. Typically, ontologies are represented using Description Logic [2,9], where subsumption typifies the semantic relationship between terms, or Frame Logic [18], where a deductive inference system provides access to semi-structured data.

Recent work has focused on ontology creation and evolution and in particular on schema matching. Many heuristics were proposed for the automatic matching of schemata (*e.g.*, Cupid [23], GLUE [8], and OntoBuilder [11]), and several theoretical models were proposed to represent various aspects of the matching process [22,27,10].

The realm of information science has produced an extensive body of literature and practice in ontology construction, *e.g.*, [44]. Other undertakings, such as the DOGMA project [41], provide an engineering approach to ontology management. Work has been done in ontology learning, such as Text-To-Onto [24], Thematic Mapping [6], OntoMiner [7], and TexaMiner [15] to name a few. Finally, researchers in the field of knowledge representation have studied ontology interoperability, resulting in systems such as Chimaera [26] and Protège [31].

Our model of an ontology is based on Bunge's terminology. We aim at formalizing the mapping between contexts and ontologies and provide an uncertainty management tool in the form of concept ranking. When experimenting with our model we assume an ontology is given, designed using any of the tools mentioned above.

2.3   Topology

In recent years researchers have applied principles from the mathematical domain of topology in different fields of Artificial Intelligence. One work uses topological localization and mapping for agent problem solving [5]. Other researchers have implemented topology in metrical information associated with actions [38,20]. In another method of topological mapping, which describes large scale static environments using a hybrid topological metric model, a global map is formed from a set of local maps organized in a topological structure, where each local map contains quantitative environment information using a local reference frame [40]. Remolina and Kuipers present a general theory of topological maps whereby sensory input, topological and local metrical information are combined to define topological maps explaining such information [33].

Following the success of these works, in this work we use topologies and topology theory as a tool of choice for integrating contexts and ontologies. While the tools we use are inherently different from those of [33] and [40], we follow their basic theme of using topology to integrate local views into a global one.

3   A Model of Context and Ontology

In this section we formally define our model of contexts and ontologies (Section 3.1) and propose a topology-based model to specify the relationships between them (Section 3.2). We conclude in Section 3.3 with a discussion and a few examples from the QUALEG project.

3.1   Contexts and Ontologies

We define a descriptor c_i from domain $\mathcal{D}$ as an index term used to identify a record of information [29]. It can consist of a word, phrase, or alphanumerical term. A weight $w_i \in \Re$ identifies the importance of descriptor c_i in relation to the record of information. For example, we can have a descriptor $c_1 = Musik$, and $w_1 = 6$. A *descriptor set* $\{\langle c_i, w_i \rangle\}_i$ is defined by a set of pairs, descriptors and weights. Each descriptor can define a different point of view of the concept. The descriptor set defines all the different perspectives and their relevant weights, which identify the relative importance of each perspective.

By collecting all the different view points delineated by the different descriptors we obtain a *context*. A *context* $\mathcal{C} = \left\{ \{\langle c_{ij}, w_{ij} \rangle\}_i \right\}_j$ is a set of finite sets of descriptors. For example, a context $\mathcal{C}$ may be a finite set of words describing each document Doc (hence $\mathcal{D}$ is a set of all possible documents) and the weights can represent the relevance of a descriptor to Doc. In classic Information Retrieval, $\langle c_{ij}, w_{ij} \rangle$ may represent the fact that the word c_{ij} is repeated w_{ij} times in Doc.

Another example which represents a context from a different perspective can be seen if we take two different descriptor sets of a published article: first, the publication information of the article, such as article title and author, and second, a set of keywords representing the classification topics of the paper. Both descriptor sets refer to the same paper, but each descriptor set provides a different viewpoint of it. An example of a

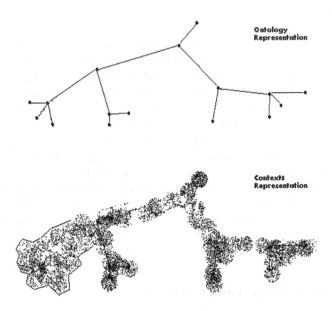

Fig. 1. Contexts and Ontology Concepts

descriptor set based on the publication information of a document can be the title and category (press release): $\{\{\langle \text{Theater im Grenzbereich}, 2\rangle\}, \{\langle \text{Pressemitteilung}, 1\rangle\}\}$. In addition, the document can be described by a descriptor set: $\{\{\langle \text{Musik}, 8\rangle\}, \{\langle \text{Open Air}, 1\rangle\}\}$. It is worth noting that the context above has two descriptor sets, each with two pairs of a descriptor and a weight.

An *ontology* $O = (V, E)$ is a directed graph, with nodes representing concepts (*things* in Bunge's terminology [3,4]) and edges representing relationships (See Figure 1 (top) for a graphical illustration). A single concept is represented by a name and a context $\mathcal{C}$.

Example 1 (Contexts and ontologies). To illustrate contexts and ontologies, consider the local government of Saarbrücken. Two ontology concepts in the ontology of Saarbrücken are Perspective du Theatre and Long Day School. The first concept, Perspective du Theatre, is associated with a context that contains descriptor sets such as:

(Perspectives du Theatre, $\{\{\langle \text{Öffentlichkeitsarbeit}, 2\rangle\}, \{\langle \text{Multimedia}, 1\rangle\}, \{\langle \text{Kulturpolitik}, 1\rangle\}, \{\langle \text{Musik}, 6\rangle\}, ...\}$)

and Long Day School is associated with the following context descriptor sets:

(Long Day School, $\{\{\langle \text{Förderbedarf}, 1\rangle\}, \{\langle \text{Mathematik}, 2\rangle\}, \{\langle \text{Musik}, 2\rangle\}, \{\langle \text{Interkulturell}, 1\rangle\}\}$).

A context, which was generated from an email message using the algorithm in [35] (to be described in Section 4.1) is $\{\{\langle \text{Musik}, 8\rangle\}, \{\langle \text{Open Air}, 1\rangle\}\}$. Intuitively, this email may be related to both concepts, possibly with a stronger connection to Perspective du

Theatre (due to the higher weight). In this work we demonstrate how such a context can be mapped to ontology concepts.

3.2 Modeling Context-Ontology Relationships

The relationships between ontologies and contexts can be modeled using topologies as follows. A *topological structure (topology)* in a set X is a collective family $\vartheta = (G_i / i \in I)$ of subsets of X satisfying

1. J finite; $\Rightarrow \bigcup_{i \in J} G_i \in \vartheta$
2. $J \subset I \Rightarrow \bigcap_{i \in J} G_i \in \vartheta$
3. $\emptyset \in \vartheta, X \in \vartheta$

The pair (X, ϑ) is called a *topological space* and the sets in ϑ are called *closed sets*.

We now define a context to be a closed set in a topology, representing a family ϑ of all possible contexts in some set X with the subset relation $\subseteq$. X is a set of sets of pairs $\langle c, w \rangle$, where c is a word (or words) in a dictionary and w is a weight. Note that ϑ is infinite since descriptors are not limited in their length and weights are taken from some infinite number set (such as the real numbers $\Re$).

The topology is defined by the following subset relation on the context: $\forall \mathcal{C}_a \; \exists \mathcal{C}_b$ such that $\mathcal{C}_a = \left\{ \{ \langle c_{ij}, w_{ij} \rangle \}_i \right\}_j \subseteq \mathcal{C}_b = \left\{ \{ \langle c_{kp}, w_{kp} \rangle \}_k \right\}_p$. Stating that for each context there exists another context that includes the existing context. Identity between contexts is defined as follows: $\mathcal{C}_a = \mathcal{C}_b$ if $c_{kp} = c_{ij}, w_{kp} = w_{ij}, \forall k, p$. Contexts are identical if all descriptors and their matching weights are identical.

The empty set and X are also contexts. Contexts as sets of descriptor sets are closed under intersection and union.

We previously defined contexts as closed sets. Next we define the notion of order of contexts using a *directed set*. A *directed set* is a set S together with a relation $\geq$, which is both transitive and reflexive, such that for any two elements $a, b \in S$, there exists another element $c \in S$ with $c \geq a$ and $c \geq b$. In this case, the relation $\geq$ is said to "direct" the set.

We define a specific directed set using contexts. A context directed set is formally defined by:

$$\mathcal{C}_0 = \{\emptyset\}$$
$$\mathcal{C}_n = \{DS_i, DS_i \cup DS_n | \forall DS_i \in \mathcal{C}_{n-1}\}$$

The definition is illustrated in Figure 2. The different descriptor sets can be viewed as a collection in a bag. We randomly select one descriptor set DS_1. Let Context $\mathcal{C}_1$ define all the descriptor sets that can be created out of one given context - this is only one descriptor set. Let Context $\mathcal{C}_2$ be the sets of descriptors that can be created from two given descriptor sets. Context $\mathcal{C}_2$ contains three descriptor sets: DS_1 from the previous context, DS_2 which is another descriptor set we select, and the union of both descriptor sets, therefore, $\mathcal{C}_1 \leq \mathcal{C}_2$. We can continue and build this directed set by adding another descriptor set to $\mathcal{C}_2$ forming a new Context $\mathcal{C}_3$, where $\mathcal{C}_1 \leq \mathcal{C}_3$ and $\mathcal{C}_2 \leq \mathcal{C}_3$. This process of creating the directed set can continue indefinitely.

This directed set forms a sequence where: $\mathcal{C}_1 \leq \mathcal{C}_2 \leq \mathcal{C}_3 \leq ... \leq \mathcal{C}_n \leq ...$

Whenever a directed set contains contexts that describe a single topic in the real world, such as school or festival, we would like to ensure that this set of contexts con-

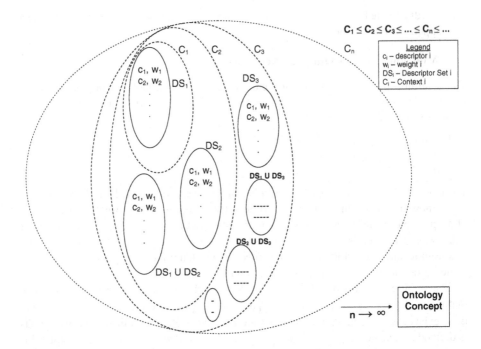

Fig. 2. Contexts Sets Converging to an Ontology Concept

verges to one ontology concept v, representing this topic, *i.e.*, $C_n \to_{n \to \infty} v$. In topology theory, such a convergence is termed an *accumulation point*, a point which is the limit of a sequence, also called a *limit point*. Figure 1 (bottom) and Figure 2 illustrate ontology concepts as points of accumulation. The concept can be viewed as delineating a growing set of descriptors forming the context. The borders outline all of the separate descriptors sets which belong to a specific concept. An overlap between descriptors belonging to different concepts is possible, similarly to dynamic taxonomies [34].

To demonstrate the creation of an ontology concept let a context be a set containing a singleton descriptor set $\{\langle \text{Mathematik}, 2 \rangle\}$. If we add another singleton descriptor set of $\{\langle \text{Musik}, 2 \rangle\}$ we form a new context which contains three descriptor sets: $\{\{\langle \text{Mathematik}, 2 \rangle\}, \{\langle \text{Musik}, 2 \rangle\}, \{\langle \text{Mathematik}, 2 \rangle, \langle \text{Musik}, 2 \rangle\}\}$. As the possible sets of descriptors describing documents increase we advance towards the coverage of the accumulation point. The directed set comprising of these contexts becomes more descriptive. We can converge to an ontology concept, such as *Long Day School*, defined by a set, to which the context set belongs. Basically the accumulation point forms the context which includes all the descriptor sets required to define a concept.

With infinite possible contexts, can we ensure the existence of ontology concepts to which these contexts converge? The answer is yes. Looking at the topological definitions, we defined contexts as a subset of a topological space. All of the subsets forming the contexts were defined to be closed sets. According to [17], the following theorem holds in regards to closed sets:

Theorem 1. *A subset of a topological spaces is closed if and only if it contains the set of its accumulation point.*

According to this theorem, any subset of contexts, being closed sets, will necessarily include an accumulation point. If we look at a finite set of descriptor sets, when each time we add another descriptor set, we will obviously reach an accumulation point, which includes all of the descriptors forming the ontology concepts. However, the above theorem guarantees that even if we have an infinite number of descriptors sets, we will eventually reach an accumulation point, which will also be a context. This context will include all of the descriptor sets defining our concept.

The proposed model employs topological definitions to delineate the relationships between contexts and ontologies. A context is a set of descriptors and their corresponding weights. A directed set is a relation of contexts that includes all of their possible unions of sets of descriptors. An ontology concept is the accumulation point of the directed set of contexts.

3.3   Discussion and Examples

A context can consist of multiple descriptor sets. Each descriptor set can belong to several ontology concepts simultaneously. For example, a descriptor set $\{\langle \text{Musik}, 2 \rangle\}$ can be shared by many ontology concepts that have interest in culture (such as schools, after school institutes, non-profit organizations, *etc.*) although it is not in their main role definition (and hence the low weight assigned to it). Such overlap of contexts in ontology concepts affects, for example, the task of email routing. The appropriate interpretation of a context of an email that is part of several ontology concepts is that the email is relevant to all such concepts. Therefore, it should be delivered to multiple departments in the local government.

In comparison, prior work [16] has focused on semantic similarity, which is essentially an abstraction / mapping between the domains of the two objects associated with the context of comparison. The work presented here uses points of accumulation to define ontology concepts to be the union of contexts rather than the intersection, as suggested in earlier works.

Of particular interest are ontology concepts that are considered "close" under some distance metric. As an example, consider the task of opinion analysis. With opinion analysis, a system should not only judge the relevant area of interest of a given email but also determine the opinion that is expressed in it. Consider an opinion analysis task, in which opinions are partitioned into two categories (*e.g.*, "for" and "against"). We can model such opinions using a common concept ontology (say, that of Perspectives du Theatre), with the addition of words that describe positive and negative opinions. An email whose context fits with the theme of Perspective du Theatre will be further analyzed to be correctly classified as "close" to the "for" or "against" category. Opinion analysis can be extended to any number of opinions in the same manner.

4   Ranking Ontology Concepts

Up until now, the proposed model assumed perfect knowledge in the sense that a context is a true representative of a local view and an ontology concept (and its related context) is a true representative of a global view. In the real world, however, this may not be the case. When a context is extracted automatically from some information source (*e.g.*, an email message), it may not be extracted accurately and descriptors may be erroneously added or eliminated. Also, even for manually crafted ontology concepts, a designer may err and provide an inaccurate context for a given concept. In [12] we also argued that even a well-crafted ontology may vary slightly between organizations within the same domain, such as local governments. Therefore, contexts are bound to vary as well.

In this section we highlight the uncertainty involved in automatic knowledge extraction and propose a method for managing such uncertainty. In particular, we discuss the impact of uncertainty on the three tasks presented above, namely email routing, opinion analysis, and public agenda in the QUALEG project. As a basis for our discussion, we first present the principles of a context recognition algorithm. Details of the algorithm are provided in [35] and the description here is given for the sake of completeness.

4.1   A Context Recognition Algorithm

Several methods were proposed in the literature for extracting context from text. A class of algorithms were proposed in the IR community, based on the principle of counting the number of appearances of each word in a text, assuming that the words with the highest number of appearances serve as the context. Variations on this simple mechanism involve methods for identifying the relevance of words to a domain, using methods such as stop-lists and inverse document frequency. For illustration purposes, we next provide a description of a context recognition algorithm that uses the Internet as a knowledge base to extract multiple contexts of a given situation, based on the streaming in text format of information that represents situations. This algorithm was adapted from [35] and is currently part of the QUALEG solution. We use the work in [35] to demonstrate the feasibility of our model. However, other models, such as [21] and [13], can be adopted for context recognition as well.

Let $\mathcal{D} = \{P_1, P_2, ..., P_m\}$ be a set of textual propositions representing a document, where for all P_i there exists a collection of descriptor sets forming the context $\mathcal{C}_i = \{\langle c_{i1}, w_{i1}\rangle, ..., \langle c_{in}, w_{in}\rangle\}$ so that $ist(\mathcal{C}_i, P_i)$ is satisfied. That is, the textual proposition P_i is true for context $\mathcal{C}_i$. The granularity of the textual propositions varies, based on the case at hand, and may be a single sentence, a single paragraph, a statement made by a single participant (in a chat discussion or a Shakespearian play), *etc.* The context recognition algorithm identifies the outer context $\mathcal{C}$ defined by

$$ist(\mathcal{C}, \bigcap_{i=1}^{m} ist(\mathcal{C}_i, P_i)).$$

The input to the algorithm is a stream, in text format, of information. The context recognition algorithm output is a set of contexts that attempts to describe the current scenario most accurately. The algorithm attempts to reach results similar to those achieved by a human when determining the set of contexts that describe the current scenario.

The context recognition algorithm consists of the following major phases: collecting data, selecting contexts for each text, ranking the contexts, and declaring the current contexts. The phase of data collection includes parsing the text and checking it against a stop-list. To improve this process, text can be checked against a domain-specific dictionary. The result is a list of keywords obtained from the text. The selection of the current context is based on searching the Internet for relevant documents according to these keywords and on clustering the results into possible contexts. The output of the ranking stage is the current context or a set of highest ranking contexts. The set of preliminary contexts that has the top number of references, both in number of Internet pages and in number of appearances in all the texts, is declared to be the current context. The success of the algorithm depends, to a great extent, on the number of documents retrieved from the Internet. With a greater number of relevant documents, less preprocessing (using methods such as Natural Language Processing) is needed in the data collection phase.

4.2 From an Automatically Extracted Context to Ontology Concepts

Given the uncertainty involved in automatically extracting contexts, adhering to a strict approach according to which a context belongs to an ontology concept only if it is an element in its associated point of accumulation may be too restrictive. To illustrate this argument, let C be a context that is an accumulation point and let C' be an automatically extracted context. The following three scenarios are possible:

$C \subset C'$: In this case the context extraction algorithm has identified irrelevant descriptors to be part of the context (false positives). Unless the set of descriptors in C' that are not in C is a context in x as well, C' will not be matched correctly.

$C' \subset C$: In this case the context extraction algorithm has failed to identify some descriptors as relevant (false negatives). Therefore, C' will only be matched correctly if C is a context in the same directed set.

$C \not\subseteq C' \wedge C' \not\subseteq C$: This is the case in which both false positives and false negatives exist in C'.

A good algorithm for context extraction generates contexts in which false negatives and false positives are considered to be the exception, rather than the rule. Therefore, we would like to measure some "distance" between an extracted context and various points of accumulation, assuming a "closer" ontology concept to be better matched. To that end, we define a metric function for measuring the distance between a context and ontology concepts, as follows.

We first define distance between two descriptors c_i and c_j with their associated weights w_i and w_j to be:

$$d(c_i, c_j) = \begin{cases} |w_i - w_j| & i = j \\ \max(w_i, w_j) & i \neq j \end{cases}$$

This distance function assigns greater importance to descriptors with larger weights, assuming that weights reflect the importance of a descriptor within a context. To define the best ranking concept in comparison with a given context we use Hausdorff metric. Let A and B be two contexts and a and b be descriptors in A and B, respectively. Then,

$$d(a, B) = \inf\{d(a, b) | b \in B\}$$
$$d(A, B) = \max\{\sup\{d(a, B) | a \in A\}, \sup\{d(b, A) | b \in B\}\}$$

The first equation provides the value of minimal distance of an element from all elements in a set. The second equation identifies the furthest elements when comparing both sets.

Example 2. Going back to our case study example, the context$\{\{\langle \text{Musik}, 8\rangle\}$, $\{\langle \text{Open Air}, 1\rangle\}\}$ may be relevant to both Perspective du Theatre and Long Day School, since in both, a descriptor Musik is found, albeit with different weights. The distance between $\langle \text{Musik}, 8\rangle$ and $\langle \text{Musik}, 6\rangle$ in Perspective du Theatre is 2 and between $\langle \text{Musik}, 8\rangle$ and $\langle \text{Musik}, 2\rangle$ in Long Day School is 6. Assume that $\{\langle \text{Open Air}, 1\rangle\}$ is a false positive, which does not appear in either Perspective du Theatre or in Long Day School. Therefore, its distance from each of the two points of accumulation is 1 (since $\inf\{d(a, b)|b \in B\} = 1, e.g.,$ when comparing $\{\langle \text{Open Air}, 1\rangle\}$ with $\{\langle \text{Kulturpolitik}, 1\rangle\}$). We can therefore conclude that the distance between the context and Perspective du Theatre is 2, which is smaller than its distance from Long Day School (computed to be 6). Therefore, Perspective du Theatre will be ranked higher than Long Day School.

Although a normalization step can be used to prevent descriptors with large frequencies from influencing the results - in the previous example this will lead to lowering the value of the weight of Musik - there is an advantage in leaving the higher value descriptors so as to give these descriptors more weight in the process, in order to better represent the weights of the contexts. A higher value means that these descriptors carry higher importance.

We next show how the proposed ranking mechanism can be utilized for the various tasks of eGovernment, as presented in Section 3.3.

Email routing: The user provides QUALEG with a distance threshold t_1. Any ontology concept that matches with a context, automatically generated from an email, and its distance is lower than the threshold $(d(A, B) < t_1)$, will be considered relevant, and the email will be routed accordingly.

Opinion analysis: The relevant set of ontology concepts is identified, similarly to email routing. Then for each ontology concept, the relative distance of the different opinions of that concept is evaluated. If the difference in distance is too close to call (given an additional threshold t_2), the system refrains from providing an opinion (and the email is routed accordingly). Otherwise, the email is marked with the opinion with minimal distance.

Public agenda: If all ontology concepts (of the n relevant concepts) satisfy that $d(A, B) \geq t_1$, the email is considered to be part of a new topic on the public agenda and is added to other emails under this concept. Periodically, such emails are clustered and provided to decision makers to determine the addition of new ontology concepts.

5   Experiences and Experiments

In this section we first present the QUALEG project as a test platform for the implementation of the model that maps context to ontology in Section 5.1. We also share our experiences with QUALEG pilots. Next, in Section 5.2 we empirically evaluate various aspects of the proposed model using two real-world data traces, taken from Reuters and news RSS.

5.1 QUALEG Experiences

The section begins with a description of the QUALEG architecture, followed by experiences with e-mail routing and opinion analysis.

QUALEG Architecture. The aim of the QUALEG project is to support the electronic interactions between civil servants and citizens. The QUALEG system aims at allowing local governments to maintain a direct connection with citizens through the ongoing adjustment of their policies according to the assessment of citizen needs. This implies that local governments should be able to measure the performance of the services they offer, assess citizen satisfaction, and re-formulate policy orientations on such elements with the participation of citizens.

These tasks are achieved through the implementation of an agent oriented QUALEG architecture, which consists of the following main seven components: (1) Agora - A Web interface to the system through which a citizen interacts via emails, chats and forums with the civil servant. (2) Datamart - The component that stores QUALEG data. (3) QUALEG ontology - A multilingual ontology describing the public and e-Government issues. (4) Knowledge Extractor - The previously described context extraction algorithm activated by the software agents. (5) QUALEG Workflow - The component that handles the flow of processes relevant to the public servants and administrations. (6) A set of agents, which in the backstage handle the main control of the QUALEG system, acting asynchronously and handling the data to be communicated among various modules. (7) A set of Web services offered for seamless data handling to and from the Datamart.

The Knowledge Extraction Agent (KE Agent) has the responsibility to trigger the Knowledge Extraction Module so that the context of the stored information is regularly analyzed. The Knowledge Extraction architecture is illustrated in Figure 3. There are four types of documents that should be analyzed: documents uploaded to AGORA, text in forums, chats, and incoming e-mail messages. In particular, the KE Agent performs periodical searches in the platform's databases for new information to be analyzed. Every transaction with the database is carried out by means of Web services. If new documents are found, the agent triggers the previously described knowledge extraction algorithm on them. Hence, the KE Agent parses all the required information - such as document id, document name, document url - to the KE module. The KE module performs the mapping with reference to an ontology, which defines the set of concepts and their relationships. After the KE process is completed, the context of the document is stored in a database.

Similarly to the KE Agent, the Opinion Analysis Agent (OA Agent) regularly searches in QUALEG's databases to find which documents have to be analyzed by the Opinion Analysis Module (OA Module). Once again, all the agent's database transactions are carried out through Web service calls. If documents requiring analysis are found, the agent triggers the opinion analysis algorithm on them in the same way as the KE agent. Opinion Analysis output is an ontology concept related to an opinion and a list of words representing the context extracted.

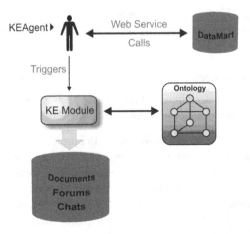

Fig. 3. Knowledge Extraction Architecture

The platform for analyzing the information was written in Java running on a standard PC. The processing time was divided into several intervals over a few days to avoid excessive use of the Internet resources employed by the algorithm: Looksmart, Wisenut, Open Directory, Ask, Sponsored Listings, MSN Search, and Vivísimo.

QUALEG Email Routing. Our first experience involved the Perspectives du Theatre Festival held during May every year in Saarbrücken, located at the French border of Germany. The festival includes contemporary French theatre, films, street events, music, *etc*. Our challenge was to analyze the festival material and provide a useful set of classifications so that the materials could be rapidly understood and routed to the appropriate civil servants.

The data we received included daily communications (in German) about this event, for a total of 104 emails, primarily emails from citizens to the city hall and press releases and announcements from the city outward. The festival is an annual event and we were given data from 2004 and 2005.

The goal of the topic classification experiment was to identify the topic of an email according to a predefined set of ontology concepts as supplied by Saarbrücken for organizing cultural events. The concepts were Organisation, Veranstalter, Finanzen, Besucher, Informationen, Rahmenprogramm, Spielplan, and Other. Each ontology concept was accompanied by a (manually designed) context that describes it.

To evaluate the proposed model we used a single ontology and two different methods to define and extract contexts. One method was that described in Section 4.1. This method used the technique of mapping contexts to ontology concepts (C2O), as detailed in Section 4.2. The other method was based on conventional Natural Language Processing (NLP) techniques, enhanced by a language domain expert to build a set of rules for identifying relevant words and grammar relevant to the German language. The NLP technique was evaluated with the support of researchers from the University of Southern California's Information Sciences Institute (ISI).

The two techniques are very different. The former is language independent, making it more suitable for multilingual environments at the possible cost of lacking language specific analysis tools used by the latter. The C2O technique uses the Internet as a knowledge base for extracting contexts. These contexts were searched against a list of descriptors that describe concepts in the ontology. The technique was based on a per sentence analysis. For each sentence a classifier was used, automatically trained on keywords and morphological variants (based on the initial list of topics from Saarbrücken). Each sentence in the input was searched against the list of keywords and morphological variants. The NLP technique started from an identical contexts list as the C2O and used the morphological variants of each context.

For both methods the input was parsed at the granularity of sentences. The C2O preprocessing included only partitioning of long sentences according to the search engine requirements. The NLP preprocessing included a Tokenizer, a tool for breaking up compound nouns, and a German Demorpher (Morphy engine), downloaded from the University of Stuttgart (http://www.lezius.de/wolfgang/morphy/). The Demorpher removes case markings, tense markings, *etc.*

Two different experiments were performed. The first experiment was to analyze our model based on the German data. The C2O method achieved a Precision of 85.37%, a Recall of 84.34%, and a total F-Score of 84.85%. This is based on the comparison of the results of the Context Recognition component to that of a human expert. The German input data was classified by two German Language experts and by Saarbrücken local government civil servant employees.

The second experiment analyzed the performance of C2O compared to the NLP technique. In this experiment a subset of 72 emails representing data from a single year was used for comparison. The results showed that C2O achieved an F-Score of 81% while the NLP technique achieved an F-Score of 78%. The results therefore show that the proposed topology-based model of contexts and ontology achieved comparable performance to the NLP technique, with the added value of being language independent.

Opinion Analysis. Opinions can be viewed as perspectives expressed in the input information. We modeled opinions to be included in the ontology as concepts, associated with context that provide the local interpretation of each opinion.

There is a difference between the email routing task based on the knowledge extraction and opinion analysis. The knowledge extraction avoids the language specific implementation and bases its analysis techniques on the use of a large corpus of relevant documents taken from the Internet, while the opinion analysis uses techniques from IR and NLP to improve content understanding. As in the knowledge extraction, the results of the opinion analysis are mapped to concepts in the ontology, in this case, opinion concepts. Opinions can be divided into an array of possibilities from extreme positive to very negative. The opinions selected for the experiment were defined in only three categories of concepts - positive, negative, and neutral.

The experiment included 72 emails in German. A set of approximately 6000 opinion verbs and 6000 opinion adjectives taken from ISI [19] were analyzed in English and translated using an online dictionary translation to German. These opinion words are associated with the three opinion concepts. Two possibilities were examined: first, to translate the emails into English and then analyze the texts for opinion, and second, to translate opinion words. The latter alternative was found to achieve better results, since considerably fewer words are translated, reducing the impact of natural language ambiguity.

The opinion analysis experiments reached a precision of 78.95%, recall of 69.23%, and F-score of 73.77%. The results indicate that it is feasible to use the model to perform opinion analysis, albeit at a lower accuracy than that of routing.

5.2 Experiments

This paper models the relationship between contexts and ontologies as a topology. We experimented with data from Reuters corpus and from news RSS. We start with a description of the two real world data traces and experiment set-up, followed by description of our experiments and an empirical analysis of the results.

The following experiments analyze the model to show how fast the contexts accumulate to a concept, the quality of the context attributed to a high number of descriptors from a single context vs. multiple contexts, and how concept overlap influences the context representation. The following experiments demonstrate model performance with multiple concepts and analyze the model performance in a dynamic setting, where a context can be associated with more than a single concept.

Data Sets and Metrics. In this paper we present a model of context and ontology relationships. When analyzing our model, we compare it to similar methods of text analysis, which belong to the field of text categorization. This field includes analysis methods to identify the category to which a given text belongs. Text categorization usually allows text to belong to only one category. Since this classification is rigid and less relevant to our requirements, the model developed in this paper allows a text to be classified into multiple categories.

The two data traces we used come from Reuters and CNN RSS. In these data traces data are partitioned to topics with no ontological relationships. The experiments focus on the concepts/contexts relationships, for which these data sets serve adequately. Research and experiments on ontological relationships using contexts are reported in [36].

The Reuters data set was taken from a publicly available trace (http://about.reuters.c om/researchandstandards/corpus/). We chose 10 news topic categories (referred to hereafter as concepts), for a total of 3,125 data, where a datum is a Reuters news article. The RSS trace was collected during August 2005 from the CNN Web site. Here, we also chose 10 news topic categories including 1,130 data, where a datum is an RSS news header or a news descriptor. The main difference between the Reuters trace and the RSS trace is the datum size. Table 1 describes the two data sets. Concept overlap is explained shortly.

We generated a context for each concept using the C2O algorithm. This context is referred to as context* and the data that was used for this context generation is referred to hereafter as the context* data. The number of data items that were used for generating context* data varies, ranging from one datum to 170 data items for Reuters and from one datum to 61 for RSS. We also varied the number of context descriptors that were generated from each datum in the context* data, ranging from 1 to 70 descriptors.

Table 1. Reuters and RSS Data Set Statistics

Data Set	Reuters	RSS
Size	3,125	1,130
Categories	10	10
Datum per Category	126 - 510	113
Minimum Concept Overlap	21.6%	12.1%
Maximum Concept Overlap	75.5%	86.7%

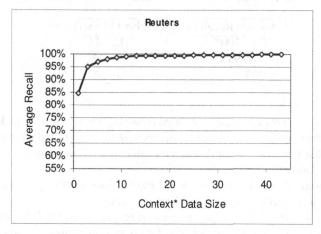

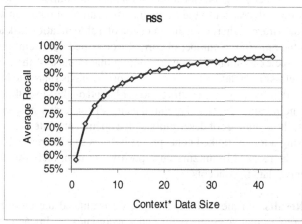

Fig. 4. Number of Contexts for Concept

A varying number of concepts was used, ranging from 1 to 10 concepts depending on the experiment. We use the C2O algorithm, adapted from [35], as an example of a context generator. C2O is known to have generated reasonable contexts in the past (see experiments in [35]).

Table 2. Average Recall Level vs. Number of Descriptors - Reuters

Average Recall Level	Number of Descriptors
100%	5 - 43
[95% - 100%)	1 - 11
[90% - 95%)	1 - 5
< 90%	1 - 3

Table 3. Average Recall Level vs. Number of Descriptors - RSS

Average Recall Level	Number of Descriptors
[95% - 100%)	15 - 43
[90% - 95%)	9 - 43
< 90%	1 - 35

Given two concepts and their associated contexts, *concept overlap* is defined to be the ratio of the number of common descriptors in both contexts and the minimum context size. Table 1 presents statistics about the minimum and maximum concept overlap found in the data sets.

As a measure of evaluation we use recall and precision metrics. Given a context* C, the recall of a context C' is defined as the ratio of the number of common descriptors and the size of context* C. A high recall measure means that the C2O algorithm was able to identify correctly a good portion of a context, minimizing false negative. We measure precision with respect to the original classification of data items to categories as given in the data traces. Therefore, the precision of a classification task using contexts is measured as the ratio of the number of correctly classified data items and the number of data items in the experiments. It is worth noting that in most of the experiments the C2O algorithm classifies a datum to a concept whose contexts share the highest number of descriptors with its context, thus setting a lower bound on the algorithm performance. It is also worth noting that QUALEG required using all concepts whose context* shares more than a threshold number of descriptors with a document context. A middle ground may require using a top-K ranked concepts. This leads to a decrease in the precision, yet it increases the recall. Minimizing false positive, in turn, increases the chances of correctly matching data to concepts.

Experiment Results. In the first experiment, we evaluated the algorithm ability to generate good representative contexts for concepts (context*). In each experiment we selected a single concept and generated a context using context* data. For each of the remaining data in this category a context was generated and compared with the context*. For each context* data size we repeated the experiment 10 times, each time choosing randomly the context* data. In this setting the average recall and precision over all experiments with the same context* data size are the same.

A graphic illustration of our results is given in Figure 4, which displays the average recall, computed over 10 different ontology concepts in Reuters and news RSS. The

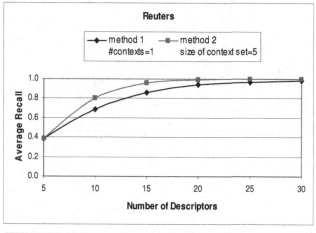

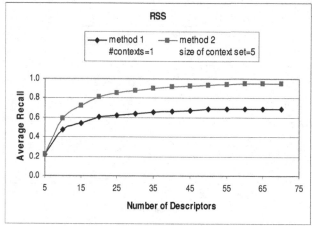

Fig. 5. Comparison of Context Collection Methods Recall

horizontal axis displays the context* data size. In this experiment each context was limited to 10 descriptors. The vertical axis displays the average recall.

The experiment results indicate that as the number of contexts defining each ontology concept increases, the concept definition improves. While this is to be expected, we also observe that the average recall quickly approaches 100%, although at a different rate for the two data sets. We attribute this different behavior to the sensitivity of the C2O algorithm to different datum length in the two data sets. While Reuters datum is a complete news article, RSS datum contains a header or a short description. Our experience shows that the C2O algorithm we use generates better contexts when given longer texts.

A per concept analysis shows an average recall ranging from 98.86% to 100% in the Reuters data set and from 91.67% to 99.62% in the news RSS data set, when context* is defined using up to 43 descriptors. Table 2 and Table 3 present a per-concept analysis

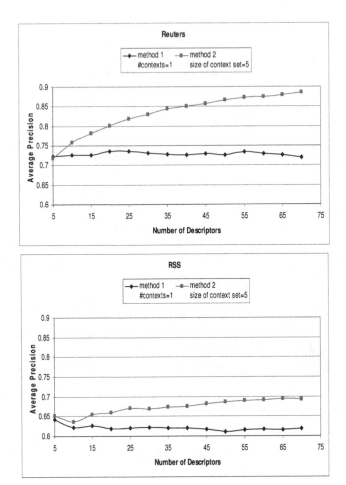

Fig. 6. Comparison of Context Collection Methods Average Precision for Varying Context Sizes

showing the range of the number of descriptors required to achieve a certain average recall level. It is worth noting that for the Reuters data set some concepts require a training data set of size 5 to achieve 100% recall. There was only one concept that did not reach 100% using a training data set of 43 data items.

We next compare two different methods for collecting context descriptors. Method 1 is based on collecting an increasing number of descriptors from a single textual datum. As we increase the number of descriptors, we add to the single context more descriptors with lower relevance value, possibly increasing uncertainty. Method 2 is based on using different descriptors sets, each one based on a different textual datum. In this set of experiments, we chose a single concept for which a context was generated based on a context* and then compared against the remaining data items associated with this category. For Method 1 to achieve a context of size M, the M top descriptors are chosen.

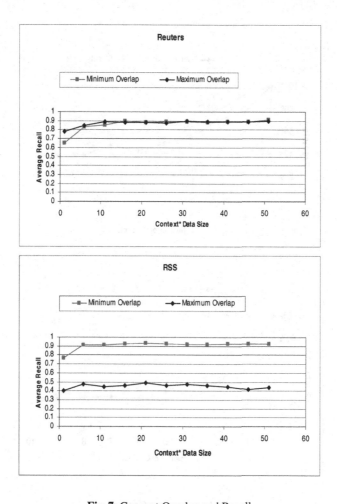

Fig. 7. Concept Overlap and Recall

For Method 2 the context* was increased, each datum adding up to 5 descriptors to the context*, until the desired number of descriptors was reached.

The results are displayed in Figure 5. As the number of descriptors defining a single context grows, the average recall improves for both methods, yet Method 2 converges faster than Method 1. For the Reuters data, both methods approach 100% recall, while for the RSS data Method 1 performs significantly worse than Method 2. We also observe that recall reaches 100% for 30 descriptors in the Reuters data set while not reaching 100% even for 70 descriptors for the news RSS data set. This is again attributed to the sensitivity of the C2O algorithm to the length of the processed text.

Comparing further the two context generation methods, we took concept pairs and generated contexts* for each concept. We then classified each of the remaining data items to one of the two concepts.

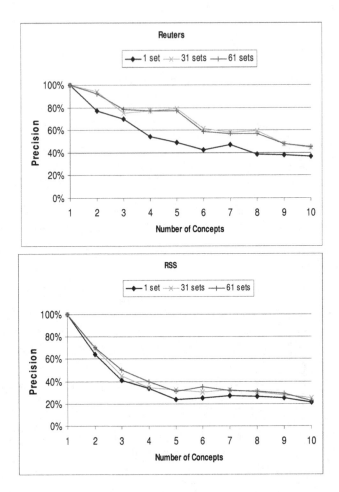

Fig. 8. Number of Concepts

Figure 6 displays the average precision rate for all pairwise combinations of concepts. The horizontal axis displays the number of descriptors in the context* data set and the vertical axis displays the average precision. For both data sets average precision generally increases for Method 2 while remaining unchanged or even decreasing for Method 1. We can conclude that Method 2 performs better and therefore we shall use this method in the remaining experiments.

To evaluate the impact of concept overlap on precision we compared two concept pairs, namely the pair with minimum concept overlap (21.6% for Reuters and 12.1% for RSS) and the pair with maximum concept overlap (75.5% for Reuters and 86.7% for RSS). For each concept in a pair we randomly chose a context* data set and generated a context* for this concept. Then, we classified the remaining data similarly to what was described earlier. The experiments were repeated for various context* data set sizes.

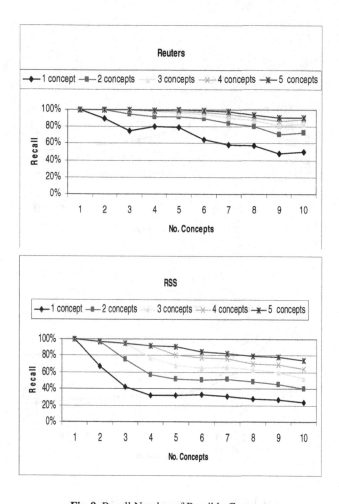

Fig. 9. Recall Number of Possible Concepts

The results of these experiments are illustrated in Figure 7. We observe different phenomena for each of the data sets. For the Reuters data the average recall converges for a training set of size 30, while for the RSS data the concept pair with a high overlap shows a significantly lower average recall for all tested training sizes. At this time we are unable to explain these differences. For the news RSS data set there is a wider difference between the minimum overlap pair and maximum overlap pair, which may partially explain this phenomenon.

Next, we analyze the impact of the number of concepts on the classification procedure. We repeated the experiment discussed earlier for an increasing number of concepts, varying the size of the context* data set as well. For this set of experiments we have enforced a rigid classification scheme, in which each document is forced to be classified to a single concept. The experiment results are summarized in Figure 8. The horizontal axis displays the number of concepts and the vertical axis presents the

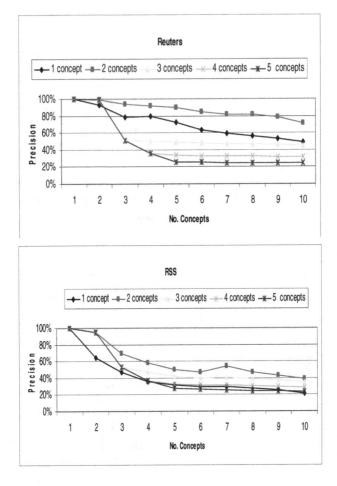

Fig. 10. Precision Number of Possible Concepts

classification precision. Each curve represents a different context* data set size. As the number of concepts increases, the precision declines. It can also be seen that precision improves as we increase the training set size. The marginal effect of increasing the training set size becomes, however, less significant as we increase the training set size. We note again that these precision curves serve as a lower bound on the algorithm efficiency. By using top-K ranked concepts, rather than a single concept, precision decreases toward a lower bound.

To analyze a document belonging to multiple concepts, a random set of concepts and documents was selected as training set. Each descriptor set included ten descriptors. From the ten possible concepts the number of concepts each document can belong to was increased from one to five concepts. The number of concepts used is the X axis. The number of concepts that can be selected is each line (1 to 5) - number of possible concepts. The recall results are presented in Figure 9. For a given K of classified concepts, recall decreases as the number of available concepts increases, as expected. However, an increase from 50% to 91.1% in recall is observed as we increase from one to up to five, out a total of ten, the number of top ranking concepts selected per document. Similarly, for the RSS data set, recall increased from 24.2% to 73.8%.

The precision results for both Reuters and RSS are presented in Figure 10. Both Reuters and RSS results show that the best precision results occur when the number of concepts to which each document can belong is two.

Finally, as a point of reference, we chose a pure vector-space technique [14], [21] of the LSI approach. The two approaches share some similarity in the goal of classifying text into predefined categories. There are also differences. First, the method we used is not based on predefined word-based vectors but rather on a bag of words. This bag of words is determined using words that are not necessarily extracted from the text itself but are associated with a possible context. The size of the word comparison set is not predetermined as in the vector-space method. Another advantage we see to C2O is the use of the Internet as a knowledge base. The Internet allows a set of descriptors to be constantly and automatically updated.

When analyzing our results and the results of the LSI approach, the emphasis on the recall should be taken into consideration. The approach presented here achieved good results in the recall. Although the statistics analysis is not identical in both approaches, the F-score achieved in [21] was 71.1% to 85.3%. The approach presented here with identical weights to the recall and precision, similar to the LSI approach, was from 58% to 100%. The results seem to be especially high when the top five concept categories for recall and top two concepts for precision are used.

6   Discussion and Conclusion

The paper presents a topological framework for combining contexts and ontologies in a model that maps contexts to ontology. Contexts, individual views of a domain of interest, are matched to concepts of an ontology, often considered to be the "golden standard," for various purposes such as email routing and opinion analysis. The model provides a conceptual structure, based on topological definitions, which delineates how and when contexts can be mapped to ontologies. The uncertainty, inherent in automatic context extraction, is managed through the definition of distance among contexts and a ranking of ontology concepts with respect to a given context.

The proposed model has been implemented as part of QUALEG, an eGovernment project. In this project, information that flows into a local government system is automatically examined, and based on its context, its positioning within the ontology is determined. Since the project involves different countries and different languages, a multilingual ontology system is used. According to the model, different descriptor sets, representing the same concept, can be mapped to the multilingual ontology. To support opinion analysis, each ontology concept was divided into positive and negative citizen opinions about the topics discussed in the email messages. This classification allows the local government to make decisions according to the citizen opinions, which are derived from the information received by email and analyzed only by the algorithm and not by a civil servant.

During our experiments with the model, we identified several factors that may contribute to uncertainty. The main reason for errors in ontology concept identification pertains to the preprocessing of the input, which was limited to a minimal and naïve dissection of text. Most of the emails consisted of a few sentences only, resulting in a one-shot attempt to determine the correct context. These results could be improved by using different preprocessing methods and utilizing "soft" NLP tools. The ontology definition, which is currently restricted to a small number of words, also contributed to a lower recall rate.

To evaluate empirically the model properties in a controlled environment, we used two real-world data traces, Reuters news reports and RSS news headlines. In these experiments we measured the effectiveness of generating contexts automatically for different concepts. We tested various methods for context extraction and examined the impact of concept overlap and number of concepts on classification quality. We can conclude that the proposed model associating a context with each ontology concept is feasible and the amount of data needed for automatically generating contexts for concepts is relatively small. Context generation can be improved, and we leave such improvements for future research.

In QUALEG the availability of a predefined ontology is assumed. Therefore, ontology concepts and their relationships are provided beforehand, and newly extracted contexts are mapped to existing concepts. A possible direction for further research would be to utilize the partial overlapping among contexts to identify ontological relationships, such as generalization-specialization relationships. An initial step in this direction is presented in [37].

Acknowledgments

The work of Segev and Gal was partially supported by two European Commission 6th Framework IST projects, QUALEG and TerreGov, and the Fund for the Promotion of Research at the Technion. We thank Amir Teller for his assistance in integrating the Knowledge Extraction component with QUALEG infrastructure and Yulia Turchin for her assistance in experimenting with Reuters and RSS data sets.

References

1. Assadi, H.: Construction of a regional ontology from text and its use within a documentary system. In: Proceedings of the International Conference on Formal Ontology and Information Systems (FOIS-98) (1998)
2. Borgida, A., Brachman, R.J.: Loading data into description reasoners. In: Proceedings of the 1993 ACM SIGMOD international conference on Management of data, pp. 217–226. ACM Press, New York (1993)
3. Bunge, M.: Treatise on Basic Philosophy: vol. 3: Ontology I: The Furniture of the World. D. Reidel Publishing Co., Inc., New York (1977)
4. Bunge, M.: Treatise on Basic Philosophy: vol. 4: Ontology II: A World of Systems. D. Reidel Publishing Co., Inc., New York (1979)
5. Choset, H., Nagatani, K.: Topological simultaneous localization and mapping (slam): Toward exact localization without explicit localization. IEEE Trans. on Robotics and Automation 17(2), 125–137 (2001)

6. Chung, C.Y., Lieu, R., Liu, J., Luk, A., Mao, J., Raghavan, P.: Thematic mapping from unstructured documents to taxonomies. In: Proceedings of the 11th International Conference on Information and Knowledge Management (CIKM) (2002)

7. Davulcu, H., Vadrevu, S., Nagarajan, S.: Ontominer: Bootstrapping and populating ontologies from domain specific websites. In: Proceedings of the First International Workshop on Semantic Web and Databases (2003)

8. Doan, A., Madhavan, J., Domingos, P., Halevy, A.: Learning to map between ontologies on the semantic web. In: Proceedings of the eleventh international conference on World Wide Web, Honolulu, Hawaii, USA, pp. 662–673. ACM Press, New York (2002)

9. Donini, F.M., Lenzerini, M., Nardi, D., Schaerf, A.: Reasoning in description logic. In: Brewka, G. (ed.) Principles on Knowledge Representation, Studies in Logic, Languages and Information, pp. 193–238. CSLI Publications (1996)

10. Gal, A., Anaby-Tavor, A., Trombetta, A., Montesi, D.: A framework for modeling and evaluating automatic semantic reconciliation. VLDB Journal 14(1), 50–67 (2005)

11. Gal, A., Modica, G., Jamil, H.M., Eyal, A.: Automatic ontology matching using application semantics. AI Magazine, 26(1) (2005)

12. Gal, A., Segev, A.: Putting things in context: Dynamic eGovernment re-engineering using ontologies and context. In: Proceedings of the 2006 WWW Workshop on E-Government: Barriers and Opportunities (2006)

13. Hotho, A., Staab, S., Maedche, A.: Ontology-based text clustering. In: Proceedings of the IJCAI-2001 Workshop Text Learning: Beyond Supervision (2001)

14. Kashyap, V., Dalal, S., Behrens, C.: Professional services automation: A knowledge management approach using LSI and domain specific ontologies. In: Proceedings of the 14th International FLAIRS Conference (Florida AI Research Symposium), Special track on AI and Knowledge Management (2001)

15. Kashyap, V., Ramakrishnan, C., Thomas, C., Sheth, A.: Taxaminer: An experimentation framework for automated taxonomy bootstrapping. International Journal of Web and Grid Services, Special Issue on Semantic Web and Mining Reasoning (September 2005)

16. Kashyap, V., Sheth, A.: Semantic and schematic similarities between database objects: a context-based approach. VLDB Journal 5, 276–304 (1996)

17. Kelley, J.: General Topology. American Book Company (1969)

18. Kifer, M., Lausen, G., Wu, J.: Logical foundation of object-oriented and frame-based languages. Journal of the ACM 42 (1995)

19. Kim, S.M., Ravichandran, D., Hovy, E.: ISI novelty track system for trec 2004. In: Proceedings of the Thirteenth Text REtrieval Conference (TREC 2004) (2004)

20. Koenig, S., Simmons, R.: Passive distance learning for robot navigation. In: Proceedings of the Thirteenth International Conference on Machine Learning (ICML), pp. 266–274 (1996)

21. Liu, T., Chen, Z., Zhang, B., Ma, W.-Y., Wu, G.: Improving text classification using local latent semantic indexing. In: Perner, P. (ed.) ICDM 2004. LNCS (LNAI), vol. 3275, pp. 162–169. Springer, Heidelberg (2004)

22. Madhavan, J., Bernstein, P.A., Domingos, P., Halevy, A.Y.: Representing and reasoning about mappings between domain models. In: Proceedings of the Eighteenth National Conference on Artificial Intelligence and Fourteenth Conference on Innovative Applications of Artificial Intelligence (AAAI/IAAI), pp. 80–86 (2002)

23. Madhavan, J., Bernstein, P.A., Rahm, E.: Generic schema matching with Cupid. In: Proceedings of the International conference on very Large Data Bases (VLDB), pp. 49–58, Rome, Italy (September 2001)

24. Maedche, A., Staab, S.: Ontology learning for the semantic web. IEEE Intelligent Systems 16 (2001)

25. McCarthy, J.: Notes on formalizing context. In: Proceedings of the Thirteenth International Joint Conference on Artificial Intelligence (1993)

26. McGuinness, D.L., Fikes, R., Rice, J., Wilder, S.: An environment for merging and testing large ontologies. In: Proceedings of the Seventh International Conference on Principles of Knowledge Representation and Reasoning (KR2000) (2000)
27. Melnik, S. (ed.): Generic Model Management: Concepts and Algorithms. Springer, Heidelberg (2004)
28. Mena, E., Kashyap, V., Illarramendi, A., Sheth, A.P.: Imprecise answers in distributed environments: Estimation of information loss for multi-ontology based query processing. International Journal of Cooperative Information Systems 9(4), 403–425 (2000)
29. Mooers, C.: Encyclopedia of Library and Information Science, vol. 7, chapter Descriptors, pp. 31–45. Marcel Dekker (1972)
30. Motro, A., Rakov, I.: Estimating the quality of databases. Lecture Notes in Computer Science (1998)
31. Noy, F.N., Musen, M.A.: PROMPT: Algorithm and tool for automated ontology merging and alignment. In: Proceedings of the Seventeenth National Conference on Artificial Intelligence (AAAI-2000), pp. 450–455, Austin, TX (2000)
32. Papatheodorou, C., Vassiliou, A., Simon, B.: Discovery of ontologies for learning resources using word-based clustering. In: Proceedings of the World Conference on Educational Multimedia, Hypermedia and Telecommunications (ED-MEDIA 2002), pp. 1523–1528 (2002)
33. Remolina, E., Kuipers, B.: Towards a general theory of topological maps. Artificial Intelligence 152, 47–104 (2004)
34. Sacco, G.: Dynamic taxonomies: A model for large information bases. IEEE Trans. Knowl. Data Eng. 12(2), 468–479 (2000)
35. Segev, A.: Identifying the multiple contexts of a situation. In: Proceedings of IJCAI-Workshop Modeling and Retrieval of Context (MRC2005) (2005)
36. Segev, A., Gal, A.: Putting things in context: A topological approach to mapping contexts and ontologies. In: Proceedings of AAAI-Workshop Workshop on Contexts and Ontologies: Theory, Practice and Applications (2005)
37. Segev, A., Gal, A.: Ontology verification using contexts. In: Proceedings of ECAI-Workshop on Contexts and Ontologies: Theory, Practice and Applications (2006)
38. Shatkay, H., Kaelbling, L.: Learning topological maps with weak local odometry information. In: Proc. IJCAI-97 (1997)
39. Siegel, M., Madnick, S.E.: A metadata approach to resolving semantic conflicts. In: Proceedings of the 17th International Conference on Very Large Data Bases, pp. 133–145 (1991)
40. Simhon, S., Dudek, G.: A global topological map formed by local metric maps. In IEEE/RSJ International Conference on Intelligent Robotic Systems 3, 1708–1714 (1998)
41. Spyns, P., Meersman, R., Jarrar, M.: Data modelling versus ontology engineering. ACM SIGMOD Record 31(4) (2002)
42. Terziyan, V., Puuronen, S.: Reasoning with multilevel contexts in semantic metanetwork. In: Nossun, R., Bonzon, P., Cavalcanti, M. (eds.) Formal Aspects in Context, pp. 107–126. Kluwer Academic Publishers, Dordrecht (2000)
43. van Rijsbergen, C.J.: Information Retrieval, 2nd edn. Butterworths, London (1979)
44. Vickery, B.C.: Faceted classification schemes. Graduate School of Library Service, Rutgers, the State University, New Brunswick, NJ (1966)

Creating Ontologies for Content Representation—The **OntoSeed** Suite

Elena Paslaru Bontas Simperl[1] and David Schlangen[2]

[1] Freie Universität Berlin
Institut für Informatik
AG Netzbasierte Informationssysteme
Takustr. 9, 14195 Berlin, Germany
`simperl@inf.fu-berlin.de`
[2] Universität Potsdam
Institut für Linguistik
Angewandte Computerlinguistik
P.O. Box 601553, 14415 Potsdam, Germany
`das@ling.uni-potsdam.de`

Abstract. Due to the inherent difficulties associated with manual ontology building, knowledge acquisition approaches such as ontology reuse or ontology learning from texts are often seen as instruments that can make this tedious process easier. In this paper we present a NLP-based method to aid ontology design in a specific application scenario, namely that in which the resulting ontology is used to support the semantic annotation of text documents. The proposed method uses the World Wide Web in its analysis of the domain-specific documents, thereby greatly reducing the need for linguistic expertise and resources, and suggests ways to specify domain ontologies in a "linguistics-friendly" format in order to improve further ontology-based natural language processing tasks such as semantic annotation. We present a thorough evaluation of the method, using corpora from three diverse real-world settings (medical information, tourism, and recipes). Additionally, for the first scenario we compare the costs and the benefits of the NLP-based ontology engineering approach against a similar, reuse-oriented experiment.

1   Introduction[1]

Ontologies are widely recognized as a key technology to realize the vision of the Semantic Web and Semantic Web applications. In this context, ontology engineering is rapidly becoming a mature discipline which has produced various tools and

---

[1] The present paper is a revised and extended version of [29]. In particular, we pointed out how our approach can complement existing methodologies and methods in the areas of ontology engineering and knowledge acquisition, and addressed its operationalization as a dedicated tool or in relation with general-purpose ontology management environments. Further on, a new section discussing the approach has been added (3.4), references have been updated, and many of the figures have been revised.

S. Spaccapietra et al. (Eds.): Journal on Data Semantics IX, LNCS 4601, pp. 141–166, 2007.

methodologies for building and managing ontologies. However, even with a clearly defined engineering methodology, building a large ontology remains a challenging, time-consuming and error-prone task, since it forces ontology builders to conceptualize their expert knowledge *explicitly* and to *re-organize* it in typical ontological categories such as concepts, properties and axioms. For this reason, knowledge acquisition techniques such as ontology reuse, ontology learning from texts or ontology lifting from semi-structured resources like databases are often seen as ways to make this tedious process more efficient: though all methods cannot currently be used to *automatically* generate a domain ontology satisfying a specific set of requirements, they can be used to *guide* or *accelerate* the modeling process.

Natural language processing techniques have proven to be particularly useful for these purposes [4,9,11,17,25,32]. However, existing systems are still knowledge or resource intensive: they may not require much prior knowledge about the *domain* that is to be modeled, but they require in-depth *linguistic expertise*—as for configuring and using the underlying techniques and tools—or *linguistic resources* such as thesauri and lexica. In this paper we present a method to aid ontology building—within a certain setting, namely that of semantic annotation of texts— by using NLP techniques to analyze texts from the target domain.[2] These techniques are comparably "knowledge-lean": they make use of the WWW as a text collection against which the domain texts are compared during analysis, which makes them easy to employ even if no linguistic expertise and resources are available, and reduces the engineering costs since it avoids building an application-specific lexicon. The method carefully describes how the results of the natural language processing techniques can be used in the context of an ontology engineering process, thus decreasing the need for additional expert support. Finally, the approach not only aids the ontology engineers in taking specific modelling decisions, but it also suggests ways to specify the ontology in such a way that it fits ideally into further NLP-based processing steps, e.g. the extraction of information from domain-specific texts. Describing these specification issues and giving some example use cases of ontologies thus created is the second aim of this paper.

The remainder of this paper is organized as follows: we motivate our approach and discuss previous work in Section 2. Section 3 gives details about our approach to using NLP to aid ontology design, which is evaluated from a technical and application perspective in Section 4. We close with a discussion of the results and an outline of future work in Section 5.

2 Motivation

2.1 Ontology Engineering

Due to the difficulties and costs involved in building an ontology from scratch, ontology engineering methodologies often recommend to rely on available

---

[2] "Semantic annotation" is understood in this paper as the process through which the contents of information items—textual documents, but also multimedia—are linked to concepts and relations whose semantics is formally defined using an ontology.

domain-related structured or unstructured data sources.[3] In conjunction with knowledge acquisition techniques they are considered a valuable input for major ontology development activities such as the requirements analysis and the conceptualization of the domain knowledge, as stated in many ontology engineering methodologies such as [15,19,38,40].

In our own experience in a Semantic Web project in the medical domain (see [30,41] for a longer discussion of this issue, and Section 4.2 below for the project setting), we found that just selecting and extracting relevant sub-ontologies, for example from a comprehensive medical ontology like UMLS,[4] was a very time-consuming process. Besides, this approach still resulted in a rather poor domain coverage and limited application-oriented usability as determined by the semantic annotation task. The ontology generated in this way could not be used optimally in NLP-based processes, while the acceptance by its intended users was extremely low because of substantial difficulties in comprehending and evaluating it (cf. Section 4); this was our motivation to develop the techniques described here.

An alternative to reusing available ontologies or related knowledge sources (e.g. classifications, thesauri) is to employ text documents as an input for the conceptualization process. The most basic way to use texts is to extract *terms* from them, i.e. to determine words that denote domain-specific concepts (e.g. "lymphocyte" in a medical text) as opposed to general concepts (e.g. "telephone" in the same text). While this is often seen as a problem that is more or less solved ([10]; see [21] for a review of methods), the methods employed still rely on the presence of linguistic resources (e.g. corpora of non-domain-specific texts, lexica; our approach differs in this respect, see below), and in any case are only the first step in a text-based analysis: ideally, the goal is to get a collection of terms that is further structured according to semantic relationships between the terms. There are several systems that go in this direction [4,9,11,17,25,32], which however still require the availability of linguistic knowledge and resources, and moreover do not seem to work on all kinds of texts.[5] In general, there is a trade-off between the cost of getting or producing these resources and the simplification these methods offer. Hence our aim was a more modest, but at the present state of the art of the Semantic Web and in the given application scenario [30,41] a more realistic one: to aid the ontology engineer as far as possible (both at methodological and technological level), while requiring as little additional linguistic resources and expertise as possible. Before we come to a description of our approach, however, we briefly review the use of ontologies in NLP, and derive some requirements for "NLP-friendly" ontologies. These requirements are crucial for the development of high-quality domain ontologies, which should combine a precise and expressive domain conceptualization with a feasible fitness of use (i.e. in our case, fitness of use in language-related tasks).

---

[3] Refer to [15,39] for recent overviews of the ontological engineering field.

[4] http://www.nlm.nih.gov/research/umls last visited in July, 2006.

[5] These methods rely on relational information implicitly encoded in the use of verbs; one of the domains we tested our approach is marked by a reduced, "telegram"-like text style with an almost complete absence of verbs, as elaborated in [33].

2.2 Ontologies in NLP

Ontologies have been used for a long time in many NLP applications, be that machine translation [27], text understanding [18], or dialogue systems (some recent examples are [16,37]), and are of course central to information-extraction or Semantic Web-related NLP applications [3].[6]

Despite all differences in purpose, a common requirement for an ontology to be considered "linguistics-friendly" (or "NLP-friendly") is that the path from lexical items (e.g. words) to ontology concepts should be as simple as possible.[7] On a more technical level, this requires that access to ontology concepts is given in a standardized form—if access is via names, then they should be in a predictable linguistic form. To give an example of this *not* being the case, the medical ontology UMLS contains concept names in the form "noun, adjective" (e.g. "Asthma, allergic") as well as "adjective noun" (e.g. "Diaphragmatic pleura"), and also concept names that are full phrases or even clauses (e.g. "Idiopathic fibrosing alveolitis chronic form"). Below we describe a method to avoid these problems during the ontology engineering process, by making the engineering team aware of the requirements of NLP applications; we also describe the concrete use of an ontology in the task of semantic annotation of text documents. A more concrete list of requirements for "NLP-friendliness" is presented in Section 3.2.

3 Using the **OntoSeed** Suite in Ontology Engineering

This section describes the suite of tools we have developed to aid the design of ontologies used in language-related tasks such as semantic annotation. We begin by giving a high-level description of the NLP-aided ontology engineering process, illustrating this with examples from the medical domain and explain the technical realization of the tools.

3.1 Overview and Examples

The OntoSeed suite consists of a number of programs that produce various statistical reports (as described below) given a collection of texts from a certain domain, with the aim to provide guidance for the ontology engineer on which concepts are important in this domain, and on the semantic relationships among these concepts. More specifically, it compiles five lists for each given collection of texts, as follows:

1. a list of nouns (or noun sequences in English texts; we will only write "noun" in the following) occurring in the collection, ranked by their "termhood" (i.e. their relevance for the text domain; see below);
2. nouns grouped by common prefixes and
3. suffixes, thereby automatically detecting compound nouns; and

---

[6] See [20] for a critical view on the use of ontologies in NLP.

[7] See [2] for a still relevant discussion of these interface issues.

4. adjectives together with all nouns they modify; and
5. nouns with all adjectives that modify them.

Figures 1 to 3 show excerpts of these files for a collection of German texts from the medical domain of lung pathology (the LungPath-Corpus (see [33]), consisting of 750 reports of around 300 words each; during ontology construction we used a "training-subset" of 400 documents). Our examples are from German texts due to the application scenario in which this work was initiated (cf. Section 4.2). While we have used those for our *systematic* evaluations, we have also tested the tools on English texts and in general we do not expect any principled differences when working with languages other than German (or at least closely related languages — languages with different writing systems like Chinese pose different problems).[8]

As illustrated in Figure 1, terms like "Tumorzelle/tumor cell" or "Lungengewebe /lung tissue" get assigned a relatively high weight by our analysis methods (the highest weight is 112.666), which suggests that these terms denote relevant domain concepts that need to be modeled. Terms related to domain-independent concepts (e.g. terms like "System/system" or "Zeit/time" in Figure 1) tend to be ranked with significantly lower value. When a decision is made on which terms to model, clusters in which these terms occur can be looked up, as shown in Figure 2. The overview of the data afforded by ordering phrases in prefix and suffix clusters can be very useful in deciding how to model complex concepts, since there is no general, established way to model them. For example, a noun phrase like "Tumorzelle/tumor cell" can be modeled as a single concept subclass of Zelle (cell), while in other settings it can be advantageous to introduce a property like Zelle infectedBy Tumor . The suffix clustering offers valuable information about subclasses or types of a certain concept (in our example in Figure 2 several types of cells). The prefix clustering can be utilized to identify concept parts or properties (e.g. in Figure 2 Lungengewebe (lung tissue) or Lungengefaess (lung vessel) as parts of the Lunge (lung)).

Linguistically, this pre- and suffix-clustering of course results in an (approximation of a) decomposition of compound nouns; following our general strategy, we leave it to the ontology engineer to specify the semantic relation between the parts of the compound, as this task requires domain knowledge. However, while the tool does not provide any guidance for the accomplishment of this task, it speeds-up its operation by propagating manually defined semantic relationships across the concept hierarchy. Once the ontology engineer has specified a link between ontological concepts/classes (for example he introduces the property infectedBy between the classes Lunge (lung) and Tumor) the tool suggests additional concepts in the hierarchy which are likely to act as domain or range of the property as well (in this case the tool takes a look at classes in the hierarchy which are more general than Lunge (lung) and Tumor and recommends them as domain and range of the property infectedBy). This will lead to a definition of the original property at BodyPart and Finding , respectively, and to a subsequent propagation of the property to all sub-classes of the two.

---

[8] Indeed, the POS-tagger we are using comes with a model of English and Italian in addition to German.

Lungenparenchym	96.515
Schnittfläche	90.993
Tumorzelle	90.951
Pleuraerguß	89.234
Entzündung	88.476
Bronchialsekret	87.711
Lungengewebe	84.918
Entzündungsbefund	83.631
....	....
Wert	1.825
System	1.761
Neuß	1.448
Bitte	1.296
Zeit	1.085
Seite	1.018

Fig. 1. Excerpt of the weighted term list (step 1)

B-Zellen	Lunge
Carcinom-Zellen	Lungen-PE
Schleimhautlamellen	Lungenabszeß
Plasmazellen	Lungenarterienembolie
Epitheloidzellen	Lungenbereich
Rundzellen	Lungenbezug
Alveolardeckzellen	Lungenbiopsat
Epithelzellen	Lungenblutung
Plattenepithelzellen	Lungenembolie
Karzinomzellen	Lungenemphysem
Schaumzellen	Lungenerkrankung
Riesenzellen	Lungenfibrose
Tumorzellen	Lungengefäße
Alveolarzellen	**Lungengewebe**
Zylinderzellen	Lungengewebsareal
Becherzellen	Lungengewebsprobe
Herzfehlerzellen	Lungengewebsstücke
Bindegewebszellen	Lungeninfarkt
Entzündungszellen	Lungenkarzinom
Pilzzellen	Lungenlappen

Fig. 2. Excerpt of the prefix (left, step 2) and suffix lists (right, step 3)

Finally, we look at ways in which the relevant terms are modified by adjectives in the texts, by inspecting the lists shown in Figure 3. These lists give us information that can be used in making a decision for one of two ways of modeling the meaning of modifiers: as properties of a concept (e.g. "gross/large" as in "grosse Tumorzelle/large tumor cell"), or as part of a single concept (e.g. "link/left" in linke Lunge (left lung)). The decision for either of the modeling alternatives cannot be made automatically, since it depends strongly on the context of the application. However, analyzing a text corpus can support the decision process: modifiers which occur mostly together with particular noun phrases or categories of concepts, respectively, could be candidates for the single concept variant, while

Tumorzelle:		92					gross:		
	beschrieben	1	1%	10	10%		Absetzungsrand	1
	einzeln	1	1%	60	1%		Abtragungsfläche	1
	epithelialer	1	1%	1	100%		Biopsate	1
	gelegen	1	1%	16	6%		Bronchus	2
	gross	4	4%	129	3%		Lungengewebsprobe	3
	klein	1	1%	88	1%		Lungenlappen	3
	mittelgross	1	1%	6	16%		Lungenteilresektat	1
	pas-positive	1	1%	6	16%		Lungenunterlappen	5
	spindeligen	2	2%	2	100%		Lymphknoten	1
	vergroessert	1	1%	9	11%		Nekroseherde	13
	zahlreich	1	1%	47	2%		Oberlappenresektat	1
							Ossifikationen	1
							PE	1
							Pleuraerguß	4
							Raumforderung	1
							Rippe	15
							Rundherd	1
							Stelle	5
							Tumor	1
							Tumorknoten	10
							Tumorzelle	4
							Vene	4

Lunge:		85					link:		
	link	9	10%	53	16%		Bronchus	7
	recht	7	8%	66	10%		Hauptbronchus	6
	tumorferne	2	2%	2	100%		**Lunge**	9
							Lungenlappen	1
							Lungenoberlappens	1
							Lungenunterlappen	4
							Mittellappen	2
							Oberlappen	9
							Oberlappenbronchus	3
							Seite	1
							Thoraxseite	3
							Unterlappen	4
							Unterlappenbronchus	2
							Unterlappensegment	1
							Unterschenkels	1

Fig. 3. Excerpt of modifier list (steps 4 and 5)

those used with a broad range of nouns should usually be modeled as a property. As Figure 3 shows, in our corpus the noun "Tumorzelle/tumor cell" occurs 92 times, 4 times modified with "gross/large" (i.e. approximately 4% of all modifiers). The modifier, on the other hand, occurs 129 times, so the co-occurrences of the two terms are 3% of all its occurrences, which indicates that "gross/large" is a property that is ascribed to many different concepts in the corpus. In contrast, the modifier "link/left" (the normalized form of "links/left") seems to be specific in the corpus to concepts denoting body organs like Lunge (lung) and its parts. A possible next step in specifying possible ontology properties could be to consider verbs in correlation with noun phrases. Our tool does not tackle this problem yet (cf. discussion below in Section 5).

To summarize, the classifications of the noun phrases and their modifiers are used as input to the conceptualization/implementation phase of the ontology building process, which is ultimately still performed *manually* in compliance to some ontology engineering methodology (Figure 4). Nevertheless, compared to a fully manual process, preparing the text information in the mentioned form offers important advantages in the following ontology engineering sub-tasks:

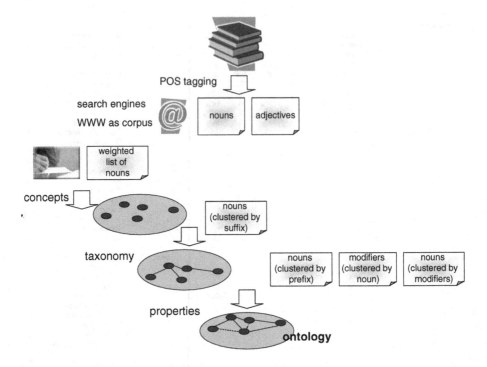

Fig. 4. The OntoSeed process

- selecting relevant concepts: the ontology engineer uses the list of nouns that are ranked according to their domain specificity as described above and selects relevant concepts and relevant concept names. Domain-specific and therefore potentially ontology-relevant terms are assigned higher rankings in the noun list (see Section 4.1 for the evaluation of the ranking function). First simple concept names from the noun list are identified as being relevant for the ontology scope. Then the ontology engineer uses the prefix and suffix clusters to decide which compound concept names should be as well included to the target ontology.
- creating taxonomy: suffix clusters can be used to identify potential sub-classes.
- creating properties/relationship: the ontology engineer uses the modifier classification and the generated taxonomy to decide about relevant properties (denoted by adjectives) and about the taxonomy level the corresponding property could be defined. For example in Figure 3 most of the concepts modified by "link/left" are subsumed by RespiratorySystem —therefore if the ontology engineer decides to define a property corresponding to this adjective, this property will be assigned the domain RespiratorySystem . However since "link/left" occurs in the corpus mostly in correlation with "Lunge/lung" an alternative conceptualization is to introduce the concept LinkeLunge (left lung) as a subclass of Lunge (lung). Further relationships are

induced by the decision to conceptualize relevant compound nouns as two or more related concepts in the ontology. For example if "Tumorzelle/tumor cell" is to be conceptualized in the ontology as `Zelle locationOf Tumor` the relationship `locationOf` should also be included to the ontology. Relationships between concepts (e.g. `locationOf`) are not suggested explicitly; however, on the basis of the taxonomy which was specified in the previous step OntoSeed is able to identify clusters of compound terms implying a similar relational semantics. For example given the fact that `Lunge` (lung) and `Herz` (heart) are both subsumed by `BodyPart` , the system suggests that the relationship correlating `Lunge` (lung) and `Infarkt` (attack) in the compound noun "Lungeninfarkt/lung attack" is the same as the one in the case of the compound "Herzinfarkt/heart attack", thus simplifying this conceptualization step even when no linguistic knowledge w.r.t. verbs is available.

From an implementation perspective, the application of our approach can be operationalized in several ways. On one hand one can implement a dedicated tool providing ease-to-use graphical interfaces to the information compiled by OntoSeed from texts, and guiding the usage of this information towards the realization of the final ontology according to the workflow described above. On the other hand such functionality could be added to existing ontology engineering environments such as Protégé, SWOOP or WebODE.[9] These tools allow users to create ontologies, by manually defining classes, properties, axioms and instances and storing the results in specific implementation languages. The information generated by OntoSeed from the document corpus could be used as an additional input for this task, thus partially automatizing the conceptualization. From a methodological perspective, OntoSeed is in compliance with established ontology engineering methodologies [15,39]. It can be understood as a knowledge acquisition activity supporting the main ontology development process (cf. [15] for a classification of ontology engineering activities and their interdependencies). Hence its outcomes can be integrated with intermediary ontologies obtained from alternative engineering activities such as manual building, ontology reuse or ontology merging.

We are following the first of the aforementioned implementation alternatives; screenshots of the current release of the OntoSeed GUI are illustrated in Appendix B. The tool allows the user to incrementally use the results of the generated reports and to adjust the content of the prospected ontology using a graphical interface.

3.2   OntoSeed and NLP-Friendly Ontologies

It is well accepted that NLP-driven knowledge acquisition on the basis of domain-specific text corpora is a useful approach in aiding ontology building [4,9,11,17,25,32]. Looking at the flow of requirements in the other direction,

---

[9] http://protege.stanford.edu/,http://www.mindswap.org/2004/SWOOP/
http://webode.dia.fi.upm.es/WebODEWeb/index.html last seen in July, 2006.

language-related tasks such as semantic annotation can be performed more efficiently if the used ontology has already been built in a "linguistics-friendly" manner, as described in the following set of operations.

– Logging Modeling Decisions: The relationship between extracted terms (resulting from the knowledge acquisition process) and the final modeled concepts should be recorded. For example the term `Klatskin tumor` will be probably modeled as a single concept, while `lung tumor` might be formalized as `tumor hasLocation lung`. These decisions should be encoded in a predefined form for subsequent NLP tasks, so that the lexicon that has to be built for these tasks knows about potential compound noun suffixes.

– Naming Conventions for Ontology Primitives: Since semantic annotation requires matching text to concept names, it is necessary that the concept names are specified in a uniform, predictable manner.[10] Typically concept names are concatenated expressions—where the first letter of every new word is capitalized— or lists of words separated by delimiters (e.g. `KlatskinTumor` or `Klatskin_Tumor`). Furthermore it is often recommended to denominate relationships in terms of verbs or predicative structures (e.g. `diagnosedBy`, `part_of`) and attributes / properties in terms of adjectives (e.g `left`).

If the names become more complex, they should be stored in a format that is easily reproducible, and allows for variations. E.g., should there be a need to have a concept name that contains modifiers ("untypical, outsized lung tumor with heavy side sequences"), the name should be stored in a format where the order of modifiers is predictable (e.g. sorted alphabetically), and the modification is disambiguated (`((lung tumor (with ((side sequences), heavy))), (untypical, outsized))`). NLP-tools (chunk parsers) can help the ontology designer to create these normalized names in addition to the human-readable ones.

We now turn to a description (3.3) and discussion (3.4) of the technical details of OntoSeed.

3.3   Technical Details

In the first processing step, the only kind of linguistic analysis proper that we employ is performed: determining the part of speech (e.g., "noun", "adjective", etc.) of each word token in the collection. Reliable systems for performing this task are readily available; we use the TreeTagger [34] developed at IMS in Stuttgart, Germany,[11] but other systems could be used as well.

This enables us to extract a list of all occurring nouns (or, for English, noun sequences, i.e., compound nouns; German compound nouns are, as is well known, written as one orthographic word). The "termhood" of each noun is determined

---

[10] This requirement, for example, is *not* fulfilled in UMLS and other medical ontologies.

[11] Freely available for academic research purposes from `http://www.ims.uni-stuttgart.de/projekte/corplex/TreeTagger/DecisionTreeTagger.html`

by the usual *inverted document frequency* measure (tf.idf), as shown in the formula below—with the added twist, however, of using a WWW-search engine to determine the document frequency in the comparison corpus.[12] In the formula, $tf(w)$ stands for the frequency of word w in our collection of texts; $wf(w)$ is the number of documents in the corpus used for comparison, i.e., the number of hits for query w reported by the search engine used— in our experiments, both www.google.com (through the API made available by Google inc.) and www.yahoo.com. N is the size of the collection, determined in an indirect way (as the search engines used do not report the number of pages indexed) by making a query for a high-frequency word such as "the" for English or "der" for German. This of course is just an approximation, and also the hits reported for normal queries get progressively less exact the more frequent a term is; for our purposes, this is precise enough, since for "Web-frequent" terms (where wf ranges from 10^3 to 10^6) rough approximations already have the desired effect of pushing the weight down.

$$weight(w) = (1 + \log tf(w)) * (\log \frac{N}{wf(w)})$$

Sorting by this weight results in lists like those shown partially in Figure 1 above; a quantitative description of the effect of this weighing procedure is given in Section 4.1.

In the next step after weighing the terms, nouns are clustered, to find common pre- and suffixes. We use a linguistically naïve (since it only looks at strings and ignores morphology), but efficient method for grouping together compound nouns by common parts. This step is performed in two stages: first, preliminary clusters are formed based on a pre- or suffix similarity of three or more letters (i.e., "lung" and "lung pathology" would be grouped into one cluster, but also "prerogative" and "prevention"). These preliminary clusters are then clustered again using a hierarchical clustering algorithm [26], which determines clusters based on maximized pre- or suffix length (see Figure 2 above). The accuracy of the suffix clustering procedure is anew improved by using the Web to eliminate suffixes that do not denominate concepts in the real world, but are simply common endings of the clustered nouns (such as the ending "ight" in "light" or "night" in English or the German ending "tion" in "Reaktion/reaction", "Infektion/infection").

The compilation of the adjective lists (Figure 3) from the tokenized and POS-tagged text collection is straightforward and need not be explained here.

3.4 Discussion of the Methods

As described above, POS-tagging is the first of the processing steps, and hence, any errors made there impact on the further steps. [34] reports an accuracy of 97.5% for the tagger we used, on texts of the same sort as those it has been trained on (newspaper text). Our LungPath corpus is characterized by a high

---

[12] See [26] for a textbook description of the family of tf.idf measures.

proportion of fragmentary sentences; this deviation from the training text sort brings accuracy down to 93.7%. This illustrates a general caveat when applying the method: *completeness* of term extraction cannot be guaranteed, as nouns may in unfortunate circumstances (misclassification at this stage) not enter the ranking list. However, as our results on coverage reported below suggest, in practice this risk seems slight, even if the corpus contains many instances of non-standard structures. Similarly one can not fully guarantee the completeness of the domain coverage, since the quality of the term extraction is highly dependent of the domain relevance of the corpus used.

Using the Web as a corpus in linguistic analysis has become a hot topic recently in computational linguistics (see e.g. a current special issue of *Computational Linguistics* [22]), and has also been used in Ontology Learning and Population and in Semantic Annotation. [6] use information automatically collected from the Web to annotate text with concepts, *given an ontology*; [1] describe methods to cull a domain specific corpus from the Web, *given a list of seed terms*). To our knowledge, the system presented here is the first to use the Web in this kind of ontology-building support application.

Nevertheless, the Web-based tf.idf method also has some potential problems, which stem from the fact that *concepts*, which is what we are really interested in, are only "imperfectly" represented by natural language expressions. Such expressions may denote more than one concept, or concepts with a more relaxed meaning than the one intended in the domain. This in turn can lead to "false positives" in the comparison corpus. An example shall make this clearer. In the medical domain, the expression "sex" may legitimately denote an important concept; however, in our comparison corpus, the Web, this term will also be frequent—for altogether different reasons. The sense we are interested in (the one from our domain corpus) is *narrower* than the one that generates the surplus hits. The effect of this is that the computed weight for the expression is lower than it ideally should be. Similarly, in a technical domain (e.g., Unix programming), the expression "cat" may be important (it is the name of a Unix *command*), but will be pushed down in the metric through the many instances in the comparison corpus where the same string denotes something completely different (a mammal).[13] As aforementioned, this so far has not been a problem in our test corpora, but we are currently experimenting with techniques that weigh not only individual words but sets of words with similar meaning (*synsets*), computed via distributional similarity [24]. Another obvious approach would be to use lexical resources such as the Princeton WordNet [12]. However, this would violate our goal of producing a "linguistically knowledge-lean" (and accessible for non-experts) suite of tools.

---

[13] The first example was of something that would be called in linguistics "sense narrowing" or perhaps "polysemy" (one word with a spectrum of senses or several discrete ones), the latter "homography" (different words that happen to be spelled in the same way). Clearly classifying lexemes into these categories is difficult and to some extent theory-dependent [8]; for us, the differences do not really matter, and we only mention them for completeness.

4   Evaluation

In this section we present the evaluation of our approach from a technical and an application-oriented perspective. We first compare the results of the NLP techniques on three different corpora against a naïve baseline assumption (Section 4.1). The whole suite of tools is then evaluated within a real-world application setting in the medical domain. For this purpose we will compare two experiments aiming at developing the same ontology using alternative knowledge acquisition strategies— a OntoSeed-aided engineering approach and a reuse-oriented one based on UMLS— in terms of development costs and suitability of the outcomes in the target application context (Section 4.2).

4.1   Technical Evaluation

For the technical evaluation of our methods we examined the weighing function described above and the results of the prefix and suffix clustering against human expertise.

A simple concept of the importance of a term would just treat its position in a frequency list compiled from the corpus as an indication of its "termhood". This ranking, however, is of little discriminatory value, since it does not separate frequent *domain-specific* terms from other frequent terms, and moreover, it does not bring any structure to the data: Figure 5 (left) shows a doubly logarithmic plot of frequency-rank vs. frequency for the LungPath data set; the distribution follows closely the predictions of Zipf's law [42], which roughly states that in a balanced collection of texts there will be a low number of very frequent terms and a high number of very rare terms.

In comparison, after weighing the terms as described above, the distribution looks like Figure 5 (right), again doubly logarithmically rank (this time: rank in weight-distribution) vs. weight. There is a much higher number of roughly similarly weighted terms, a relatively clear cut-off point, and a lower number of low-weighed terms. A closer inspection of the weighed list showed that it distributed the terms from the corpus roughly as desired: the percentage of general terms within each 10% chunk of the list (sorted by weight) changed progressively from 5% in the first chunk (i.e., 95% of the terms in the highest ranked

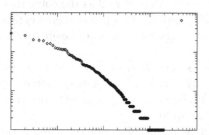 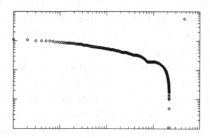

Fig. 5. Rank (x-axis) vs. frequency (left), and rank vs. weight (right); doubly logarithmically

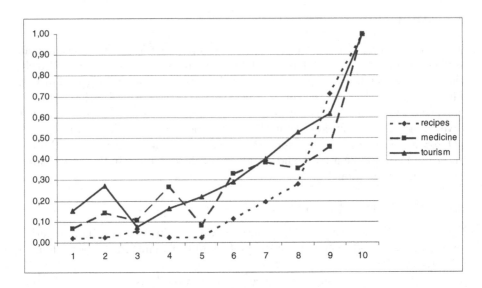

Fig. 6. The ratio of general terms / domain terms per 10% chunk of weighted term list (highest weight to the left) for the three corpora

10% denoted domain-specific terms) to 95% in the last chunk (with the lowest weights). We repeated this process (weighing, and manually classifying terms as *domain-specific* or *general*) with two further corpora and found a similar correlation between weight and "termhood" (the results for both corpora are shown in Figure 6). The first was a collection of 244 English texts (approximately 80500 word tokens altogether) describing environmental aspects of world countries. The second corpus contained 500 XML-formatted cooking recipes (approximately 45000 tokens) in German language.

In all corpora, however, there was one interesting exception to this trend: a higher than expected number of terms in one 10% chunk in the middle of the weight distribution which were classified as irrelevant by the experts. These turned out to mostly be misspellings of names for general concepts—a kind of "noise" in the data to which the termhood measure is vulnerable (since in the misspelled form they will be both rare in the analyzed collection as well as the comparison corpus, the Web, pushing them into the middle ground in terms of their weights). While this is not a dramatic problem, we are working on ways of dealing with it in a principled manner.

Further on, the comparison of the clusters generated as described in Section 3.3 with the results of the human classification revealed an average percentage of approximately 14% of irrelevant suffix/prefix clusters — a satisfactory result given the linguistically naïve algorithms employed.

We now turn to a qualitative evaluation of the usefulness of OntoSeed within a real-world Semantic Web application we are developing for the medical domain.

4.2 Application-Based Evaluation

In order to evaluate the costs and the benefits of the OntoSeed approach, we examined two subsequent semi-automatic experiments which aimed at building the same application ontology using different engineering strategies based on knowledge acquisition: the re-usage of existing medical ontologies and the OntoSeed-guided acquisition of application-relevant knowledge from texts. The evaluation procedure focused on two criteria: the efficiency of the ontology engineering process (i.e. the associated development efforts) and the usability of the ontology in the application setting (i.e. as regarding the semantic annotation of medical reports). A second objective of the evaluation was targeted at the methodological background of our approach i.e. at the question whether the approach can guide the engineering team towards the creation of an application ontology.

Application Scenario. The aim of the project SWPATHO - A Semantic Web for Pathology was to investigate the potential of semantic technologies, particularly ontologies, for the realization of a content-based retrieval system for the domain of *lung pathology* [30,41].[14]The ontology-based application operates upon an archive of medical reports (the LungPath-Corpus mentioned above) consisting of both textual and image-based data, which are semantically annotated in order to transform them into a valuable resource for diagnosis and teaching, which can be searched in a fast, *content-based* manner [30,41]. The semantic annotation of the data is realized by linguistically extracting semantic information from medical reports and lists of keywords associated with each of the digital images (both reports and keyword lists are available in textual form). The search is content-based in that it can make use of semantic relationships between search concepts and those occurring in the text (cf. Appendix A. In the same time the medical information system can provide quality assurance mechanisms on the basis of the semantic annotations of the patient records. The annotated patient records are analyzed on-the-fly by the quality assurance component, and potential inconsistencies w.r.t. the background domain ontology are spotted.

Extracting semantic information from the medical text data is realized automatically using LUPUS—Lung Pathology System [33]. LUPUS consists of a NLP component (a robust parser) and a Semantic Web component (a domain ontology represented in OWL, and a Description Logic reasoner), which work closely together, with the domain ontology guiding the information extraction process. The result of the linguistic analysis is a (partial) semantic representation of the content of the textual data in form of an OWL semantic network of instances of concepts and properties from the domain ontology. This ontology is used in three processing stages in LUPUS, all of which can profit from a good coverage (as ensured by building the ontology bottom-up, supported by OntoSeed) and a "linguistics-friendly" specification (as described above). The most obvious step where NLP and ontology interface is concept lookup: the ontology defines the vocabulary of the semantic representation. Since LUPUS cannot "know"

---

[14] http://swpatho.ag-nbi.de

whether a phrase encountered (e.g. "anthrakotischer Lymphknoten/anthracotic lymph node") is modelled as a simple or complex concept (i.e., as a concept AnthrakotischerLymphknoten or as a concept Lymphknoten having the property anthrakotisch) it has to first try the "longest match". For this to work, the system has to be able to construct a form that would be the one contained in the ontology. To stay with this example, an inflected occurrence of these terms, e.g. in "die Form des anthrakotischen Lymphknotens" ("the form of the anthracotic lymph node"), would have to be mapped to a canonical form, which then can be looked up. As mentioned above, in ontologies like UMLS there is no guarantee that a concept name would be in a particular form, if present at all. In a second step, the ontology is used to resolve the meaning of compound nouns and prepositions [33].

OntoSeed experiment vs. UMLS experiment. During this project we examined two alternatives for the semi-automatic generation of an ontology for lung pathology which suits the application functionality mentioned above. The two experiments were similar in terms of engineering team (and of course, of the application context). In the first one the ontology was compiled on the basis of UMLS, as the largest medical ontology available. The engineering process was focused on the customization of pre-selected UMLS libraries w.r.t. the application requirements and resulted in an ontology of approximately 1200 concepts modeling the anatomy of the lung and lung diseases [28,30]. Pathology-specific knowledge was found to not be covered by available ontologies to a satisfactory extent and hence was formalized manually. In the second experiment the ontology was generated with the help of the OntoSeed tools as described in Section 3.1.[15]

We compared the efforts invested in the corresponding engineering processes and analyzed the fitness of use of the resulting ontologies, in our case the results these ontologies achieved in semantic annotation tasks. The main advantages of the OntoSeed-aided experiment compared to the UMLS-based one are the significant cost savings in conjunction with the improved fitness of use of the generated ontology.

Development efforts. From a resource point of view, building the first ontology involved four times as many resources as the second approach (5 person-months for the UMLS-based ontology with 1200 concepts vs. 1.25 person-months for the "text-close" ontology of a similar size). We note that the customization of UMLS [16]required over 45% of the overall effort necessary to build the target ontology in the UMLS experiment (cf. Figure 7). Further 15% of the resources were spent on translating the input representation formalisms to OWL. The reuse-oriented approach gave rise to considerable efforts to evaluate and extend the outcomes: approximately 40% of the total engineering effort were necessary

---

[15] The knowledge-intensive nature and the complexity of the application domain convinced us to not pursue the third possible alternative, building the ontology from scratch.

[16] Customization includes getting familiar with, evaluating and extracting relevant parts of the source ontologies.

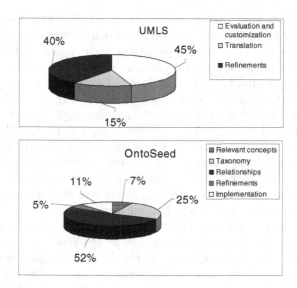

Fig. 7. Efforts distribution for the UMLS-based (top) and the OntoSeed (bottom) ontology engineering experiments

for the refinement of the preliminary ontology. The effort distribution for the second experiment was as follows (cf. Figure 7): 7% of the overall effort was invested in the selection of the relevant concepts. Their taxonomical classification required 25% of the resources, while a significant proportion of 52% was spent on the definition of additional semantic relationships. Due to the high degree of familiarity w.r.t. the resulting ontology, the evaluation and refinement phase in the second experiment was performed straight forward with 5% of the total efforts. The OWL implementation necessitated the remaining 11%.

In comparison with a fully manual process the major benefit of OntoSeed according to our experiences would be the pre-compilation of potential domain-specific terms and semantic relationships. The efforts invested in the taxonomical classification of the concepts are comparable to building from scratch, because in both cases the domain experts still needed to align the domain-relevant concepts to a pre-defined upper-level ontology (in our case the Semantic Network core medical ontology from UMLS). The selection of domain-relevant terms was accelerated by the usage of the termhood measure as described above since this avoids the manual processing of the entire domain corpus or the complete evaluation of the corpus vocabulary. The efforts necessary to conceptualize the semantical relationships among domain concepts were reduced by the clustering methods employed to suggest potential subclass and domain-specific relationships. However the OntoSeed approach assumes the availability of domain-narrow text sources and the quality of its results depends on the quality/domain relevance of the corpus (cf. the discussion in Section 3.4.

Quality of the Outcomes. In order to evaluate the quality of the outcomes (i.e. the ontologies resulted from the experiments mentioned above) we compared their usability within the LUPUS system by setting aside a subset (370 texts) of the LungPath corpus and comparing the number of nouns matched to a concept. Using the ontology created by using OntoSeed (on a different subset of the corpus) as compared to the ontology derived from UMLS resulted in a 10 fold increase in the number of nouns that were matched to an ontology concept—very encouraging results indeed, which indicate that our weighting method indeed captures concepts that are important for the whole domain, i.e. that the results generalize to unseen data. However, this evaluation method does of course not tell us how good the recall is w.r.t. all potentially relevant information, i.e., whether we not still miss relevant concepts—this we could only find out using a manually annotated test corpus, a task which is currently performed. In a preliminary evaluation, domain experts selected the most significant (w.r.t their information content) concepts from an arbitrary set of 50 patient reports. These concepts are most likely to be used as search terms in the envisioned system because of their high domain relevance (as assigned by human experts). The ontology derived from UMLS contained 40% of these concepts (cf. Figure 8). However, only 8% of them were directly found in the ontology,[17] while the usage of the remaining 32% in the automatic annotation task was practically impossible because of the arbitrary concept terminology used in UMLS. As underlined before, UMLS contains concept names in various forms ("noun, adjective", "adjective noun", full phrases—to name only a few). In comparison, the OntoSeed-generated ontology was able to deliver 80% of the selected concepts with an overall rate of 61% directly extracted concepts. In contrast to the UMLS-oriented case, the 19% of the remaining, indirectly recognized concepts could be de facto used in automatic annotation tasks, due to the NLP-friendly nature of the ontology. In the second ontology the concepts were denominated in an homogeneous way and critical modeling decisions were available in a machine-processable format.

The results of the evaluation can of course not be entirely generalized to arbitrary settings. Still, due to the knowledge-intensive character of its processes, medicine is considered a representative use case for Semantic Web technologies [23]. Medical ontologies have already been developed and used in different application settings: GeneOntology [7], NCI-Ontology [14], LinKBase [5] and finally UMLS. Though their modeling principles or ontological commitments have often been subject of research [36,31,35,13], there is no generally accepted methodology for how these knowledge sources could be *efficiently* embedded in real Semantic Web applications. At the same time, the OntoSeed results could be easily understood by domain experts, enabled a rapid conceptualization of the application domain whose quality could be efficiently evaluated by the ontology users. Though OntoSeed was evaluated in a particular application setting, that of

---

[17] Directly extracted concepts are the result of simple string matching on concept names or their synonyms. The indirect extraction procedure assumes that a specific concept available in the text corpus is formalized "indirect" in the ontology i.e. as a set of concepts and semantical relationships; see Section 3.

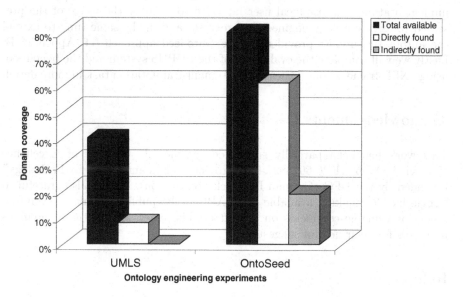

Fig. 8. Fitness of use of the two ontologies

semantically annotating domain-narrow texts using NLP techniques, we strongly believe that the tools and the underlying approach are applicable to various domains and domain-specific corpora with similar results. This assumption was in fact confirmed to some degree by the technical evaluation of the tools on two additional corpora (cf. Section 4.1).

5   Conclusions and Future Work

In this paper we presented methods to aid the ontology building process. Starting from a typical ontology-driven application setting—the semantic annotation of text documents—we introduced an approach that can aid ontology engineers and domain experts in the ontology conceptualization process, the only requirement being a collection of domain-specific text to kick-start the ontology building. We evaluated the analysis method itself on three corpora, with good results, and its methodological background within a specific application setting, where it resulted in a significant reduction of effort as compared to adaptation of existing resources. Additionally, the method suggests guidelines for building "linguistics-friendly" ontologies, which perform better in ontology-based NLP tasks like semantic annotation.

As future work, we are investigating to what extent analyzing verbs in domain specific texts can be used to aid ontology building, and ways to extract more taxonomic information from this source (e.g. information about hyponym (is-a) relations, via the use of the copula (x is a y)), while still being as linguistically knowledge-lean as possible. Second, we are currently finalizing the implementation of a graphical user interface to simplify the usage of the presented tools in ontology engineering processes and in the same time to extend the automatic support provided by the OntoSeed approach (cf. Appendix B. Lastly we will complete the evaluation of the LUPUS system and the benefits of using "NLP-friendly" ontologies for the semantic annotation task in more detail.

Acknowledgements

This work has been partially supported by the EU Network of Excellence "KnowledgeWeb" (FP6-507482). The project "A Semantic Web for Pathology" is funded by the DFG (German Research Foundation). We are also grateful to Google Inc. for making available their API to the public. Thanks to Manfred Stede for valuable comments on a draft of this paper, and to the anonymous reviewers for their helpful suggestions.

References

1. Baroni, M., Bernardini, S.: BootCaT: Bootstrapping Corpora and Terms from the Web. In: Proceedings of the International Language Resources Conference (LREC04), May 2004, Lisbon, Portugal, pp. 1313–1316 (2004)
2. Bateman, J.A.: The Theoretical Status of Ontologies in Natural Language Processing. In: Preuβ, S., Schmitz, B. (eds.) Proceedings of the Workshop on Text Representation and Domain Modelling, Technische Universität, Berlin (1992)
3. Bontcheva, K., Cunnigham, H., Tablan, V., Maynard, D., Saggion, H.: Developing Reusable and Robust Language Processing Components for Information Systems using GATE. In: Proceedings of the 3rd International Workshop on Natural Language and Information Systems (NLIS02), pp. 223–227. IEEE Computer Society Press, Los Alamitos (2002)
4. Buitelaar, P., Olejnik, D., Sintek, M.: A Protege Plug-In for Ontology Extraction from Text Based on Linguistic Analysis. In: Bussler, C.J., Davies, J., Fensel, D., Studer, R. (eds.) ESWS 2004. LNCS, vol. 3053, Springer, Heidelberg (2004)
5. Ceusters, W., Smith, B., Flanagan, J.: Ontology and Medical Terminology: Why Description Logics are Not Enough. In: Proceedings Towards An Electronic Patient Record TEPR2003, CD–ROM (2003)
6. Cimiano, P., Handschuh, S., Staab, S.: Towards the Self-Annotating Web. In: Proceedings of the 13th International World Wide Web Conference (WWW-2004), New York, USA, pp. 462–471 (2004)
7. The Gene Ontology Consortium: Gene Ontology: Tool for the Unification of Biology. Nature Genetics 25, 25–30 (2000)
8. Cruse, D.A.: Lexical Semantics. Cambridge University Press, Cambridge (1986)
9. Dittenbach, M., Berger, H., Merll, D.: Improving Domain Ontologies by Mining Semantics from Text. In: Proceedings of the 1st Asian-Pacific Conference on Conceptual Modelling, pp. 91–100. Australian Computer Society, Inc. (2004)
10. Drouin, P.: Detection of Domain Specific Terminology Using Corpora Comparison. In: Proceedings of the International Language Resources Conference LREC04, May 2004, Lisbon, Portugal (2004)

11. Faure, D., Poibeau, T.: First Experiments of Using Semantic Knowledge Learned by ASIUM for Information Extraction Task Using INTEX. In: Proceedings of the Ontology Learning ECAI-2000 Workshop, pp. 7–12 (2000)
12. Fellbaum, C. (ed.): WordNet: An Electronic Lexical Database. MIT Press, Cambridge, USA (1998)
13. Gangemi, A., Pisanelli, D.M., Steve, G.: An Overview of the ONIONS Project: Applying Ontologies to the Integration of Medical Terminologies. Data Knowledge Engineering 31(2), 183–220 (1999)
14. Golbeck, J., Fragoso, G., Hartel, F., Hendler, J., Parsia, B., Oberthaler, J.: The National Cancer Institute's Thesaurus and Ontology. Journal of Web Semantics 1(1) (2003)
15. Gómez-Pérez, A., Fernández-López, M., Corcho, O.: Ontological Engineering. Springer, Heidelberg (2003)
16. Gurevych, I., Porzel, R., Slinko, E., Pfleger, N., Alexandersson, J., Merten, S.: Less is more: using a single knowledge representation in dialogue systems. In: Proceedings of the HLT-NAACL 2003 Workshop on Text Meaning, Morristown, NJ, USA, pp. 14–21, Association for Computational Linguistics (2003)
17. Hahn, U., Schnattinger, K.: Towards Text Knowledge Engineering. In: Proceedings of the AAAI/IAAI, pp. 524–531 (1998)
18. Hobbs, J.R., Croft, W., Davies, T., Edwards, D., Laws, K.: Commonsense metaphysics and lexical semantics. Compuational Linguistics 13(3–4), 241–250 (1987)
19. Jarrar, M., Meersman, R.: Formal Ontology Engineering in the DOGMA Approach. In: Meersman, R., Tari, Z., et al. (eds.) CoopIS 2002, DOA 2002, and ODBASE 2002. LNCS, vol. 2519, pp. 1238–1254. Springer, Heidelberg (2002)
20. Junichi, T., Ananiadou, S.: Thesaurus or logical onotology, which do we need for mining text? Language Resources and Evaluation 39(1), 77–90 (2005)
21. Kageura, K., Umino, B.: Methods of Automatic Term Recognition. Terminology 3(2), 259–289 (1996)
22. Kilgarriff, A., Grefenstette, G.: Introduction to the Special Issue on the Web as Corpus. Computational Linguistics 29(3), 333–348 (2003)
23. KnowledgeWeb European Project: Prototypical Business Use Cases (Deliverable D1.1.2 KnoweldgeWeb FP6-507482) (2004)
24. Lee, L.: Measures of Distributional Similarity. In: Proceedings of the 37th Annual Meeting of the Association for Computational Linguistics, Maryland, USA, pp. 25–32 (1999)
25. Maedche, A., Staab, S.: Semi-automatic Engineering of Ontologies from Text. In: Proceedings of the 12th International Conference on Software Engineering and Knowledge Engineering SEKE2000, pp. 231–239 (2000)
26. Manning, C.D., Schütze, H.: Foundations of Statistical Natural Language Processing. MIT Press, Cambridge, Massachusetts, USA (1999)
27. Nirenburg, S., Raskin, V.: The Subworld Concept Lexicon and the Lexicon Management System. Computational Linguistics 13(3–4) (1987)
28. Paslaru Bontas, E., Mochol, M., Tolksdorf, R.: Case Studies in Ontology Reuse. In: Proceedings of the 5th International Conference on Knowledge Management IKNOW05 (2005)
29. Paslaru-Bontas, E., Schlangen, D., Schrader, T.: Creating Ontologies for Content Representation – the OntoSeed Suite. In: Meersman, R., Tari, Z. (eds.) On the Move to Meaningful Internet Systems 2005: CoopIS, DOA, and ODBASE. LNCS, vol. 3761, pp. 1296–1313. Springer, Heidelberg (2005)

30. Paslaru Bontas, E., Tietz, S., Tolksdorf, R., Schrader, T.: Generation and Management of a Medical Ontology in a Semantic Web Retrieval System. In: Meersman, R., Tari, Z. (eds.) On the Move to Meaningful Internet Systems 2004: CoopIS, DOA, and ODBASE. LNCS, vol. 3290, pp. 637–653. Springer, Heidelberg (2004)
31. Pisanelli, D.M., Gangemi, A., Steve, G.: Ontological Analysis of the UMLS Metathesaurus. JAMIA 5, 810–814 (1998)
32. Reinberger, M.L., Spyns, P.: Discovering Knowledge in Texts for the Learning of DOGMA-inspired Ontologies. In: Proceedings of the ECAI-2004 Workshop Ontology Learning and Population, August 2004, Valencia, Spain, pp. 19–24 (2004)
33. Schlangen, D., Stede, M., Paslaru Bontas, E.: Feeding OWL: Extracting and Representing the Content of Pathology Reports. In: Proceedings of the NLPXML Workshop 2004 (2004)
34. Schmid, H.: Probabilistic part-of-speech tagging using decision trees. In: Proceedings of the International Conference on New Methods in Language Processing (1994)
35. Schulze-Kremer, S., Smith, B., Kumar, A.: Revising the UMLS Semantic Network. In: Proceedings of the Medinfo 2004 (2004)
36. Smith, B., Williams, J., Schulze-Kremer, S.: The Ontology of GeneOntology. In: Proceedings of the AMIA (2003)
37. Stede, M., Schlangen, D.: Information-Seeking Chat: Dialogues Driven by Topic-Structure. In: Proceedings of Catalog (the 8th Workshop on the Semantics and Pragmatics of Dialogue SemDial04), pp. 117–124 (2004)
38. Sure, Y., Staab, S., Studer, R.: Methodology for Development and Employment of Ontology based Knowledge Management Applications. In: Meersman, R., Sheth, A. (eds.) SIGMOD Record – Web Edition, vol. 31(4), Special Section on Semantic Web and Data Management (December 2002), Available at http://www.acm.org/sigmod/record/
39. Sure, Y., Tempich, C., Vrandecic, D.: Ontology Engineering Methodologies. In: Semantic Web Technologies: Trends and Research in Ontology-based Systems, Wiley, UK (2006)
40. Tempich, C., Pinto, H.S., Sure, Y., Staab, S.: An Argumentation Ontology for DIstributed, Loosely-controlled and evolvInG Engineering processes of oNTologies (DILIGENT). In: Gómez-Pérez, A., Euzenat, J. (eds.) ESWC 2005. LNCS, vol. 3532, Springer, Heidelberg (2005)
41. Tolksdorf, R., Paslaru Bontas, E.: Organizing Knowledge in a Semantic Web for Pathology. In: Proceedings of the NetObjectDays Conference, pp. 39–54 (2004)
42. Zipf, G.K.: Human Behaviour and the Principle of Least Effort. Addison-Wesley, Cambridge, MA, USA (1949)

A   The **SWPATHO** System

SWPATHO is an ontology-based information system for pathology, which prototypically realizes the eHealth application scenario introduced above. An online demo of the system is available at http://swpatho.ag-nbi.de/english/software.html

The screenshots should give an idea about the underlying implementation. Figure 9 depicts the way the domain ontology is used as an instrument for content- and structure-based search in the pathology report archive. Queries can

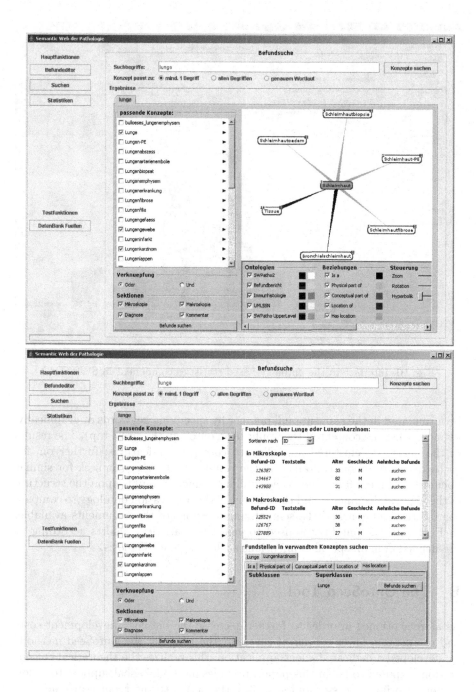

Fig. 9. Interfaces to the ontology-based retrieval component in SWPATHO

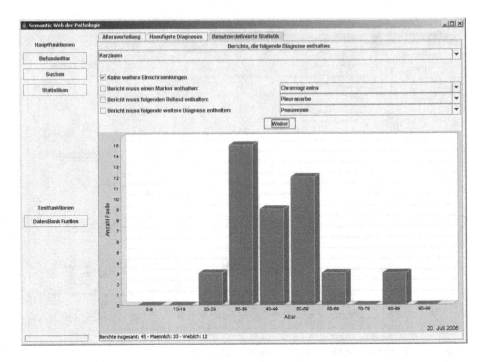

Fig. 10. Interface to the ontology-based statistics component in SWPATHO

be formulated in the conventional manner by specifying keywords or graphically, by navigating the content of the application ontology (Figure 9 top). The results of the query are clustered according to core patient features; further on, for each pathology report contained in the result set, the user can seek for similar documents (Figure 9 bottom). The similarity function builds upon the structure of the medical documents and the content of the application ontology to compare the full text content and the semantic annotations of the documents available. In Figure 10 the ontology is used to generate statistical reports according to pre-defined domain-specific dimensions such as age or diagnosis.

B   The OntoSeed Tool

As aforementioned in order to further decrease the ontology development costs and to ensure a lower barrier of entry for the usage of the OntoSeed methods we developed a dedicated client application; this realizes the theoretical considerations exposed so far in this paper, provides methodological support to ontology engineering processes and simplifies the access to the reports produced by OntoSeed using a graphical user interface.

Figure 11 depicts the interface to the weighed list of corpus terms. The user specifies the concepts of the final ontology in that she can modify the labels of the

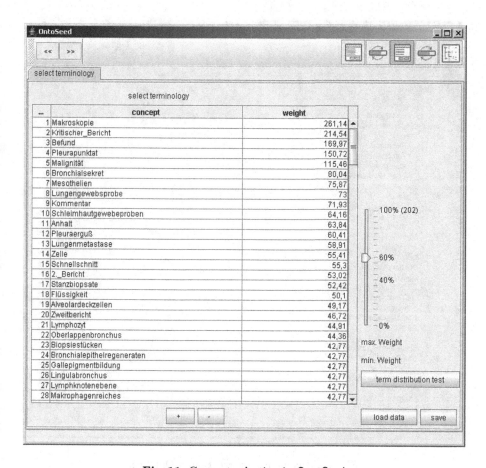

Fig. 11. Concept selection in OntoSeed

potential concepts and decide to eliminate individual terms or the percentages of the total result set.

Figure 12 shows the creation of the taxonomy, which is performed after the specification of the domain-relevant concepts with the help of the prefix clusters computed by OntoSeed (cf. Section 3.1). The user can modify the suggested taxonomical structure by moving concepts throughout the hierarchy and modifying individual labels.

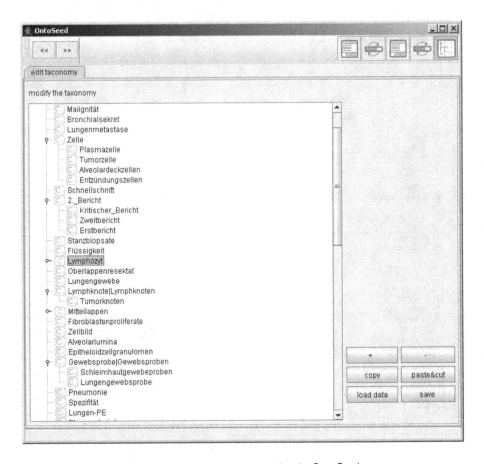

Fig. 12. Taxonomy construction in OntoSeed

Security Ontology to Facilitate Web Service Description and Discovery

Anya Kim, Jim Luo, and Myong Kang

Center for High Assurance Computer Systems
Naval Research Laboratory
Washington, DC 20375
{kim,luo,mkang}@itd.nrl.navy.mil

Abstract. Annotation with security-related metadata enables discovery of resources that meet security requirements. This paper presents the NRL Security Ontology, which complements existing ontologies in other domains that focus on annotation of functional aspects of resources. Types of security information that could be described include mechanisms, protocols, objectives, algorithms, and credentials in various levels of detail and specificity. The NRL Security Ontology is more comprehensive and better organized than existing security ontologies. It is capable of representing more types of security statements and can be applied to any electronic resource. The class hierarchy of the ontology makes it both easy to use and intuitive to extend. We applied this ontology to a Service Oriented Architecture to annotate security aspects of Web service descriptions and queries. A refined matching algorithm was developed to perform requirement-capability matchmaking that takes into account not only the ontology concepts, but also the properties of the concepts.

1 Introduction

In today's network-centric computing environment, automatic discovery of resources and the ability to share information and services across different domains are important capabilities [1]. The first step in providing these capabilities is to markup these resources with various metadata in a well-understood and consistent manner. Such annotation will enable resources to be machine-readable and machine-understandable.

Using metadata to find distributed resources that meet one's functional requirements is only the first step. Resource requestors may have additional requirements such as security, survivability, or quality of service (QoS) specifications. For example, they may require resources to possess a certain military classification level, to originate from trusted sources, or to be handled according to a specified privacy policy. Therefore, resources need to be sufficiently annotated with security-related metadata so that they can be correctly discovered, compared, and invoked according to security as well as functional requirements of the requestor.

In this paper, we introduce a set of security-related ontologies collectively referred to as the NRL Security Ontology [2, 3]. The NRL Security Ontology provides the ability for precisely describing security concepts at various levels of detail. This ontology complements existing ontologies that mainly focus on functional aspects of

S. Spaccapietra et al. (Eds.): Journal on Data Semantics IX, LNCS 4601, pp. 167–195, 2007.

capability, content, and parameters. Marking up security aspects of resources is a crucial step toward deploying a secure Service Oriented Architecture (SOA) system.

Other groups have recognized the need for security annotation of services and proposed a set of security-related ontologies [4-6]. However, these ontologies possess certain limitations, discussed in Section 2. The NRL Security Ontology was created to address these limitations. We expect this work to serve as a catalyst in the development of standardized security-related ontologies with contributions from both the security community and the semantic Web community.

The rest of the paper is organized as follows. Section 2 examines previous work in security ontologies and discusses the need for improvements. Section 3 presents the NRL security ontology, including design objectives, domain and scope, and detailed descriptions of each ontology. Section 4 gives examples of how to use these ontologies to annotate and query for resources particularly in a Web service context. It also discusses an algorithm for matchmaking between queries and resource descriptions. Section 5 presents future work and our conclusion.

2   Existing Security-Related Ontologies

Realization of the need for security ontologies is not new. Denker et al. have created several ontologies for specifying security-related information in Web services [4] using Daml+OIL [7] and later OWL [8]. We refer to this set of ontologies as the DAML Security Ontology for the rest of the paper. The authors state that the goal of these ontologies is to enable high-level markup of Web resources, services, and agents, while providing a layer of abstraction on top of various Web service security standards such as XML-Enc [9], XML-Dsig [10], and SAML (Security Assertion Markup Language) [11].

While we realize that these ontologies are works-in-progress and provide a great foundation for describing security-related concepts, we found two issues with them. First, they are not intuitive to understand especially in terms of the organization of subclass relationships. Second, they cannot express all the security information that we want to describe or be easily extended to do so.

The intuitiveness issue is particularly true for the main Security Mechanisms ontology which we depict simplified in Figure 1. Certain unrelated concepts are defined as sibling classes, which does not make sense from either a security perspective or an ontology perspective. For example, the two subclasses Syntax and KeyFormat are defined as sibling classes under the Security Mechanism class. These two subclasses are not security mechanisms, so they should not be children of the Security Mechanism class. Also, they are totally unrelated concepts that should not be siblings. As another example, two individuals, Kerberos and SSH are both declared as instances of the KeyProtocol class, however these are not key protocols. Also, a Security Notation class is defined with various instances, but from a computer security perspective, it does not make sense to group these individuals together. Some instances (such as Confidentiality and Authorization) are security objectives, while Policy is an abstract concept that is used to describe a high level set of rules to achieve these security objectives, and Policy Languages are those that are used to represent policies in some mathematical or logical format [12, 13]. That these various

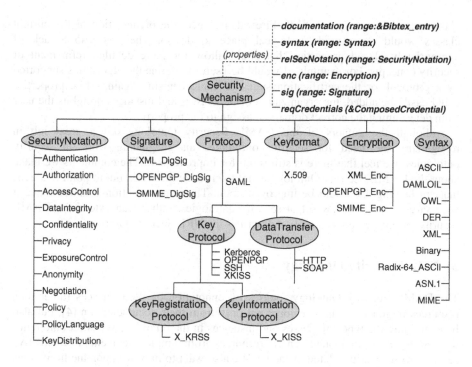

Fig. 1. Graphical Representation of a DAML Security Ontology

concepts are grouped together as instances of the same class is puzzling. Additionally, all properties have the top class as their domains. However, those properties do not apply to most of the subclasses.

The second issue we mentioned is the lack of expressiveness. The DAML security ontology includes many classes and instances that are not directly relevant for security annotation while lacking others that are necessary. For example, syntax and data transfer protocols are useful concepts in another domain, but are not particularly relevant for describing security-related information, yet are included in the DAML security ontology. Furthermore, the only encryption instances defined in the ontology are S/MIME, OpenPGP, and XML encryption. In fact, S/MIME and OpenPGP standards do not only deal with encryption, but have additional capabilities such as key exchange and digital signatures, so how these instances would be used to describe actual encryption mechanisms is unclear. For example, there is no way to state a concept such 'SSH with DES encryption algorithm'. We do realize that more instances and properties could be added as the need arises and is so stated by the DAML Security Ontology authors. However, the way in which the concepts within the DAML Security Ontologies are organized makes it difficult to extend them to add concepts in locations that make sense. For example, there should be classes to represent military as well as commercial security devices and security policies, but there is no appropriate location in the class hierarchy to create, for example, a Security Policy class. If a user wanted to add an instance of XML Firewall to the ontology, it would not fit within any of the current classes. If the user tried to create a class under which to place XML Firewall instance, the organization of the current classes would not provide a logical place to do so. There is also a lack of appropriately placed properties that could allow for more detailed refinement of security concepts. For example, it would be useful to define the algorithms supported by a protocol, or the certification status of a mechanism. Again, while properties could easily be added, the organization of the classes and instances prohibits the user from determining the correct domain to assign to the property.

Although the authors of the DAML Security Ontology did a great job in recognizing the need for security ontologies and beginning work in security ontologies, we feel that there is still room for improvement. The comments we make about the DAML Security Ontology is not to criticize the work, but to point out areas that are lacking and could be improved upon. The issues mentioned above make it necessary to create a new set of security ontologies, rather than extend the DAML security ontology. The next section describes the NRL Security Ontology in detail.

3   NRL Security Ontology

The DAML Security Ontology focuses on annotation of Web services rather than resources in general. This is evident not only from their documentation [4], but also by examining the types of classes and instances in the ontology. We want ontologies that can be used to annotate generic resources from simple documents to interactive services with security-related metadata. We also want to improve upon the limitations of the DAML Security Ontology outlined in the previous section. The NRL Security Ontology was designed with the following objectives in mind:

1. Describe security related information applicable to all types of resources
2. Provide the ability to annotate security related information in various levels of detail for various environments (both commercial and military)
3. Create ontologies that are easy to extend and provide reusability
4. Bridge the gap between the operational people that understand the business logic and the security people that understand the security requirements, particularly in the context of enterprise applications

3.1   Domain and Scope of the Ontology

When creating an ontology, one of the most important factors is the domain and scope in which it will be used [14]. While our objectives outlined above are a good starting point, in order to create ontologies that will be truly useful, we need to understand the types of questions that the ontology will be expected to answer.

These ontologies will be used by both the resource provider and the requestor to express their security requirements and capabilities. We must consider the various ways that the same statement can be expressed. Furthermore, we need to consider statements that are unlikely in order to limit the scope of the ontology. Statements that are either too broad or too specific are unlikely to be used and provide no useful information.

Noy et al. [14] state that one of the best ways to determine the scope of the ontology is to list a set of *competency questions* that can be answered using the ontology. For our purposes we did the same by composing a list of security requirements and capabilities for both the resource requestor and the provider. From the requestor's perspective, security requirements can be stated in terms of specific mechanisms or in terms of abstract security objectives. From the resource provider's perspective, security requirements are similar to the notion of policy and can express concepts such as authentication and access control. The provider's capabilities include protocols and mechanisms that the provider possesses and security policies it adheres to. The actual list of the requirements and capabilities statements we created can be found in [3]. The most current OWL files for the ontology are located at [15].

3.2 Brief Introduction to OWL

We chose OWL to represent our ontologies because of its power to express meaning and semantics and complex relationships. This section gives a very broad overview of OWL to assist readers in understanding the following sections. Readers that are familiar with OWL concepts should skip this section. Readers that are interested in further details of OWL should refer to [8, 16] for additional information.

The basic concepts in OWL are classes, individuals and properties. The basic construct in OWL are classes. Classes describe concepts in the knowledge domain. For example, the class Soda could refer to all classes of carbonated beverages. Individuals or instances are specific members of the class. For example, Mountain Dew and Dr. Pepper can be instances of the Soda class. The Soda class itself can have subclasses that represent concepts that are more specific than its parent class. The classes Diet Soda and Decaf Soda can represent classes of sodas that are diet and contain no caffeine, respectively.

Properties can further define relationships between classes, constrain classes or describe various attributes of classes. There are two types of properties; object properties and datatype properties. Object properties relate instances of one class to instances of another class. An example of an object property can be *manufacturedBy* to represent the ownership relationship between various Soda instances and Soda Manufacturer instances. The *manufacturedBy* property can be defined to have a domain of the class Soda, and a range of the class Soda Companies. Then, an instance such as Mountain Dew can be declared to be manufactured by the Pepsi Corporation. Datatype properties relate instances of a class to RDF literals or XML Schema Datatypes. An example of a datatype property can be *hasSugar* to determine whether a soda instance contains sugar or not. In this case, the domain for the property would be the Soda class, and the range would be a Boolean.

Similar to the Subclass relationship, properties can also be defined as subproperties of other properties. Subproperties have domains and ranges that are subsets of the parent property. Properties themselves can also contain further information by being defined as being transitive, symmetric, etc using constructs such as TransitiveProperty, Symmetric Property, etc.

Restrictions can be placed on these properties so that classes can only contain a specific number of instances (minCardinality, maxCardinality) of a property. For example, we can restrict the Soda class so that it can possess only one *manufacturedBy* property value. Property restrictions can also be placed on values so that the range of the property must contain all values, some values or a particular value from a class. For example, we can restrict the *manufacturedBy* property to only contain values from the class of Soda Companies.

Additional expressive powers of OWL come from OWL Class Constructors and OWL Axioms. For example, the unionOf construct can be used to represent the class of all sodas that are diet and contain no caffeine. Other constructs defined in OWL include IntersectionOf, ComplementOf, etc. An example of a class axiom is the equivalentClass. The equivalentClass construct defines two classes to have the same instances. A class defined as Pop can be declared as an equivalentClass of Soda, to address the terminology of the Midwestern U.S. region. Similarly, the sameAs construct can be used to create different names for the same individual or instance.

Throughout this paper, we represent classes as text within a circle, instances as regular text, properties as italicized text, with the relationship between domain and range of the property shown with a dotted line.

OWL has three sublanguages, OWL-Lite, OWL-DL, and OWL-Full with increasing levels of expressiveness. We use OWL-DL to develop our ontologies since OWL DL provides strong expressiveness sufficient for what we intend to express, while retaining computational completeness and decidability for reasoning systems.

3.3 Organizational Structure of NRL Security Ontology

We chose OWL to create our ontologies because it provides a rich vocabulary for describing classes and properties [8, 16]. It is widely used in many communities that have begun to develop ontologies of their own knowledge domains [17].

There are seven separate ontologies that make up the NRL Security Ontology:

1. Main Security ontology: an ontology to describe security concepts that are the starting point in which users begin to identify various security components
2. Credentials ontology: an ontology to specify various authentication credentials such as passwords or PIN numbers for user authentication
3. Security Algorithms ontology: an ontology to describe various security algorithms such as algorithms for encryption, digital signatures, and key exchange
4. Security Assurance ontology: an ontology to specify different assurance standards used to specify the level of trust that can be placed on a security component or product
5. Service Security ontology: an ontology to facilitate security annotation of semantic Web services using OWL-S (Profile), an ontology to describe Web services
6. Agent Security ontology: an ontology to enable querying of security information from the agent (consumer) prospective used as an alternative method of querying with the OWL-S Profile particularly when the agent is not a Web service and cannot use the OWL-S profile
7. Information Object ontology: an ontology to describe security of input and output parameters of Web services used specifically to specify whether an input/output parameter is encrypted, what algorithm is used for the encryption, etc.

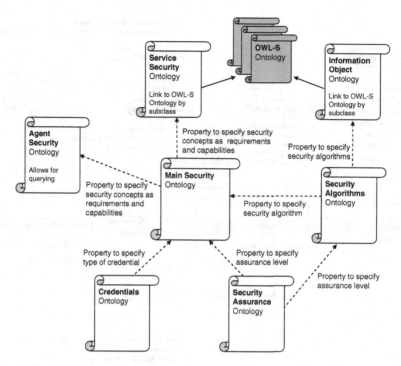

Fig. 2. Graphical Representation of Security-Related Ontologies and Their Relationships

The Service Security, Agent Security, and Information Object ontologies are based closely on corresponding DAML Security ontologies while the others are new. The Credentials, Security Algorithms, and Security Assurance ontologies provide values for properties defined for concepts in the Main Security ontology. They enable concepts from the Main Security ontology to be described in more detail with respect to types of credentials used, supported algorithms, and associated levels of assurance. For example, a concept such as Security Protocol in the Main Security ontology can be further refined by properties that take as range values algorithms, credentials, and assurance levels. The Service Security ontology provides the means to use security concepts from the Main Security ontology in the Web services framework. The Agent Service ontology enables creation of security-related queries using security concepts from the Main Security ontology for consumers that are not themselves Web services. The Information Object ontology allows for annotation of Web service inputs and outputs using the Security Algorithms ontology. The relationship among these ontologies is represented in Figure 2. The ontology depicted in gray represents OWL-S, a set of core ontologies created specifically to describe Web services. We chose to use OWL-S since it uses OWL constructs and provides rich semantic description of Web services.

Next, we present a brief explanation of classes, properties and relationships in each ontology. The actual OWL files for the NRL Ontology can be found in [3, 15].

Main Security Ontology (securityMain.owl). The core ontology in the NRL security ontology set is the Main Security ontology (Figures 3a and 3b). It imports the Credentials

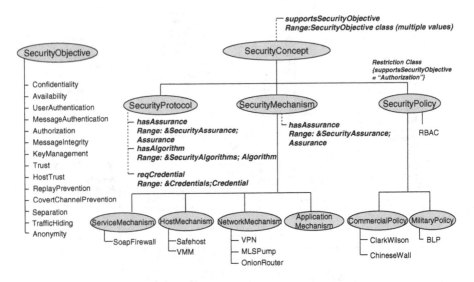

Fig. 3a. Main Security Ontology

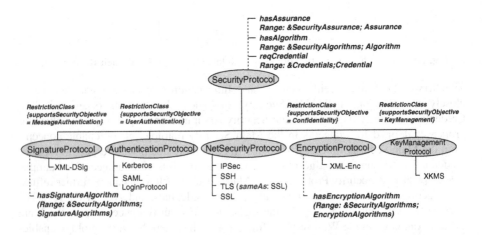

Fig. 3b. Security Protocol Class of the Main Security Ontology

ontology, Security Algorithms ontology, and Security Assurance ontology as object properties. The top class, 'SecurityConcept' possesses three subclasses: 'Security Protocol', 'SecurityMechanism' and 'SecurityPolicy'. Due to space limitat-ions, the SecurityProtocol class, along with its children and properties are depicted separately in Figure 3b.

In the computer science literature, security objectives are goals that attempt to minimize risks and vulnerabilities to assets, policies partition the system into secure and insecure states (while stating which security objectives are to be upheld), and mechanisms and protocols enforce the policy [12, 13]. While some may argue that the distinction between security protocols and security mechanisms is blurred, we define security protocols as an agreed upon series of steps to accomplish a task while security mechanisms are implementations of protocols [18]. We specifically differentiate them here to provide the ability to describe security concepts in both manners.

The Main Security ontology has a separate class called 'SecurityObjective' that enables users to specify security objectives for the 'SecurityConcept' class using the *supportsSecurityObjective* property. For example, IPSec is declared to have Confidentiality, MessageAuthentication, and TrafficHiding as its *supportsSecurity Objective* property values. Security objectives also enable users to search for protocols, mechanisms, or policies based on the security objective they require. For example, users can query, "find all instances that provide confidentiality" and receive a list of all the security concepts that have a value of Confidentiality in their *supportsSecurityObjective* property.

Another way we can use 'SecurityObjective' is to enable security descriptions when concrete security information is unavailable at the time. For instance, assume that an enterprise application planner designs two applications, App1 and App2, and the military requirement states that these two should have separation between them. However, at the planning stage, it is unknown in what (security) environment these applications will be deployed. In computer security, the environment is a factor in determining the type of security mechanism to be used. The enterprise application planner can still use the ontology to specify the security objective of Separation as a requirement. When the application is moved to a real system and ready to be deployed, the application deployer can then search for instances in the 'SecurityConcept' class that provide Separation, and choose one that is available in his environment. In this case, VPN happens to be the only mechanism that provides separation, so he can replace the Separation requirement with a VPN requirement.

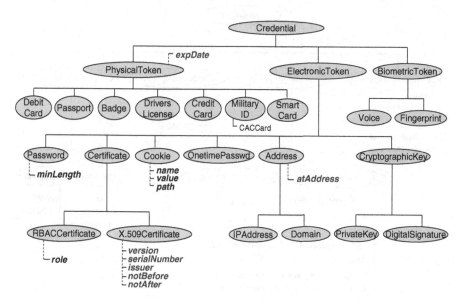

Fig. 4. Credentials Ontology

Credentials Ontology (credentials.owl). Authentication is one of the most fundamental security requirements in a networked environment. The Credentials ontology allows for specification of credentials used for authentication purposes (Figure 4). Concepts in the Security Main ontology can refer to a specific credential through their *reqCredential* property. While we adopted some of the notations in the DAML Credential ontology, we improved upon it by reorganizing and creating classes to be more intuitive from a computer security perspective, categorizes credentials into physical token, electronic token, and biometric token, using the basic 'what you have', 'what you know', and 'what you are' concepts of authentication [18]. Arranging the subclasses in this manner allows for easily extending the ontology if the need arises, since all basic authentication mechanisms fall into one of these three categories.

Under the 'PhysicalToken' class, we kept many of the classes from the DAML Credential ontology under their 'IDCard' class. In addition, we created a class to describe military IDs and an instance to represent CAC (Common Access Card) cards used in the military. The ontology can be extended to add properties such as issuing agency, expiration date, issue date, etc. Under the 'ElectronicToken' class, we provide subclasses that enable authentication based on host address, certificates, passwords, and cryptographic keys to name a few. Additional properties were added to describe certificates including the issuer, version and serial number under the Certificate class. In order to support role-based (RBAC) certificates [19], an 'RBACCertificate' class was created as a subclass of the Certificate class with a *role* property. The 'BiometricToken' class represents credentials that pertain to human traits. For now, only 'Voice' and 'Fingerprint' subclasses are defined here.

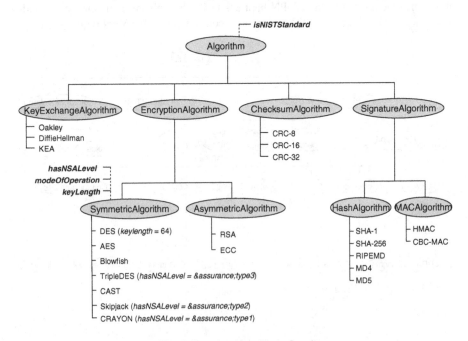

Fig. 5. Security Algorithms Ontology

When the Security Main ontology uses the Credentials ontology through its *reqCredential* property, there is no cardinality restriction. Therefore, multifactor credential requirements (cases where two or more types of authentication is required, such as the use of a smart card with a PIN) can easily be represented by specifying two or more credentials for the *reqCredential* property values.

Security Algorithms Ontology (securityAlgorithms.owl). The Security Algorithms ontology was created to enable description of various security algorithms (Figure 5). The Security Main ontology can use the Security Algorithms ontology to specify the types of algorithms that are supported by various security protocols and mechanisms. The algorithms are classified into key exchange algorithms, encryption algorithms, checksum algorithms, and signature algorithms. In particular, the symmetric encryption algorithms can further be described by the type of certification level it received from the NSA (*hasNSALevel* property), the modes of operation that the algorithm can support, and the various key lengths that are available.

Security Assurance Ontology (securityAssurance.owl). The Security Assurance ontology provides a way to describe standardized assurance methods for security protocols, mechanisms, and algorithms (Figure 6). They can be described in terms of their assurance level using the *hasAssurance* property from the Main Security ontology. The 'Assurance' class is classified according to different assurance methods: 'Standard', 'Accreditation', 'Evaluation', and 'Certification'. This ontology is the least compete of all our ontologies. However, we have added classes to describe the Common Criteria and TCSEC evaluations, and the FIPS and NSA standards [20].

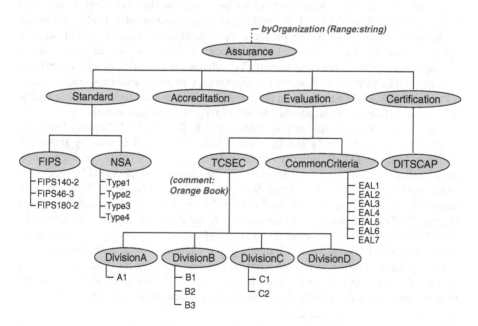

Fig. 6. Security Assurance Ontology

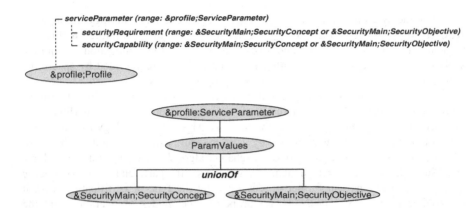

Fig. 7. Service Security Ontology

Service Security Ontology (serviceSecurity.owl). OWL-S [21] is an OWL-based semantic markup description language that provides a core set of constructs for describing Web services specifically. It provides a set of ontologies called Profile, Process, and Grounding to describe Web services. The Profile describes services in terms of what the service does (and can also be used to describe what is requested of a service), the Process describes how to use it, and the Grounding specifies how to interact with it.

In order for the NRL Security Ontology to be used in the Web service context, a link must be made to the OWL-S ontologies so that security related information can be included in an OWL-S specification. Specifically, we decided to add security specifications to the OWL-S Profile since it provides features to specify characteristics of a service, and security is a characteristic. Additionally, clients can also use OWL-S Profile to describe the service they request, without having to create a Process or Grounding as well. In the future, we may expand the ontology to enable security specifications to be attached to other OWL-S ontologies as well.

The Service Security ontology was developed to link the NRL Security Ontology to the OWL-S Profile in a similar manner that to the Service Security Extension ontology from the DAML security ontology. In the Service Security ontology, a new class called ParamValues is defined as the union of 'SecurityConcept' and 'SecurityObjective' from the Main Security ontology. This ParamValue is then defined as a subclass of the 'ServiceParameter' class in the OWL-S Profile ontology (Figure 7). This enables security annotations to be described as service parameters. The OWL-S Profile also contains a *serviceParameter* property that can have ServiceParameter as its value[1]. Extending the definition of the Profile class by declaring two properties, *securityRequirement* and *securityCapability* as subproperties of the *serviceParameter* property enables the OWL-S Profile to include security requirements and security capabilities in its service description. We continue the use

---

[1] Note that the OWL-S Profile ontology has a property and class of the same name, service parameter. However, the property starts with a lowercase letter, while the class starts with an uppercase letter. Thus, *serviceParameter* refers to a property while ServiceParameter refers to a class.

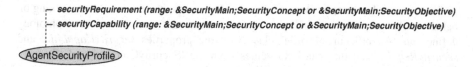

securityRequirement (range: &SecurityMain;SecurityConcept or &SecurityMain;SecurityObjective)

securityCapability (range: &SecurityMain;SecurityConcept or &SecurityMain;SecurityObjective)

AgentSecurityProfile

Fig. 8. Agent Security Ontology

of the terminology of 'security capability' and 'security requirement' from [4]. Furthermore, we defined the range for these subproperties as ParamValues so they accept values from 'SecurityConcept' or 'SecurityObjective' classes. This allows security requirements and capabilities to be stated in terms of either a particular security objective, or a specific security mechanism.

Agent Security Ontology (agentSecurity.owl). Not only do Web services have security capabilities and requirements that need to be described, but the service consumer also possesses its own set of security capabilities and requirements. The Agent Security ontology allows consumers to describe this security-related information to query Web services to find ones that have compatible requirements and capabilities (Figure 8). The DAML Security Ontologies have an agent security ontology as well that ours is based upon. We decided to maintain the use of a separate agent security ontology to describe consumer-side security specifications for two reasons. First, when the consumer itself is also a Web service, it can still use the OWL-S Profile to describe its security requirements and capabilities. However, we cannot expect the consumer to always be a Web service. It can be a Web browser or end-user application. In these cases, it makes sense to have a separate ontology for consumer-side specifications. Second, when consumers describe their security specifications, they can either describe them as their own requirements and compare that to the service's capabilities, or they can describe the capabilities they want from their ideal service, and match that against various service capability descriptions. Using the agent security ontology allows users to easily differentiate between these two methods of security specification. For the latter case, the consumer can use the OWL-S profile to describe its ideal service. For the former case, they use the agent security ontology to describe their own requirements, and matchmaking is done accordingly. This issue is further discussed in Section 4.2.

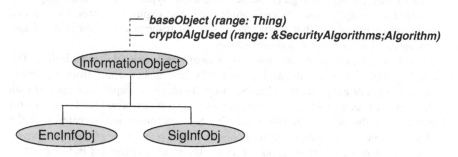

baseObject (range: Thing)

cryptoAlgUsed (range: &SecurityAlgorithms;Algorithm)

InformationObject

EncInfObj   SigInfObj

Fig. 9. Information Object Ontology

Since in a truly semantic Web, a semantically-aware program would be working on behalf of the user, we use the term 'agent' to represent this concept. The ontology defines an 'AgentSecurityProfile' class with the properties *securityCapability* and *securityRequirement* that can hold values from the 'SecurityConcept' and 'Security Objective' classes.

Information Object Ontology (InfObj.owl). The Information Object ontology is based very closely on a DAML ontology of the same name, created to capture encrypted or signed input/output data of Web services. It has an 'InfObj' class and two subclasses, 'EncInfObj' (Encrypted Information Object) and 'SigInfObj' (Signed Information Object) (Figure 9). The 'InfObj' class is used as the range for input and output parameters of services described with OWL-S. The ontology has the *cryptoAlgUsed* property to specify the algorithm used to encrypt or sign the object. In the original DAML ontology, the *cryptoAlgUsed* property pointed to a set of algorithms defined within the DAML Information Object ontology. However, we felt that the two concepts of information object and security algorithms were so dissimilar that they did not belong within the same ontology file. Hence, in the NRL Information Object ontology, the *cryptoAlgUsed* property points to classes in the Security Algorithms ontology.

3.4   Design Objectives Revisited

At the beginning of Section 3 we outlined a set of objectives expected to be achieved by the NRL Security Ontology. This subsection discusses whether those design objectives were met and to what degree.

1. **Describe security related information not only for Web services, but for all types of resources:** The NRL Security Ontology enables us to describe security information of various types of resources. We can describe security protocols that are specific to Web services such as XML-enc and SAML, but also include many protocols and mechanisms such as IPSec, Kerberos and SSH that are generally applied to any resource.
2. **Provide the ability to annotate security related information in various levels of detail for various environments:** The ontology can provide specific details of security mechanisms through properties such as the types of algorithms supported, required key length, types of credentials used, and expiration dates. Classes and instances were created that enable description of resources relevant to a military environment as well as for commercial use.
3. **Create ontologies that are easy to extend and provide reusability:** The ontologies are created with a class hierarchy that makes sense from a security perspective. For example, the Main Security Ontology concepts were created with the notion of security objectives, policies that support objectives, and mechanisms that enforce the policy. Classes in the Credential ontology were created with the classification of authentication mechanisms ('what you know', 'what you have', and 'what you are') kept in mind. Because classes were organized in this manner, following the convention of computer security professionals, it is easier to extend the ontologies. For example, when a new instance needs to be created, it is simple to figure out which class it should belong to. It is also easier to create properties with the correct domain and range values.

4. **Bridge the gap between the operational people that understand the business logic and the security people that understand the security requirements, particularly in the context of enterprise applications:** Both parties may want to add security requirements into the enterprise application but from different perspectives. The operational people can specify security requirements on the enterprise application from a high-level perspective (e.g. security objectives) even if they're not familiar with the technical aspects or know what environment the application will be running in and what mechanisms will be available. This allows the operational people to still communicate the basic security requirements they need to the security people. The security people can view these security specifications, and along with their knowledge of deployment environment and available mechanisms, provide more specific security requirements in a context-appropriate manner that can later be viewed by the operation people if necessary.

In the next section, we will provide some examples of how to apply these ontologies to annotate resources with security information.

4 Application of NRL Security Ontology to a Service Oriented Architecture

The NRL Security Ontology was designed to describe security-related information of resources in general. In this section, we demonstrate how to annotate Web services in a Service Oriented Architecture. In particular, we focus on:

- How to annotate Web services with security requirements and capabilities
- How to create queries for finding Web services with given security requirements and capabilities
- How to perform matchmaking between queries and service descriptions in the SOA context

4.1 Annotating Web Services with Security Descriptions

OWL-S introduces a set of ontologies to provide "essential knowledge about a service." In particular, the OWL-S Profile ontology is used to describe "what does a Web service require of the user(s) or other agents and provide for them" [22]. The semantic annotation of Web services can be extended with the NRL Security ontology to describe the security specifications of the services. Thus, we extended the definition of the Profile class in the OWL-S Profile ontology. The Service Security ontology that was described in section 3.3 shows the linkage between OWL-S Profile ontology and NRL Security ontology.

In this manner, security requirements and capabilities are attached as properties to the service profile. Security capabilities are defined as security features that the service is capable of while security requirements are features that must be satisfied by any entity using the service. Security requirements and capabilities can possess values from the Security Main ontology. The values may be abstract notions, such as a security objective, or detailed mechanisms, such as a specific protocol with a given algorithm.

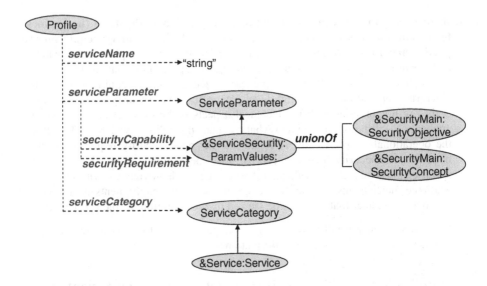

Fig. 10. Graphical Depiction of Relationship between Profile, Service and Security Main

In describing security capabilities and security requirements, we make some basic assumptions. Security requirements are those that need to be satisfied by the other party. Therefore, if an entity (service or consumer) has a service requirement, it is implied that they also have that particular capability, so it does not need to be restated as a capability. For instance, if a service requires the consumer to use SSL, it implies that the service is capable of using SSL as well. Therefore, if the service states the use of SSL as a requirement, it does not need to state it as a capability. On the other hand, just because an entity lists a capability, it does not mean that this is a requirement of that entity. For example, many security protocols such as SSH, SSL, and IPSec provide a list of encryption algorithms that they support (i.e. are capable of), but do not require the other party to possess.

We created a simple Service ontology to semantically describe the category of the business service. The concepts in the Service ontology are defined as subclasses of the ServiceCategory concept in the OWL-S Profile ontology so that they can be used in conjunction with the Profile. Having the Service ontology described in this manner enables users to use the ServiceCategory concept in two ways; describing service categorizations based on some classification scheme, or using the Service ontology provided here. This Service ontology was created ad-hoc, in order to provide a semantic business service description and is no where near complete. Therefore, it is not worth describing here. Figure 10 shows the relationship between the OWL-S Profile, NRL Service Security Ontology, NRL Security Main Ontology and the sample Service ontology.

Next, we provide two example service profiles for some imaginary services, Acme Stock Quotes and Anya's Rare Books, using all these ontologies. A graphical depiction of the service profiles are shown in Figure 11. As can be seen in the figure, security capabilities and requirements are attached to the service profile through the use of properties (i.e., *securityRequirement* and *securityCapability*). These take concepts from the Security Main ontology, which in turn may use concepts from other ontologies in the NRL Security Ontology. A snippet of the OWL code for these service profiles can be found in the Appendix.

As can be noted in Figure 11, when credentials are used as range values for the *reqCredential* property, the class values are attached. Credentials are so varied for each organization and individual, that it is not possible to represent all instances of them. For example, an X.509 Certificate is one mechanism used for authentication. Each user can have at least one, and each can be issued by a trusted 3rd party organization. To create possible instances of X.509 certificates for each user with property annotations such as *issuedBy* was deemed unreasonable. Therefore, when creating service profiles, we simply allow various credentials (classes) to be used as property range values.

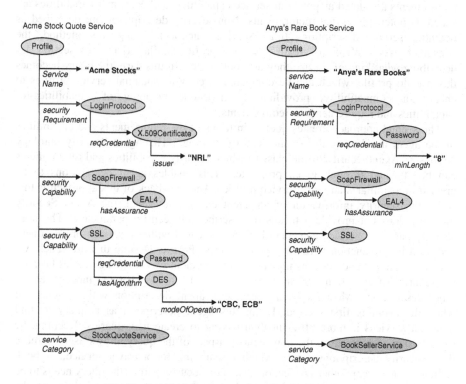

Fig. 11. Graphical Depiction of Profiles for Two Services

4.2 Creating Queries to Find Services

To query for a resource, there are two parts to be considered. One is the security description and the other is the non-security description. We define everything not related to security as non-security descriptions. If an agent is looking for a travel reservation service or a book buying service, this would fall under the non-security description category. Under this definition, specific objects within the service description such as price and credit card number are also part of the non-security description. These objects may require security specifications to be attached to them, such as adding the requirement of confidentiality to a credit card number, but the objects themselves are not security related (although they may contain private or sensitive information). Security requirements for such objects can be specified using the Information Object ontology. The security descriptions are the security capabilities and requirements that the agent possesses (and thus should be satisfied by a potential service).

When creating these queries with security descriptions, there are two approaches that can be used depending on how the security requirements and capabilities are stated. The first approach is to state the query in terms of the security descriptions of the service profile. In other words, consumers state their security statements (capabilities and requirements) in terms of their ideal service. Thus, consumer requirements are stated as potential service capabilities and consumer capabilities are stated as potential service requirements. Non-security descriptions are described as potential service descriptions (e.g., service category). Using this method, the consumer uses OWL-S to create a service profile similar to that of section 4.1 describing what kind of service they are looking for. In this case, the query becomes this pseudo profile, which can be compared directly to potential service profiles to check for compatibility, providing a one-to-one mapping of capabilities-to-capabilities and requirements-to-requirements.

The second approach creates queries in terms of the requirements and capabilities of the agent itself using the Agent Security ontology. The Agent Security ontology defines an AgentSecurityProfile class to which security capabilities and requirements can be attached through given properties. This enables agent descriptions to be created in a similar manner to service profiles. The drawback of this approach is that while the security information of an agent can be described, the Agent Security ontology does not provide a means to describe non-security parameters. The non-security part (i.e., service category) has to be created within a service profile query and used in conjunction with the Agent Security Profile. Despite this drawback, we believe that in many cases, this may be a more efficient way to create queries because the security specifications (of an agent or service) can be generated independent of other descriptions. Most likely, a consumer's agent description will be generated when the agent is first created. Using this agent description as a query to find potential services is more efficient than having to create new queries. Keeping the security part separate from the non-security aspect of the query allows users to reuse their security descriptions. Thus, whether searching for a travel service, or book selling service or any other service, only the non-security part of the query needs to be changed, and as long as the agent's capabilities and requirements remain the same, the security part of the query need only be created once and remain intact. Figure 12 shows an example query created using the AgentSecurityProfile class.

We have also created a prototype system and set of tools that facilitate ontology browsing, query creation and matchmaking. In our prototype, OWL documents (ontologies and service descriptions) are imported into the registry (UDDI) data structures using a lossless translation scheme that fully supports property annotations and allows for semantic query processing [23, 24]. The associated tools support both methods of creating queries. However, the prototype and tools are not the scope of this paper. Interested readers are directed to [25] for further information.

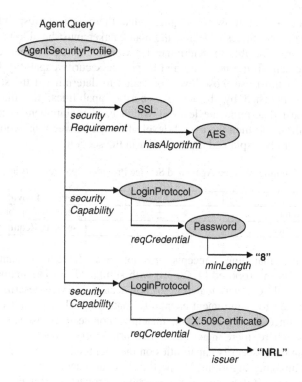

Fig. 12. Graphical Depiction of Example Agent Security Profile

4.3 Reasoning and Matching Algorithm

We have stated that both resource consumers (i.e., agents) and providers may have security requirements and capabilities. Matchmaking looks for a two-way correspondence between these requirements and capabilities. When querying for services using the first method described in section 4.2, the matching algorithm is quite simple. It is just a matter of the pseudo profile being a subset of the actual service profiles. However, when describing agent security information with the latter approach, the matching algorithm is more complex. The service security requirements are compared to agent security capabilities and service security capabilities are compared to agent security requirements. In order for a match of security concepts to occur between a service provider and an agent, two conditions should be met. First, the service provider's security capabilities should satisfy all the agent's security requirements. Second, the service provider's security requirements should all be satisfied by the agent's security capabilities. This implies that the list of capabilities from one side should subsume the list of requirements from the other (Table 1).

Every single agent security requirement must have a corresponding security capability on the service provider side to satisfy it. Likewise, every single server security requirement must have a corresponding security capability on the agent side that satisfies the requirement. This also implies that the security capabilities of each side do not need to be satisfied: there may be many security capabilities that a service or agent possesses, but it is not required that there is a corresponding security requirement that necessitates it. Hence the matchmaker must be able to perform two tasks. First, it must be able to determine the level of match between each specific security requirement from one entity and a specific security capability from another entity. Second, it must use those levels of match to determine if the set of security requirements is matched by the set of security capabilities. In other words, the matchmaker must determine the level at which each requirement is matched to a security capability, and then the overall level of match between the requester and the provider. This will be explained in detail later in the section.

Table 1. The Matching between Agent and Service Provider Requirements and Capabilities

Agent		Service Provider
Security Requirements	$\subseteq$	Security Capabilities
Security Capabilities	$\supseteq$	Security Requirements

These specific matching concepts are not new. Several semantic matching algorithms have been proposed [4, 26-30] with similar ideas. The majority of these [26-30] support only one-way matching of non-security service descriptions to agent queries as opposed to requirement-capability matching. They do not consider two-way matching since their focus is on matching non-security aspects; they do not consider cases where there may be non-security requirements from the service provider-side and non-security capabilities on the agent-side to be expressed. The last proposed matchmaking algorithm [4] performs requirement-capability matching for both sides. However, it does not take into account property attributes. Consequently, it will not support cases where both the requirement and capability point to the same concept but the concepts are annotated with different properties. For example, the agent and service provider may both use SSH (stated as a requirement on one side and a capability on the other), but if the agent requires SSH using TripleDES and the service provider is only capable of SSH with AES then these two should not match. Our matchmaker extends their matching algorithm by performing requirement-capability matching, taking into account property annotations.

Specifically, when describing security information of resources, the ability to include properties in the matching algorithm is very important. This is due to the fact that security information can require detailed descriptions that make extensive use of properties. Complex statements can be made with multiple layers of properties. For example, there could be a security requirement that requires the use of XML-enc (*securityRequirement* property) with a symmetric encryption algorithm (*hasAlgorithm* property) that has been declared a type 3 algorithm from the NSA (*hasNSALevel* property).

In particular, when a concept is annotated with properties, we consider it to be more restrictive than the same concept with no (or less) property annotations. For example, a requirement for a user to input a password is not as restrictive as a requirement for a password that is at least 8 characters long. A requirement to use SSH is less restrictive than one that states using SSH with a specific encryption algorithm such as DES.

There are four possible levels of match for each requirement-capability pair: perfect match, close match, possible match, and no match in decreasing order of matching. The first task of the matchmaker is to determine the kind of match.

Perfect Match cases. Perfect matches occur when both one's capability and the other's requirement point to the same concept. The same concept can mean the exact same concept, or two concepts declared as equivalent in the ontology. There are two ways this can occur:

- **Case 1.** Both the requirement and capability specify the exact same ontology concept. The instances and property values specified by both sides are identical. This is the trivial case. For example, if an agent query states that it requires the service to possess a VPN (Virtual Private Network) that possesses a Common Criteria EAL4 rating and a service describes its capability as possessing a VPN with a Common Criteria rating of EAL 4 then these two are a perfect match.
- **Case 2.** The requirement and capability refer to equivalent concepts, and if properties are specified, the properties are identical or equivalent. For example, an agent's requirement specifies SSL and the service provider's capability is listed as TLS. In the Main Security ontology, these two concepts are listed as equivalent classes; hence they are identical and will produce a perfect match. We sometimes call this an equivalence match to differentiate from the first case. This case is worth noting because it shows that our matching algorithm can fully support OWL equivalence classes and the *sameAs* construct. It can also provide more matches for a given query. Another reason to treat it as a separate case is for instances where users may not be aware that some concepts have identical meaning, or that they are considered identical in an ontology.

Close Match cases. A close match occurs when one's requirement is more general (i.e., described in less detail) than the other's capability. There are three ways this can occur:

- **Case 1.** The requirement specifies a more general concept at a higher level in the ontological hierarchy. For example, the agent's capability is stated as DES while the service provider's requirement asks for a symmetric encryption algorithm. DES is an instance of the 'SymmetricAlgorithm' class and thus lower in the hierarchy. We assume that the service provider specified its requirement as a higher level concept because it does not care which specific algorithm is used as long as it is a symmetric encryption algorithm. Therefore, we can assume a match.
- **Case 2.** The requirement and capability have the same concept, but the capability is specified in more detail (i.e., property). For example, the agent's capability is specified as AES with 256 bit keys while the service provider's requirement asks for AES (with no properties). AES with 256 bit keys is a more specific instance of AES so we can assume that there is a match.
- **Case 3.** The requirement is stated in terms of a security objective while the capability is stated in terms of a security concept that supports that specific objective. For example, the agent's requirement is stated as the objective of Confidentiality and the service provider's capability is given as XML-Enc which has the *supportsSecurityObjective* value of Confidentiality. Since the requirement is looking for anything that supports Confidentiality and XML-Enc does support it, we view this as a match.

In these three cases, it may seem that the matches are indeed similar to the perfect match cases, and in most cases this may turn out to be true. However, we cannot guarantee that this will always be the situation, so we distinguish them as close matches instead. For instance, in case 2, while the AES standard specifies mandatory key lengths that must be supported, some vendors may also provide optional key lengths in addition to the standard. Therefore, while one side may specify AES as a general requirement, it does not mean it will support all possible vendor-specific key lengths. Similar arguments for close matches can be made for the other two cases.

Possible Match cases. A possible match occurs when one's requirement is more specific (i.e., defined in more detail) than the other's capability. This is the opposite of a close match. A possible match does not rule out the possibility of a match, but the information available cannot ensure the capability can match the requirement. Further negotiation between the consumer and service provider may be required. There are three ways this can occur:

- **Case 1.** The requirement specifies a more specific concept (lower in the hierarchy). For example, the agent's capability is stated as symmetric encryption algorithm while the service provider's requirement asks for DES. The symmetric encryption algorithm that the agent is capable of could be DES, but it is not certain. Therefore, it is only a partial match.
- **Case 2.** The requirement and capability refer to the same concept, but the requirement specifies a more refined concept (i.e. property). For example, the capability is stated as AES while the requirement asks for AES with 256-bit keys. The AES specified in the capability could be possible of 256-bit key encryption, but it is not certain. Therefore, it is only a partial match.
- **Case 3.** The requirement is stated in terms of a security concept while the capability is stated in terms of a security objective that is supported by the security concept. For example, the agent's requirement is stated as confidentiality while the service provider's capability is stated as XML-Enc which supports confidentiality. The agent may be capable of using XML-Enc, but it is not certain. All we can deduce is that the agent is capable of confidentiality. Therefore, it is only a partial match.

No Match cases. No match occurs when one's capability and the other's requirement are disparate without the possibility of matching. There are two ways this can occur:

- **Case 1.** The requirement and capability point to two unrelated concepts. For example, the requirement states it requires DES and the capability states its capability as RSA. These concepts have no hierarchical relationship to each other and so are unrelated. There can be no match.
- **Case 2.** The requirement and capability point to the same concept but have different specifics (i.e. properties) with respect to that concept. For example, the requirement points to AES in CBC mode while the capability states AES in CFB mode. The capability and requirement can both use AES, but they require modes of operation; one is a block cipher the other is a stream cipher so they are not compatible.

For the second task of the matchmaker, it must attempt to match every requirement on one side against every capability on the other side. The degree of match for a single requirement is its highest level of match it has against all of the possible capabilities. The overall level of match between the agent and the service provider is the same as the lowest degree of match of any of the requirement-capability pairs. There are four possibilities:

- If at least one of the requirements is not matched, then the agent is not matched to the service provider. The requestor will not be able to use the service.
- If all the requirement-capability pairs are at least possible matches, then there is a possible match between the agent and the service provider. This means there is not enough information to determine one way or the other whether the agent can use the service. Additional information or negotiation will be needed to make that determination.
- If all the requirement-capability pairs are at least close matches, then it is highly probable that the agent can indeed use the service.
- If all the requirement-capability pairs are perfect matches, then obviously the agent can use the service.

In the following section, we will provide an example of the matching process between a service description and an agent query.

4.4 Application of the Matching Algorithm

In the previous subsections we examined how to actually describe services and create queries using the security ontologies, and how the matching algorithm works. In this subsection, we will show how to apply the matching algorithm to the service and agent profiles from the previous subsections.

Recapping the previous sections, we had two service profiles (Figure 9). One for a stock quote service, and the other for a book selling service. We also created an agent security profile (Figure 10) that can be used as a query in finding a compatible service. For the purposes of this paper, we will ignore the Service Category part of the service profile and only focus on the matching of security requirements and capabilities.

Given these two service descriptions and the agent query, the matching algorithm would match the requestor's capabilities to the provider's requirements and the requestor's requirements to the provider's capabilities in the following manner (Tables 2 and 3):

Table 2. Matching Agent Capabilities to Stock Quote Service's Requirements

Service Security Requirement	Agent Security Capability	Match Level
Login with X.509 Certificate issued by NRL	Login with password that has a min. length of 8	No Match
	Login with X.509 Certificate issued by NRL	Perfect Match

Table 3. Matching Stock Quote Service's Capabilities to Agent's Requirements

Service Security Capability	Agent Security Requirement	Match Level
SOAP Firewall with Common Criteria level EAL4	SSL with AES algorithm	No Match
SSL		Possible Match

- In Table 2, there is only one service security requirement that must be satisfied. Of the two possible capabilities that the agent possesses, the first one is no match, but the second capability is a perfect match. Hence, there is an agent capability that perfectly matches the service's requirement
- In Table 3 there is one agent security requirement that has to be fulfilled. While the first service capability listed does not match at all, the second service capability possesses the same concept of SSL, but with less detail. This is Case 2 of the possible match situation. Overall, it is possible that the agent security requirement may be satisfied by one of the capabilities of the service

Since the lowest level of match in the sets of requirement-capability pairs is possible match, the matchmaker will declare the service to be a possible match. The requester is not certain whether it can use the service. It must obtain additional information or negotiate with the provider to make that decision.

Using the same query, and matching it to the second service profile, Anya's Book Service (figure 10), we get the following results summarized in Tables 4 and 5.

Table 4. Matching Agent Capabilities to Anya's Book Service's Requirements

Service Security Requirement	Agent Security Capability	Match Level
Login with password that has a min. length of 8	Login with password that has a min. length of 8	Perfect Match
	Login with X.509 Certificate issued by NRL	No Match

Table 5. Matching Anya's Book Service's Capabilities to Agent's Requirements

Service Security Capability	Agent Security Requirement	Match Level
SOAP Firewall with Common Criteria level EAL4	SSL with AES algorithm	No Match
SSL with DES, AES, and DiffieHellman algorithm		Close Match

- In Table 4, there is only one service security requirement that must be satisfied. Of the two possible capabilities that the agent possesses, the first one is a no match, but the second capability is a perfect match. Hence, there is an agent capability that perfectly matches the service's requirement
- In Table 5 there is one agent security requirement that has to be fulfilled. While the first service capability listed does not match at all, the second service capability possesses the same concept of SSL, but with less detail. This is Case 2 of the close match situation.

Since the lowest level of match in the sets of requirement-capability pairs is close match, the matchmaker will declare the service to be a close match.

Given this query and the two services, Anya's Book Service would be a better match to the agent, since it is a close match whereas the Stock Quote Service is a possible match.

5 Conclusion and Future Work

Annotating resources with metadata enables them to be machine-understandable and facilitates automatic discovery and invocation. Most work in the area thus far has focused on annotation of resources in terms of functionality. However, security is an important issue especially in a network-centric environment. Most resources on the network are protected by some sort of security mechanisms. Satisfying functional requirements alone may not guarantee access to desired resources. As a result, annotation of resources in terms of security is just as important as annotation in terms of functionality.

In this paper, we presented the NRL Security Ontology for making security annotations. It is much more comprehensive than security ontologies previously available in terms of the number of concepts, the properties of the concepts, and the type of resources that can be described. Its organization is also more intuitive so that it is easier to use as well as to extend. New properties and instances can be added without modifying the overall class hierarchy. We demonstrated how the ontology can be applied to the Web services in a Service Oriented Architecture to describe security capabilities and requirements. A matchmaking algorithm was presented to perform requirement-capability matchmaking that takes into account not just the concepts, but also the properties of the concept. This is important because security annotations make extensive use of property attributes. The ability to take them into account makes this matching algorithm much more refined than previous work. Although not presented here, we also created a set of tools that enable browsing of ontologies, composing queries, and searching the UDDI for services that match the set of queries [25].

The creation of these ontologies is an iterative process. Additional instances and properties will always be needed to express new security statements. Classes and properties may be added and deleted as the security community continues to evaluate and refine the security ontologies. Additional ontologies are still needed to address issues such as privacy policies, access control, survivability, and QoS. We hope this work will serve as a catalyst in the development of standardized security-related ontologies with contributions from both the security community and the semantic Web community.

References

1. IA Architecture and Technical Framework: Executive Summary of the End-to-End IA Component of the GIG Integrated Architecture, National Security Agency Information Assurance Directorate (2004)
2. Kim, A., Luo, J., Kang, M.: Security Ontology for Annotating Resources. In: Meersman, R., Tari, Z. (eds.) On the Move to Meaningful Internet Systems 2005: CoopIS, DOA, and ODBASE. LNCS, vol. 3761, pp. 1483–1499. Springer, Heidelberg (2005)
3. Kim, A., Luo, J., Kang, M.: Security Ontology for Annotating Resources. Naval Research Lab, NRL Memorandum Report, NRL/MR/5540-05-641, p. 51, Washington, DC (2005)

4. Denker, G., Kagal, L., Finin, T., Paolucci, M., Sycara, K.: Security for DAML Web Services: Annotation and Matchmaking. In: Fensel, D., Sycara, K.P., Mylopoulos, J. (eds.) ISWC 2003. LNCS, vol. 2870, pp. 335–350. Springer, Heidelberg (2003)
5. Denker, G., Nguyen, S., Ton, A.: OWL-S Semantics of Security Web Services: a Case Study. In: 1st European Semantic Web Symposium, Heraklion, Greece (2004)
6. Kagal, L., Paolucci, M., Srinivasan, N., Denker, G., Finin, T., Sycara, K.: Authorization and Privacy for Semantic Web Services. In: AAAI Spring Symposium, Workshop on Semantic Web Services, Stanford, California (2004)
7. W3C: DAML+OIL, Reference Description (March 2001) http:// www.w3.org/ TR/ daml+oil-reference
8. W3C: OWL Web Ontology Language Overview (2004) http://www.w3.org/TR/owl-features/
9. IETF and W3C Working Group: XML Encryption (2001) http:// www.w3c.org/ Encryption/2001
10. IETF and W3C Working Group: XML Signature (2003) http://www.w3c.org/Signature
11. OASIS SSTC: Security Assertion Markup Language (SAML) 2.0 Technical Overview, Working Draft (2005) http://www.oasis-open.org/committees/download.php/12938/sstc-saml-tech-overview-2.0-draft-06.pdf
12. Bishop, M.: Computer Security: Art and Science. Addison-Wesley, Boston, MA (2002)
13. Pfleeger, C.P., Pfleeger, S.L.: Security in Computing, 3rd edn. Prentice-Hall, New Jersey (2003)
14. Noy, N.F., McGuinness, D.L.: Ontology Development 101: A Guide to Creating Your First Ontology, Stanford Knowledge Systems Laboratory, KSL-01-05 (2001)
15. Naval Research Lab 4SEA Project: NRL Ontology Files (2005) http://chacs.nrl.navy.mil/projects/4SEA/ontology.html
16. W3C Recommendation: OWL Web Ontology Language Guide, vol. 2005, W3C (2004)
17. DAML Ontology Library: http://www.daml.org/ontologies/
18. Schneier, B.: Applied Cryptography, 2nd edn. John Wiley and Sons, Inc., New York (1996)
19. Ferraiolo, D.F., Kuhn, D.R., Chandramouli, R.: Role-Based Access Control. Artech House, Norwood, MA (2003)
20. Committee on National Security Systems: National Information Assurance (IA) Glossary, Ft. Meade, MD, p. 85 (2003) http://www.cnss.gov/Assets/pdf/cnssi_4009.pdf
21. Martin, D., Burstein, M., Hobbs, J., Lassila, O., McDermott, D., McIlraith, S., Narayanan, S., Paolucci, M., Parsia, B., Payne, T., Sirin, E., Srinivasan, N., Sycara, K.: OWL-S: Semantic Markup for Web Services (2003) http://www.daml.org/services/owl-s/1.1/overview/
22. DAML: OWL-S 1.1, DAML Program.
23. Luo, J., Montrose, B., Kang, M.: An Approach for Semantic Query Processing with UDDI. In: Meersman, R., Tari, Z., Herrero, P. (eds.) On the Move to Meaningful Internet Systems 2005: OTM 2005 Workshops. LNCS, vol. 3762, pp. 89–98. Springer, Heidelberg (2005)
24. Luo, J., Montrose, B., Kim, A., Khashnobish, A., Kang, M.: Adding OWL-S Support to the Existing UDDI Infrastructure. In: IEEE International Conference on Web Services (ICWS 2006), Chicago, USA (2006)
25. Kang, M., Kim, A., Luo, J., Montrose, B., Khashnobish, A.: Ontology-based Security Specification Tools for SOA. In: 17th Information Resource Management Association Conference (IRMA 06), Washington, DC (2006)

26. Srinivasan, N., Paolucci, M., Sycara, K.: Adding OWL-S to UDDI, Implementation and Throughput. In: Cardoso, J., Sheth, A.P. (eds.) SWSWPC 2004. LNCS, vol. 3387, Springer, Heidelberg (2005)
27. Jaeger, M., Tang, S.: Ranked Matching for Service Descriptions using DAML-S. In: Enterprise Modelling and Ontologies for Interoperability (EMOI), INTEROP 2004, Riga, Latvia (2004)
28. Paolucci, M., Kawamura, T., Payne, T.R., Sycara, K.: Importing the Semantic Web in UDDI. In: Web Services, E-business and Semantic Web Workshop (ESSW02) (2002)
29. Sivashanmugam, K., Verma, K., Sheth, A., Miller, J.: Adding Semantics to Web Service Standards. In: 1st International Conference on Web Service (ICWS'03), Las Vegas, Nevada (2003)
30. Colgrave, J., Akkiraju, R., Goodwin, R.: External Matching in UDDI. In: Proceedings of the International Conferences on Web Services (ICWS 2004), San Diego, California, USA (2004)

Appendix. OWL Files for Service Profiles and Agent Security Profiles Used in Examples

For sake of brevity, namespace declarations and other material have been omitted

- Service Profiles (From Figure 10)

```
<!-- Security Requirements -->

<!-- Requirement1: Can do a Login Protocol that accepts
passwords -->
<credentials:Password rdf:ID="userPassword">
   <credentials:minLength
rdf:datatype="&xsd;int">8</credentials:minLength>
</credentials:Password>

<security:Login_Protocol rdf:ID="Requirement1">
   <security:reqCredential rdf:resource="UserPassword"/>
</security:Login_Protocol>

<!-- Requirement2: Can do a Login Protocol that accepts
certificates signed by NRL -->
<credentials:X.509Certificate rdf:ID="X.509">
   <credentials:issuer
rdf:datatype="&xsd;string">NRL</credentials:issuer>
</credentials:X.509Certificate>

<security:Login_Protocol rdf:ID="Requirement2">
   <security:reqCredential rdf:resource="X.509"/>
</security:Login_Protocol>

<!-- Security Capabilities -->
<!-- Capability1: Possess a SOAP Firewall w/ EAL4 assurance -->
<security:SoapFirewall rdf:ID="Capability1">
    <security:hasAssurance rdf:resource="&assurance;EAL4"/>
</security:SoapFirewall>
```

```
<!-- Capability2: Can do SSL with DES, AES and DiffieHellman -->

<security:SSL rdf:ID="Capability2">
   <security:hasEncryptionAlgorithm
rdf:resource="&algorithms;DES"/>
   <security:hasEncryptionAlgorithm
rdf:resource="&algorithms;AES"/>
   <security:hasEncryptionAlgorithm
rdf:resource="&algorithms;DiffieHellman"/>
</security:SSL>

<!-- Capability3: Can do SSL with password and DES algorithm in
CBC/ECB modes -->

<algorithms:DES rdf:ID="ModedDES">
   <algorithms:modeOfOperation
rdf:datatype="&xsd;string">CBC</algorithms:modeOfOperation>
   <algorithms:modeOfOperation
rdf:datatype="&xsd;string">ECB</algorithms:modeOfOperation>
</algorithms:DES>

<security:SSL rdf:ID="Capability7">
   <security:reqCredential rdf:resource="UserPassword"/>
   <security:hasEncryptionAlgorithm rdf:resource="ModedDES"/>
</security:SSL>

<!-- Service Descriptions using Requirements and Capabilities
     defined above. -->

<profile:Profile rdf:ID="Acme Stock Purchasing">
   <profile:serviceName>Acme Stocks</profile:serviceName>
   <profile:textDescription>We pick and buy stocks
                    </profile:textDescription>
   <service:securityRequirement rdf:resource="#Requirement2"/>
   <service:securityCapability rdf:resource="#Capability1"/>
   <service:securityCapability rdf:resource="#Capability3"/>
</profile:Profile>

<profile:Profile rdf:ID="AnyaBookService">
   <profile:serviceName>Anya's Rare Books</profile:serviceName>
   <profile:textDescription>We only deal with rare books,
published before 1943</profile:textDescription>
   <service:securityRequirement rdf:resource="#Requirement1/>
   <service:securityCapability rdf:resource="#Capability1"/>
   <service:securityCapability rdf:resource="#Capability2"/>
</profile:Profile>
```

- Example Agent Security Profile (From Figure 11)

```
<!-- Security Requirements -->
<!—Requirement1: Can do SSL with AES -->
```

```
<security:SSL rdf:ID="Requirement1">
   <security:hasEncryptionAlgorithm
rdf:resource="&algorithms;AES"/>
</security:SSL>

<!-- Security Capabilities -->
<!-- Capability1: Can do LoginProtocol accepts passwords -->
<credentials:Password rdf:ID="UserPassword">
   <credentials:minLength rdf:datatype="&xsd;int">8
   </credentials:minLength>
</credentials:Password>

<security:Login_Protocol rdf:ID="Capability1">
   <security:reqCredential rdf:resource="UserPassword"/>
</security:Login_Protocol>

<!-- Capability2: Can do a Login Protocol that accepts
certificates signed by NRL -->
<credentials:X.509Certificate rdf:ID="X.509">
   <credentials:issuer rdf:datatype="&xsd;string">NRL
   </credentials:issuer>
</credentials:X.509Certificate>

<security:Login_Protocol rdf:ID="Capability2">
   <security:reqCredential rdf:resource="X.509"/>
</security:Login_Protocol>

<!-- Agent Security Profiles -->
<!—This Agent Query will find one service (from ServiceProfile)
-->
<agent:AgentSecurityProfile rdf:ID="AgentQuery">
   <agent:securityRequirement rdf:resource="#Requirement1"/>
   <agent:securityCapability rdf:resource="#Capability1"/>
   <agent:securityCapability rdf:resource="#Capability2"/>
</agent:AgentSecurityProfile>
```

Author Index

Lecture Notes in Computer Science

Sublibrary 3: Information Systems and Application, incl. Internet/Web and HCI

For information about Vols. 1– 4278
please contact your bookseller or Springer

Vol. 4541: T. Okadome, T. Yamazaki, M. Makhtari (Eds.), Pervasive Computing for Quality of Life Enhancement. IX, 248 pages. 2007.

Vol. 4537: K.C.-C. Chang, W. Wang, L. Chen, C.A. Ellis, C.-H. Hsu, A.C. Tsoi, H. Wang (Eds.), Advances in Web and Network Technologies, and Information Management. XXIII, 707 pages. 2007.

Vol. 4531: J. Indulska, K. Raymond (Eds.), Distributed Applications and Interoperable Systems. XI, 337 pages. 2007.

Vol. 4526: M. Malek, M. Reitenspieß, A. van Moorsel (Eds.), Service Availability. X, 155 pages. 2007.

Vol. 4524: M. Marchiori, J.Z. Pan, C.d.S. Marie (Eds.), Web Reasoning and Rule Systems. XI, 382 pages. 2007.

Vol. 4519: E. Franconi, M. Kifer, W. May (Eds.), The Semantic Web: Research and Applications. XVIII, 830 pages. 2007.

Vol. 4518: N. Fuhr, M. Lalmas, A. Trotman (Eds.), Comparative Evaluation of XML Information Retrieval Systems. XII, 554 pages. 2007.

Vol. 4508: M.-Y. Kao, X.-Y. Li (Eds.), Algorithmic Aspects in Information and Management. VIII, 428 pages. 2007.

Vol. 4506: D. Zeng, I. Gotham, K. Komatsu, C. Lynch, M. Thurmond, D. Madigan, B. Lober, J. Kvach, H. Chen (Eds.), Intelligence and Security Informatics: Biosurveillance. XI, 234 pages. 2007.

Vol. 4505: G. Dong, X. Lin, W. Wang, Y. Yang, J.X. Yu (Eds.), Advances in Data and Web Management. XXII, 896 pages. 2007.

Vol. 4504: J. Huang, R. Kowalczyk, Z. Maamar, D. Martin, I. Müller, S. Stoutenburg, K.P. Sycara (Eds.), Service-Oriented Computing: Agents, Semantics, and Engineering. X, 175 pages. 2007.

Vol. 4500: N.A. Streitz, A. Kameas, I. Mavrommati (Eds.), The Disappearing Computer. XVIII, 304 pages. 2007.

Vol. 4495: J. Krogstie, A. Opdahl, G. Sindre (Eds.), Advanced Information Systems Engineering. XVI, 606 pages. 2007.

Vol. 4480: A. LaMarca, M. Langheinrich, K.N. Truong (Eds.), Pervasive Computing. XIII, 369 pages. 2007.

Vol. 4471: P. Cesar, K. Chorianopoulos, J.F. Jensen (Eds.), Interactive TV: A Shared Experience. XIII, 236 pages. 2007.

Vol. 4469: K.-c. Hui, Z. Pan, R.C.-k. Chung, C.C.L. Wang, X. Jin, S. Göbel, E.C.-L. Li (Eds.), Technologies for E-Learning and Digital Entertainment. XVIII, 974 pages. 2007.

Vol. 4443: R. Kotagiri, P. Radha Krishna, M. Mohania, E. Nantajeewarawat (Eds.), Advances in Databases: Concepts, Systems and Applications. XXI, 1126 pages. 2007.

Vol. 4439: W. Abramowicz (Ed.), Business Information Systems. XV, 654 pages. 2007.

Vol. 4430: C.C. Yang, D. Zeng, M. Chau, K. Chang, Q. Yang, X. Cheng, J. Wang, F.-Y. Wang, H. Chen (Eds.), Intelligence and Security Informatics. XII, 330 pages. 2007.

Vol. 4425: G. Amati, C. Carpineto, G. Romano (Eds.), Advances in Information Retrieval. XIX, 759 pages. 2007.

Vol. 4412: F. Stajano, H.J. Kim, J.-S. Chae, S.-D. Kim (Eds.), Ubiquitous Convergence Technology. XI, 302 pages. 2007.

Vol. 4402: W. Shen, J.-Z. Luo, Z. Lin, J.-P.A. Barthès, Q. Hao (Eds.), Computer Supported Cooperative Work in Design III. XV, 763 pages. 2007.

Vol. 4398: S. Marchand-Maillet, E. Bruno, A. Nürnberger, M. Detyniecki (Eds.), Adaptive Multimedia Retrieval: User, Context, and Feedback. XI, 269 pages. 2007.

Vol. 4397: C. Stephanidis, M. Pieper (Eds.), Universal Access in Ambient Intelligence Environments. XV, 467 pages. 2007.

Vol. 4380: S. Spaccapietra, P. Atzeni, F. Fages, M.-S. Hacid, M. Kifer, J. Mylopoulos, B. Pernici, P. Shvaiko, J. Trujillo, I. Zaihrayeu (Eds.), Journal on Data Semantics VIII. XV, 219 pages. 2007.

Vol. 4365: C.J. Bussler, M. Castellanos, U. Dayal, S. Navathe (Eds.), Business Intelligence for the Real-Time Enterprises. IX, 157 pages. 2007.

Vol. 4353: T. Schwentick, D. Suciu (Eds.), Database Theory – ICDT 2007. XI, 419 pages. 2006.

Vol. 4352: T.-J. Cham, J. Cai, C. Dorai, D. Rajan, T.-S. Chua, L.-T. Chia (Eds.), Advances in Multimedia Modeling, Part II. XVIII, 743 pages. 2006.

Vol. 4351: T.-J. Cham, J. Cai, C. Dorai, D. Rajan, T.-S. Chua, L.-T. Chia (Eds.), Advances in Multimedia Modeling, Part I. XIX, 797 pages. 2006.

Vol. 4328: D. Penkler, M. Reitenspiess, F. Tam (Eds.), Service Availability. X, 289 pages. 2006.

Vol. 4321: P. Brusilovsky, A. Kobsa, W. Nejdl (Eds.), The Adaptive Web. XII, 763 pages. 2007.

Vol. 4317: S.K. Madria, K.T. Claypool, R. Kannan, P. Uppuluri, M.M. Gore (Eds.), Distributed Computing and Internet Technology. XIX, 466 pages. 2006.

Vol. 4312: S. Sugimoto, J. Hunter, A. Rauber, A. Morishima (Eds.), Digital Libraries: Achievements, Challenges and Opportunities. XVIII, 571 pages. 2006.

Vol. 4306: Y. Avrithis, Y. Kompatsiaris, S. Staab, N.E. O'Connor (Eds.), Semantic Multimedia. XII, 241 pages. 2006.

Vol. 4302: J. Domingo-Ferrer, L. Franconi (Eds.), Privacy in Statistical Databases. XI, 383 pages. 2006.

Vol. 4299: S. Renals, S. Bengio, J.G. Fiscus (Eds.), Machine Learning for Multimodal Interaction. XII, 470 pages. 2006.

Vol. 4295: J.D. Carswell, T. Tezuka (Eds.), Web and Wireless Geographical Information Systems. XI, 269 pages. 2006.

Vol. 4286: P.G. Spirakis, M. Mavronicolas, S.C. Kontogiannis (Eds.), Internet and Network Economics. XI, 401 pages. 2006.

Vol. 4282: Z. Pan, A. Cheok, M. Haller, R.W.H. Lau, H. Saito, R. Liang (Eds.), Advances in Artificial Reality and Tele-Existence. XXIII, 1347 pages. 2006.